For DUMMIES
COMPUTER
BOOK SERIES
FROM IDG

Lotus 1-2-3® Mil...
For Du...

MW01131583

The Universal SmartIcon Bar

SmartIcon	What It Does
	Creates a new workbook
	Opens an existing file
	Saves the current file
	Prints
	Displays Print Preview
	Undoes last command or action
	Cuts to Clipboard
	Copies to Clipboard
	Pastes Clipboard contents

Keyboard Combinations for Dialog Boxes

F1	Opens help for the dialog box
Alt+*hot key*	Selects the control of the hot key (underlined letter) that you press
Tab	Moves forward and activates the next control
Shift+Tab	Moves backward and activates the preceding control
Spacebar	Checks or unchecks an option button or check box
Alt+↑ or Alt+↓	Opens and closes a drop-down listbox
Arrow keys	Moves within a group of controls (such as option buttons)
End	Selects the last item in a listbox
Home	Selects the first item in a listbox
PgUp or PgDn	Moves to the top or bottom item in the list of items currently visible in a listbox and selects the item
Enter	Completes the command and closes the dialog box (just like clicking OK)
Esc	Closes the dialog box without completing the command (just like clicking Cancel)

Basic Survival Skills

What You Want to Do	How You Do It
Display InfoBox for selected object	Alt+Enter
Save your file	Ctrl+S
Quit 1-2-3	Alt+F4
Open a file	Ctrl+O
Undo last action	Ctrl+Z
Clear cell	Delete
Get the Shortcut Menu	Right-click in a selected cell or object
Activate a different window in 1-2-3	Ctrl+F6
Move to another Windows application	Alt+Tab

Formatting Shortcuts

Ctrl+B	Adds or removes boldface
Ctrl+E	Centers cell contents
Ctrl+I	Adds or removes italics
Ctrl+L	Left-aligns cell contents
Ctrl+N	Removes bold, italics, and underlining from the current selection
Ctrl+R	Right-aligns cell contents
Ctrl+U	Adds or removes underlining

...For Dummies: #1 Computer Book Series for Beginners

Lotus 1-2-3® Millennium Edition For Dummies®

Cheat Sheet

Function Keys

Key	What It Does
F1 (HELP)	Displays online help that's usually relevant to what you're doing
F2 (EDIT)	Switches the program into Edit mode so that you can change the contents of the current cell
F3 (NAME)	Lists names of files, charts, ranges, query tables, drawn objects, versions, @functions, macro key names, and macro commands
F4	In Edit, Point or Value mode, cycles the cell references in formulas from absolute to mixed to relative; in Ready mode, anchors the cell pointer so that you can select a range of cells
F5 (GOTO)	Moves the cell pointer to a cell, named range, worksheet, chart, drawn object, query table, version, or active file
F6 (PANE)	Moves the cell pointer between panes in split windows and between worksheets displayed in perspective view
F7 (QUERY)	Updates the records in a query table (equivalent to choosing Query⇨Refresh Now)
F8 (TABLE)	Repeats the last Range⇨Analyze⇨What-if Table command
F9 (CALC)	In Ready Mode, recalculates all formulas; in Edit or Value mode, converts a formula to its current value
F10 (MENU)	Activates the menu bar to use the keyboard

Selection Keys

Key Combination	What It Does
Shift+arrow key	Extends the selection to include the next cell to the left, above, or below
End, Shift+←	Expands the selection to the last nonblank cell to the left
End, Shift+→	Expands the selection to the last nonblank cell to the right
End, Shift+↑	Expands the selection to the last nonblank cell at the top
End, Shift+↓	Expands the selection to the last nonblank cell below
Shift+Home	Selects all cells from the active cell to cell A1
Ctrl+Shift+PgDn	Extends the selection to include the next sheet
Ctrl+Shift+PgUp	Extends the selection to include the previous sheet
Ctrl+Shift+Home	Selects all cells in the current worksheet

Activating Sheets

Key Combination	What It Does
Ctrl+PgDn	Activates the preceding sheet, unless you're on the first sheet, in which case it has no effect
Ctrl+PgUp	Activates the next sheet, unless you're on the last sheet, in which case it has no effect
Home	Moves to the top of the file and moves cell pointer to the upper-left cell
Ctrl+Home	Activates the first sheet and moves the cell pointer to the upper-left cell
End, Ctrl+Home	Moves to the last cell that contains data on the last sheet that contains data

IDG BOOKS WORLDWIDE

...For Dummies: #1 Computer Book Series for Beginners

TM

References for the Rest of Us! ®

BESTSELLING BOOK SERIES FROM IDG

Are you intimidated and confused by computers? Do you find that traditional manuals are overloaded with technical details you'll never use? Do your friends and family always call you to fix simple problems on their PCs? Then the *...For Dummies*® computer book series from IDG Books Worldwide is for you.

...For Dummies books are written for those frustrated computer users who know they aren't really dumb but find that PC hardware, software, and indeed the unique vocabulary of computing make them feel helpless. *...For Dummies* books use a lighthearted approach, a down-to-earth style, and even cartoons and humorous icons to diffuse computer novices' fears and build their confidence. Lighthearted but not lightweight, these books are a perfect survival guide for anyone forced to use a computer.

> *"I like my copy so much I told friends; now they bought copies."*
>
> — Irene C., Orwell, Ohio

> *"Quick, concise, nontechnical, and humorous."*
>
> — Jay A., Elburn, Illinois

> *"Thanks, I needed this book. Now I can sleep at night."*
>
> — Robin F., British Columbia, Canada

Already, millions of satisfied readers agree. They have made *...For Dummies* books the #1 introductory level computer book series and have written asking for more. So, if you're looking for the most fun and easy way to learn about computers, look to *...For Dummies* books to give you a helping hand.

LOTUS 1-2-3®
MILLENNIUM
EDITION FOR
DUMMIES®

by John Walkenbach

IDG Books Worldwide, Inc.
An International Data Group Company

Foster City, CA ♦ Chicago, IL ♦ Indianapolis, IN ♦ New York, NY

Lotus 1-2-3® Millennium Edition For Dummies®

Published by
IDG Books Worldwide, Inc.
An International Data Group Company
919 E. Hillsdale Blvd.
Suite 400
Foster City, CA 94404
www.idgbooks.com (IDG Books Worldwide Web site)
www.dummies.com (Dummies Press Web site)

Library of Congress Catalog Card No.: 98-85685

ISBN: 0-7645-0314-6

Printed in the United States of America

10 9 8 7 6 5 4 3 2 1

1O/SU/QW/ZY/IN

Distributed in the United States by IDG Books Worldwide, Inc.

Distributed by Macmillan Canada for Canada; by Transworld Publishers Limited in the United Kingdom; by IDG Norge Books for Norway; by IDG Sweden Books for Sweden; by Woodslane Pty. Ltd. for Australia; by Woodslane (NZ) Ltd. for New Zealand; by Addison Wesley Longman Singapore Pte Ltd. for Singapore, Malaysia, Thailand, Indonesia and Korea; by Norma Comunicaciones S.A. for Colombia; by Intersoft for South Africa; by International Thomson Publishing for Germany, Austria and Switzerland; by Toppan Company Ltd. for Japan; by Distribuidora Cuspide for Argentina; by Livraria Cultura for Brazil; by Ediciencia S.A. for Ecuador; by Ediciones ZETA S.C.R. Ltda. for Peru; by WS Computer Publishing Corporation, Inc., for the Philippines; by Unalis Corporation for Taiwan; by Contemporanea de Ediciones for Venezuela; by Computer Book & Magazine Store for Puerto Rico; by Express Computer Distributors for the Caribbean and West Indies. Authorized Sales Agent: Anthony Rudkin Associates for the Middle East and North Africa.

For general information on IDG Books Worldwide's books in the U.S., please call our Consumer Customer Service department at 800-762-2974. For reseller information, including discounts and premium sales, please call our Reseller Customer Service department at 800-434-3422.

For information on where to purchase IDG Books Worldwide's books outside the U.S., please contact our International Sales department at 650-655-3200 or fax 650-655-3297.

For information on foreign language translations, please contact our Foreign & Subsidiary Rights department at 650-655-3021 or fax 650-655-3281.

For sales inquiries and special prices for bulk quantities, please contact our Sales department at 650-655-3200 or write to the address above.

For information on using IDG Books Worldwide's books in the classroom or for ordering examination copies, please contact our Educational Sales department at 800-434-2086 or fax 317-596-5499.

For press review copies, author interviews, or other publicity information, please contact our Public Relations department at 650-655-3000 or fax 650-655-3299.

For authorization to photocopy items for corporate, personal, or educational use, please contact Copyright Clearance Center, 222 Rosewood Drive, Danvers, MA 01923, or fax 978-750-4470.

About the Author

John Walkenbach has been involved with spreadsheets for about 25 percent of his life (and he's over 40). He has written more than 250 spreadsheet articles and reviews for publications such as *PC World, Windows, PC/Computing,* and *InfoWorld.* In addition, he's the author of about 20 other spreadsheet books, including *1-2-3 97 For Windows For Dummies.* John is currently a contributing editor for *PC World,* and writes the monthly spreadsheet column.

John holds a Ph.D. in experimental psychology from the University of Montana, and has worked as an instructor, consultant, programmer, and market research manager for the largest S&L ever to fail (and he takes no responsibility for that). Currently, he heads JWalk and Associates, a small consulting firm in Southern California.

Besides spreadsheets, John has a growing infatuation with the World Wide Web, and he maintains "The Spreadsheet Page" (www.j-walk.com/ss/). In his spare time, he likes to annoy his neighbors with loud blues guitar playing and weird sounds from his synthesizers.

ABOUT IDG BOOKS WORLDWIDE

Welcome to the world of IDG Books Worldwide.

IDG Books Worldwide, Inc., is a subsidiary of International Data Group, the world's largest publisher of computer-related information and the leading global provider of information services on information technology. IDG was founded more than 25 years ago and now employs more than 8,500 people worldwide. IDG publishes more than 275 computer publications in over 75 countries (see listing below). More than 90 million people read one or more IDG publications each month.

Launched in 1990, IDG Books Worldwide is today the #1 publisher of best-selling computer books in the United States. We are proud to have received eight awards from the Computer Press Association in recognition of editorial excellence and three from *Computer Currents*' First Annual Readers' Choice Awards. Our best-selling *...For Dummies*® series has more than 50 million copies in print with translations in 38 languages. IDG Books Worldwide, through a joint venture with IDG's Hi-Tech Beijing, became the first U.S. publisher to publish a computer book in the People's Republic of China. In record time, IDG Books Worldwide has become the first choice for millions of readers around the world who want to learn how to better manage their businesses.

Our mission is simple: Every one of our books is designed to bring extra value and skill-building instructions to the reader. Our books are written by experts who understand and care about our readers. The knowledge base of our editorial staff comes from years of experience in publishing, education, and journalism — experience we use to produce books for the '90s. In short, we care about books, so we attract the best people. We devote special attention to details such as audience, interior design, use of icons, and illustrations. And because we use an efficient process of authoring, editing, and desktop publishing our books electronically, we can spend more time ensuring superior content and spend less time on the technicalities of making books.

You can count on our commitment to deliver high-quality books at competitive prices on topics you want to read about. At IDG Books Worldwide, we continue in the IDG tradition of delivering quality for more than 25 years. You'll find no better book on a subject than one from IDG Books Worldwide.

John J. Kilcullen
John Kilcullen
CEO
IDG Books Worldwide, Inc.

Steven Berkowitz
Steven Berkowitz
President and Publisher
IDG Books Worldwide, Inc.

Eighth Annual
Computer Press
Awards ≥1992

Ninth Annual
Computer Press
Awards ≥1993

Tenth Annual
Computer Press
Awards ≥1994

Eleventh Annual
Computer Press
Awards ≥1995

IDG Books Worldwide, Inc., is a subsidiary of International Data Group, the world's largest publisher of computer-related information and the leading global provider of information services on information technology. International Data Group publishes over 275 computer publications in over 75 countries. More than 90 million people read one or more International Data Group publications each month. International Data Group's publications include: **ARGENTINA:** Buyer's Guide, Computerworld Argentina, PC World Argentina; **AUSTRALIA:** Australian Macworld, Australian PC World, Australian Reseller News, Computerworld, IT Casebook, Network World, Publish, Webmaster; **AUSTRIA:** Computerwelt Osterreich, Networks Austria, PC Tip Austria; **BANGLADESH:** PC World Bangladesh; **BELARUS:** PC World Belarus; **BELGIUM:** Data News; **BRAZIL:** Annuário de Informática, Computerworld, Connections, Macworld, PC Player, PC World, Publish, Reseller News, Supergamepower; **BULGARIA:** Computerworld Bulgaria, Network World Bulgaria, PC & MacWorld Bulgaria; **CANADA:** CIO Canada, Client/Server World, ComputerWorld Canada, InfoWorld Canada, NetworkWorld Canada, WebWorld; **CHILE:** Computerworld Chile, PC World Chile; **COLOMBIA:** Computerworld Colombia, PC World Colombia; **COSTA RICA:** PC World Centro America; **THE CZECH AND SLOVAK REPUBLICS:** Computerworld Czechoslovakia, Macworld Czech Republic, PC World Czechoslovakia; **DENMARK:** Communications World Danmark, Computerworld Danmark, Macworld Danmark, PC World Danmark, Techworld Denmark; **DOMINICAN REPUBLIC:** PC World Republica Dominicana; **ECUADOR:** PC World Ecuador; **EGYPT:** Computerworld Middle East, PC World Middle East; **EL SALVADOR:** PC World Centro America; **FINLAND:** MikroPC, Tietoverkko, Tietoviikko; **FRANCE:** Distributique, Hebdo, Info PC, Le Monde Informatique, Macworld, Reseaux & Telecoms, WebMaster France; **GERMANY:** Computer Partner, Computerwoche, Computerwoche Extra, Computerwoche FOCUS, Global Online, Macwelt, PC Welt; **GREECE:** Amiga Computing, GamePro Greece, Multimedia World; **GUATEMALA:** PC World Centro America; **HONDURAS:** PC World Centro America; **HONG KONG:** Computerworld Hong Kong, PC World Hong Kong, Publish in Asia; **HUNGARY:** ABCD CD-ROM, Computerworld Szamitastechnika, Internetto online Magazine, PC World Hungary, PC-X Magazin Hungary; **ICELAND:** Tolvuheimur PC World Island; **INDIA:** Information Communications World, Information Systems Computerworld, PC World India, Publish in Asia; **INDONESIA:** InfoKomputer PC World, Komputek Computerworld, Publish in Asia; **IRELAND:** ComputerScope, PC Live!; **ISRAEL:** Macworld Israel, People & Computers/Computerworld; **ITALY:** Computerworld Italia, Macworld Italia, Networking Italia, PC World Italia; **JAPAN:** DTP World, Macworld Japan, Nikkei Personal Computing, OS/2 World Japan, SunWorld Japan, Windows NT World, Windows World Japan; **KENYA:** PC World East African; **KOREA:** Hi-Tech Information, Macworld Korea, PC World Korea; **MACEDONIA:** PC World Macedonia; **MALAYSIA:** Computerworld Malaysia, PC World Malaysia, Publish in Asia; **MALTA:** PC World Malta; **MEXICO:** Computerworld Mexico, PC World Mexico; **MYANMAR:** PC World Myanmar; **NETHERLANDS:** Computer! Totaal, LAN Internetworking Magazine, LAN World Buyers Guide, Macworld Netherlands, Net, WebWereld; **NEW ZEALAND:** Absolute Beginners Guide and Plain & Simple Series, Computer Buyer, Computer Industry Directory, Computerworld New Zealand, MTB, Network World, PC World New Zealand; **NICARAGUA:** PC World Centro America; **NORWAY:** Computerworld Norge, CW Rapport, Datamagasinet, Financial Rapport, Kursguide Norge, Macworld Norge, Multimediaworld Norge, PC World Ekspress Norge, PC World Nettverk, PC World Norge, PC World ProduktGuide Norge; **PAKISTAN:** Computerworld Pakistan; **PANAMA:** PC World Panama; **PEOPLE'S REPUBLIC OF CHINA:** China Computerworld, China Computer Users, China Infoworld, China Telecom World Weekly, Computer & Communication, Electronic Design China, Electronics Today, Electronics Weekly, Game Software, PC World China, Popular Computer Week, Software Weekly, Software World, Telecom World; **PERU:** Computerworld Peru, PC World Profesional Peru, PC World SoHo Peru; **PHILIPPINES:** Click!, Computerworld Philippines, PC World Philippines, Publish in Asia; **POLAND:** Computerworld Poland, Computerworld Special Report Poland, Cyber, Macworld Poland, Networld Poland, PC World Komputer; **PORTUGAL:** Cerebro/PC World, Computerworld/Correio Informático, Dealer World Portugal, Mac*In/PC*In Portugal, Multimedia World; **PUERTO RICO:** PC World Puerto Rico; **ROMANIA:** Computerworld Romania, PC World Romania, Telecom Romania; **RUSSIA:** Computerworld Russia, Mir PK, Publish, Seti; **SINGAPORE:** Computerworld Singapore, PC World Singapore, Publish in Asia; **SLOVENIA:** Monitor; **SOUTH AFRICA:** Computing SA, Network World SA, Software World SA; **SPAIN:** Communicaciones World España, Computerworld España, Dealer World España, Macworld España, PC World España; **SRI LANKA:** Infolink PC World; **SWEDEN:** CAP&Design, Computer Sweden, Corporate Computing Sweden, Internetworld Sweden, it.branschen, Macworld Sweden, MaxiData Sweden, MikroDatorn, Natverk & Kommunikation, PC World Sweden, PCaktiv, Windows World Sweden; **SWITZERLAND:** Computerworld Schweiz, Macworld Schweiz, PCtip; **TAIWAN:** Computerworld Taiwan, Macworld Taiwan, NEW ViSiON/Publish, PC World Taiwan, Windows World Taiwan; **THAILAND:** Publish in Asia, Thai Computerworld; **TURKEY:** Computerworld Turkiye, Macworld Turkiye, Network World Turkiye, PC World Turkiye; **UKRAINE:** Computerworld Kiev, Multimedia World Ukraine, PC World Ukraine; **UNITED KINGDOM:** Acorn User UK, Amiga Action UK, Amiga Computing UK, Apple Talk UK, Computing, Macworld, Parents and Computers UK, PC Advisor, PC Home, PSX Pro, The WEB; **UNITED STATES:** Cable in the Classroom, CIO Magazine, Computerworld, DOS World, Federal Computer Week, GamePro Magazine, InfoWorld, I-Way, Macworld, Network World, PC Games, PC World, Publish, Video Event, THE WEB Magazine, and WebMaster; online webzines: JavaWorld, NetscapeWorld, and SunWorld Online; **URUGUAY:** InfoWorld Uruguay; **VENEZUELA:** Computerworld Venezuela, PC World Venezuela; and **VIETNAM:** PC World Vietnam.   5/7/98

Dedication

This book is dedicated to Katlyn-Rose, and her special furry friends named Harvey and Ginger.

Author's Acknowledgments

Thanks to everyone who played a role in transforming a bunch of ideas in my head into a real live book that you can hold in your hand.

Special thanks to John Pont, my primary editor, whose gentle nudging helped me meet the deadline. I also appreciate the great work done by Constance Carlisle and Paula Lowell (copy editors) and David Medinets (technical editor). These people all make my job much easier.

Publisher's Acknowledgments

We're proud of this book; please register your comments through our IDG Books Worldwide Online Registration Form located at http://my2cents.dummies.com.

Some of the people who helped bring this book to market include the following:

Acquisitions, Editorial, and Media Development

Project Editor: John W. Pont

Acquisitions Editor: Michael Kelly

Copy Editors: Constance Carlisle, Paula Lowell, Linda S. Stark

Technical Editor: David Medinets

Editorial Manager: Mary C. Corder

Editorial Assistant: Donna Love

Production

Project Coordinators: Cindy L. Phipps, Regina Snyder

Layout and Graphics: Lou Boudreau, J. Tyler Connor, Angela F. Hunckler, Todd Klemme, Jane E. Martin, Anna Rohrer, Brent Savage, Kathie Schutte

Proofreaders: Christine Berman, Kelli Botta, Michelle Croninger, Rachel Garvey, Nancy Price, Rebecca Senninger, Robert Springer, Janet M. Withers

Indexer: Sharon Hilgenberg

Special Help

Suzanne Thomas

General and Administrative

IDG Books Worldwide, Inc.: John Kilcullen, CEO; Steven Berkowitz, President and Publisher

IDG Books Technology Publishing: Brenda McLaughlin, Senior Vice President and Group Publisher

Dummies Technology Press and Dummies Editorial: Diane Graves Steele, Vice President and Associate Publisher; Mary Bednarek, Director of Acquisitions and Product Development; Kristin A. Cocks, Editorial Director

Dummies Trade Press: Kathleen A. Welton, Vice President and Publisher; Kevin Thornton, Acquisitions Manager

IDG Books Production for Dummies Press: Michael R. Britton, Vice President of Production; Beth Jenkins Roberts, Production Director; Cindy L. Phipps, Manager of Project Coordination, Production Proofreading, and Indexing; Kathie S. Schutte, Supervisor of Page Layout; Shelley Lea, Supervisor of Graphics and Design; Debbie J. Gates, Production Systems Specialist; Robert Springer, Supervisor of Proofreading; Debbie Stailey, Special Projects Coordinator; Tony Augsburger, Supervisor of Reprints and Bluelines

Dummies Packaging and Book Design: Robin Seaman, Creative Director; Jocelyn Kelaita, Product Packaging Coordinator; Kavish + Kavish, Cover Design

◆

The publisher would like to give special thanks to Patrick J. McGovern, without whom this book would not have been possible.

◆

Contents at a Glance

Cartoons at a Glance

By Rich Tennant

page 9

page 47

page 325

page 181

page 133

page 255

Fax: 978-546-7747 • E-mail: the5wave@tiac.net

Table of Contents

Introduction

Allow me to guess your situation. . . .

You need to know how to use the latest and greatest version of 1-2-3, but you don't want to get bogged down with all sorts of technical details. I bet that you don't know all that much about computers, and you really have no aspirations of becoming a 1-2-3 guru. In other words, you're probably a bottom-line kind of person who likes to cut to the quick. And, unlike the stereotypical computer user, you also have a sense of humor. If that's true, you've come to the right place.

Welcome to *1-2-3 Millennium Edition For Dummies* — the best beginner's guide to one of the best spreadsheet programs available. Owning this book doesn't necessarily make you a dummy — that's a reputation you must earn on your own. Actually, you've already demonstrated that you're smart enough not to waste your time poring over massive, boring manuals.

If you bought this book, thanks — now I can afford to feed my goldfish this week. If you borrowed it from someone, please give it back and buy your own copy. If you're standing around in a bookstore trying to make up your mind about it, just buy it and be on your way (the clerk's getting suspicious).

Here's a sneak preview of what this book has to offer:

- Down-to-earth information about the most useful parts of 1-2-3 to get you up to speed in no time (well, actually it takes *some* time)

- Step-by-step instructions and informative examples that demonstrate things you may want to do (or things someone *else* wants you to do)

- Very few extraneous details about things that you don't really care about anyway

- Lively, entertaining, and easy-to-read text, with subtle humor sprinkled liberally throughout its pages by your adept yet humble author

- Lots of things you can say and do to make you seem smarter than you really are

- Cartoons by Rich Tennant that are guaranteed to be funnier than your average Sunday comic strip

Have no fear; this is not an advanced reference book. Don't expect the computer geek at your office to borrow this book to look up all the gory details of creating LotusScript programs.

What This Book Covers

This book is for people who are just starting out with Lotus 1-2-3 Millennium Edition — and for those who are upgrading from a previous version of the software. But anyone can buy it — I won't check.

Notice that the title of this book isn't *The Complete Guide to 1-2-3 Millennium Edition.* I don't cover everything about 1-2-3 — but then again, you don't want to *know* everything about 1-2-3, right?

1-2-3 Millennium Edition, which began shipping in 1998, is very similar to 1-2-3 97. But if you're using a previous version of 1-2-3, this book won't do you much good because 1-2-3 97 and 1-2-3 Millennium Edition are quite different from the previous versions of the product.

Read the Whole Thing?

My intention is not that you read this book from cover to cover. Frankly, the plot stinks, the character development leaves much to be desired, and you won't find any steamy sex scenes (those parts were removed by my editor).

If you do decide to read this book straight through, you'll find that the chapters *do* move along in a quasi-logical progression — but they also stand on their own. After you get up and running with 1-2-3, you can safely put this book aside until you need to move on to the next challenge. When that time comes, follow these simple steps:

1. **Scan the Table of Contents for a general topic; refer to the Index for a specific question.**

   If your problem is "How do I get rid of these stupid gridlines?" look under *gridlines,* not *stupid.* (If you don't know what a gridline is, take a side trip to the Glossary in the back of the book.)

2. **Based on what you discover in the Table of Contents or Index, turn to the page that discusses the topic.**

3. Read the informative and often jocund text that introduces the topic.

4. If reading the introductory text doesn't help, take a look at the step-by-step instructions provided and work your way through them.

Unless the task you're trying to accomplish is a fairly sophisticated or unusual one, this book can certainly shed some light on it. Even if a particular section doesn't seem to be related to what you're trying to do, you may find that working through the problem step by step provides some insights that enable you to figure out the answer on your own. But what I hope to get across more than anything is that you should feel free to play around in 1-2-3 and experiment with things. That's the best way to become comfortable with the program.

The topics in this book usually start out with some introductory comments and often include step-by-step instructions for accomplishing a task. You can skim through the introductory text to see whether it's really what you want.

If you're just starting out, I recommend that you read some of the chapters in their entirety — or at least until the subject matter exceeds the level of complexity you can stomach. For example, if you've never printed anything before, you should read Chapter 9 from the beginning.

Some topics have additional information for those overachievers who want to know even more about what they're doing. Reading these sections only increases the depth of your knowledge of 1-2-3 — and that's certainly not what this book is all about. So you may want to make a mental note: *See the Technical Stuff icon, skip the section.*

As long as you have your mental notepad out, here's another one for you: *See the Warning icon, read the section.* The Warning icon signals something that may eat your data, cause your computer to go to warp nine, suddenly turn your fingers green, or otherwise ruin your whole morning. More about icons later.

How This Book Is Organized

Personally, I think that my editors and I are the only ones who really care about how this book is organized. I started out with an outline — the part of the term paper you always hated writing, remember? The outline eventually turned into the Table of Contents, which you can peruse if you're really into organizational issues. But you may prefer the following synopsis of the book's major parts.

Part I: Introducing 1-2-3 Millennium Edition

The three chapters in this part are for people who don't have a clue as to what a spreadsheet — much less 1-2-3 — is all about. Chapter 1 contains oodles of interesting information so you can hold your own should you ever find yourself at a cocktail party populated by spreadsheet junkies (eww!). Chapter 2 tells you how to start and exit 1-2-3. In Chapter 3, I cover two basic ingredients of 1-2-3: menus and InfoBoxes.

Part II: Getting Busy

Like it or not, you can't just jump into 1-2-3 and expect to start doing meaningful things immediately; you need some basic background information. Part II imparts this knowledge in the form of four chapters. You discover how to enter data, create formulas, use built-in functions, make changes to what you've already done, and do many other things that you may or may not be interested in (but that you really ought to know about). You don't have to read everything in these chapters at once; you can always refer to them when the need arises.

Part III: Saving, Printing, and Creating New Sheets

After you create your first 1-2-3 masterpiece, you're going to want to save it for posterity. In Part III, I cover such topics as saving your work (and making sure that you don't lose it), printing your spreadsheets out for the world to see, and working with more than one sheet in a file.

Part IV: Making Yourself at Home

The five chapters in this section are full of "gee whiz" stuff (with a bit of "jeepers" stuff thrown in for good measure). You can probably get by for quite a while pretending that these topics don't exist. But sooner or later, you may want to start working smarter and getting better results. When and if that time comes, Part IV is here to show you how to perform some simple customization, make your worksheets look great, create and customize graphs, make nifty maps, and take all kinds of shortcuts that can save you valuable minutes each day, giving you more time for important things like goofing off.

Part V: Expanding Your Horizons

In this part, I tell you just enough about some of the more advanced topics so that you can get by. If you're so moved, you can spiff up your work with drawings and graphic objects, discover databases, and even find out how to record and use time-saving scripts. This part also explores some of the coolest 1-2-3 features: outlining, using the Version Manager, and going online.

Part VI: The Part of Tens

What would a *...For Dummies* book be without a collection of short chapters containing lists of ten or so things in each? In this book, these chapters are huddled together in Part VI. Turn to this part for concise lists of habits you should acquire, information you definitely must know, and useful formulas that you can use in your work.

Glossary

Hey, this is a computer book — it *has* to have a glossary. I think it's a law in some states.

Foolish Assumptions

People who write books usually have a target reader in mind. In the case of this book, my target reader is a conglomerate of dozens of beginning computer users that I've met over the years. The following points more or less describe this typical new user (and may even describe you):

- You have access to a PC at work (and maybe at home), but working on the computer isn't the most interesting part of your job.

- Your computer is running Microsoft Windows 95 or later (maybe even Microsoft Windows NT).

- You have some experience with computers (word processing, mostly) and may have gone so far as to install a program or two — most likely a game program.

- Someone just installed 1-2-3 Millennium Edition on your computer, and you have to figure out how to use the sucker.

> ✔ You've never used a spreadsheet before — or if you have, you really didn't understand what you were doing.
>
> ✔ You need to get some work done, and you have a low tolerance for boring computer books.

Conventions — Typographical and Otherwise

As you work your way through this book, you may notice that it uses different type styles. I use two typefaces not just because variety is the spice of life, but also so you can easily distinguish text that appears on-screen or that you're supposed to type.

If you have to type something, that something appears in **bold type**. Here's an example: "Enter **256** into cell A1." In this case, you type the three numbers and press the Enter key.

Occasionally, 1-2-3 graces your screen with a message. To indicate such messages, I use the monospace typeface, like so: `Ready`.

Sometimes, I tell you to press a *key combination* — which means that you hold down one key while you press another. For example, the Ctrl+Z key combination means that you should hold down the Ctrl (Control) key while you press Z once.

This book, of course, assumes that your system has a mouse (or a mouse substitute, such as a trackball) attached to it. To issue a 1-2-3 command, click the appropriate menu and then click a command from the list that drops down. If you prefer to use the keyboard to issue commands, you have to press Alt to access the menu, use the arrow keys to move to the selection you want, and then press Enter.

When I ask you to choose a command, I don't waste time giving directions for both keyboarders and mouseketeers. Rather than say something like:

> If you're using the keyboard, press Alt+F and then press S to save your file. Mouse users should click File and then click Save.

I simply underline the letters you need to press on your keyboard (called *hot keys*), like so:

> Save your file by choosing File⇨Save.

This way, you can choose your method of payment. A lot simpler, no?

Icons Used in This Book

Somewhere along the line, a high-priced market research company must have shown that computer books sell more copies if they have icons stuck inside the margins. Icons are those little pictures that are supposed to draw your attention to various features or help you decide whether something is worth reading. Whether the research is valid remains to be proven, but I'm not taking any chances. So here are the icons you encounter in this book:

This icon signals material that you really *shouldn't* care about. Read this only if you're interested in the nitty-gritty details — for the nerd in all of us.

Don't skip over material marked with this icon. It tells you about a shortcut that can save you lots of time and make you a hit at the next computer-geek party.

This icon alerts you to information you need to store away in the deep recesses of your brain for later use.

Read anything marked with this icon. Otherwise, you may lose your data, blow up your computer, cause a nuclear holocaust, or worse.

This icon alerts you to features found only in 1-2-3 Millennium Edition. If you're moving up from 1-2-3 97, these icons are for you. Otherwise, just ignore this stuff.

Now What?

If you've never used a spreadsheet, I strongly suggest that you read Chapters 1 and 2 before you do anything else. Chapter 1 tells you what a spreadsheet is and exactly what 1-2-3 can do. Chapter 2 tells you how to start the program (and how to get out of it when you've had enough).

On the other hand, it's a free country (at least it was when I wrote this book), so I won't sic the Computer Book Police on you if you opt to thumb through randomly and read whatever strikes your fancy. If you have a particular task in mind — such as "How do I sort all these numbers?" — go to the Index. Go directly to the Index. Do not pass Go; do not collect $200.

Good luck and have fun.

Part I
Introducing Lotus 1-2-3 Millennium Edition

The 5th Wave   By Rich Tennant

©RICHTENNANT

"DO YOU WANT ME TO CALL THE COMPANY AND HAVE THEM SEND ANOTHER REVIEW COPY OF THEIR DATABASE SOFTWARE SYSTEM, OR DO YOU KNOW WHAT YOU'RE GOING TO WRITE?"

In this part . . .

This part contains three chapters that provide some essential information for using 1-2-3. If you've never used a spreadsheet before, or if you need a quick refresher course on the subject, these chapters are for you. In Chapter 1, I tell you exactly what 1-2-3 can do to make your life easier. Chapter 2 provides the details on starting 1-2-3, putting it aside temporarily when you need to do something else, and exiting gracefully when you've had enough. In Chapter 3, discover the tricks of the trade when it comes to using menus, dialog boxes, and the InfoBox.

Chapter 1

So You Want to Use 1-2-3?

. . . .

. . . .

This chapter doesn't have any hands-on training stuff. In other words, it contains nothing to help you solve an immediate problem. If you're really in a hurry to get started, or if you have little tolerance for background information and historical drivel, you can safely flip ahead to Chapter 2. But if you want a good foundation for the rest of the book, you can get it right here — and you may even find what you read rather interesting.

This chapter alone gives you more information about 1-2-3 and Lotus than about 99.99 percent of the people on this planet know. That (well, and about two bucks) gets you a cup of cappuccino at your local Starbucks coffee shop. What's more, this chapter paves the way for everything that follows and gives you a feel for how spreadsheets fit into the overall scheme of the universe.

Okay, So What Is 1-2-3?

Glad you asked. *1-2-3* is a software package that functions as an electronic spreadsheet. Think of a large sheet of accountant's paper with gridlines drawn on it. Then try to envision an electronic version of this page that you can see on your computer monitor. The electronic version is huge — so big that you can see only a tiny portion on your screen at one time. But you can use the keyboard or mouse to move around in this worksheet so that you can see it all (but not all at one time). Actually, a 1-2-3 file is more like a *pad* of accountant's paper, because you can store as many as 256 pages of spreadsheets in a single file.

In place of the gridlines, the electronic spreadsheet called 1-2-3 contains rows and columns. The place where each row and column intersect is called a *cell.* You can enter numbers and words into the cells, copy and move cells around, and print the results for the world to see. At quitting time, you can save all this good stuff in a file on your hard disk and work on it later.

If you're not convinced that an electronic spreadsheet such as 1-2-3 is really better than a paper-based spreadsheet, consider the accountant who keeps tabs on all his company's accounts receivable. If Joe Accountant stores these records in 1-2-3, here's what he can do with the information:

- Easily change it if necessary (no eraser or correction fluid required).

- Sort and re-sort it any which way — by dollar amount, company name, number of days overdue, and so on.

- Use it for other purposes, such as sending the names and addresses off to a word processor to use in a mass mailing.

- Print it out with such quality that it rivals an expensive annual report.

TECHNICAL STUFF

Just how big is a worksheet?

Imagine, for a moment, that you entered a number into every cell in a 1-2-3 worksheet. We're talking 256 columns and 65,536 rows — which works out to be exactly 16,777,216.00 cells. Filling every cell is actually impossible, because your computer doesn't have nearly enough memory to hold all this information. But bear with me on this, okay?

If you entered the numbers manually into each cell, the task would take about 388 days (figuring a relatively rapid two seconds per cell, with no coffee breaks or time-outs for sleep). Hopefully, you save your work often while entering this amount of data, because having to repeat five or six months of data entry due to a power failure would be a real shame.

You don't want to lose all this work, so you'd better make a backup copy of this file. Before you start, however, make sure that you have about several thousand blank floppy disks on hand. (*Tip:* Use high-density floppies.)

Using the default column width and row height, 1-2-3 can print 50 rows and eight columns (or 400 cells) on a sheet of 8.5 x 11 paper. Therefore, printing the entire worksheet requires 41,934 sheets of paper. If you use cheap photocopier paper, this stack of pages is about seven feet tall.

Using a 4-page-per-minute laser printer, printing the whole document takes about a week (not including time spent changing paper and replacing toner cartridges).

If this worksheet contains formulas, you must take recalculation time into account. I have no way of estimating how long recalculating the formulas in such a worksheet would take. But taking that long-awaited weekend getaway after pressing the F9 key isn't a bad idea.

By the way, I used 1-2-3 to perform the calculations in this sidebar — proving that you can use 1-2-3 for completely meaningless projects, as well as, for actual, constructive work. And don't forget — these calculations apply to a single worksheet. 1-2-3 can actually have as many as 256 worksheets in a file!

But the real fun starts when you begin to enter formulas into cells. *Formulas* perform calculations on other cells. For example, you can enter a formula that displays the average of the numbers in a column, in effect saying *Add up all the numbers in this column and then divide by the number of values in the column.* But the neatest thing of all is that the formulas recalculate their results if you change the numbers in any of the cells they use. You may not appreciate this feature now, but you will later on (trust me).

But wait, there's more (he says in a late-night-infomercial tone of voice). 1-2-3 also enables you to apply slick formatting to the cells to make your worksheets and charts look as if they were created by a graphic artist. 1-2-3 offers many other features to ease your work — the most useful of which I tell you about throughout this book.

But Is 1-2-3 Any Good?

Software stores stock several spreadsheet products, so you may be curious as to how 1-2-3 stacks up against the competition (or then again, you may not care at all). Today, most software is developed for Microsoft Windows, and three popular Windows spreadsheets are available: Lotus 1-2-3, Microsoft Excel, and Corel Quattro Pro.

Although 1-2-3 isn't the best-selling spreadsheet (Excel currently holds that distinction), it's definitely no slouch. In fact, the new features in 1-2-3 Millennium Edition make the program better than ever. In any case, you can rest assured that you (or whoever was responsible) made a good purchase decision, and you're using an excellent product.

What Can This Puppy Do?

People use 1-2-3 for many things. The following sections provide a brief sampling of what you have to look forward to.

Crunch some numbers

People buy spreadsheet programs mainly to manipulate and calculate numbers. For example, if you need to create a budget (probably the most common use for spreadsheets), you enter your budget category names and values for each month into cells. Then you stick in some formulas to add up the total for each month, as well as the annual total for each category — see Figure 1-1 to get an idea of what I'm talking about. Finally, you fiddle around with the numbers until the formulas come up with the results your boss wants. It's all pretty easy, after you get the hang of it.

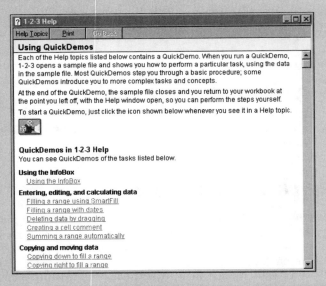

A	A B	C	D	E	F	G	H	I	J	K
		1998 Operating Budget								
1			Jan	Feb	Mar	Apr	May	Jun	Jul	A
2										
3	**Total Administration**		30,365	30,365	30,365	91,095	31,665	30,365	30,365	92,3
4		Salaries	13500	13500	13500	40,500	13,500	13,500	13,500	40,5
5		Benefits	2835	2835	2835	8,505	2,835	2,835	2,835	8,5
6	**Total Personnel**		16,335	16,335	16,335	49,005	16,335	16,335	16,335	49,0
7		Office	300	300	300	900	300	300	300	9
8		Computer	90	90	90	270	90	90	90	2
9	**Total Supplies**		390	390	390	1,170	390	390	390	1,1
10		Transportation	4000	4000	4000	12,000	4,000	4,000	4,000	12,0
11		Hotel	2200	2200	2200	6,600	2,200	2,200	2,200	6,6
12		Meals	1100	1100	1100	3,300	1,100	1,100	1,100	3,3
13	**Total Travel**		7,300	7,300	7,300	21,900	7,300	7,300	7,300	21,9
14		Computers	1600	1600	1600	4,800	2,400	1,600	1,600	5,6
15		Copiers	2000	2000	2000	6,000	2,500	2,000	2,000	6,5
16		Other	1500	1500	1500	4,500	1,500	1,500	1,500	4,5
17	**Total Equipment**		5,100	5,100	5,100	15,300	6,400	5,100	5,100	16,6
18		Lease	0	0	0	0	0	0	0	

E:\lotus\123\98budget.123

Admin \ Finance \ Operations \

Figure 1-1:
1-2-3 hard
at work
crunching
numbers.

TIP

Quick demo anyone?

While you're discovering 1-2-3, keep in mind that the program offers a number of demos that you may find helpful. To access these demos, choose Help⇨QuickDemos from the menu. You get a new window that lists the demos that you can view (see the accompanying figure). These demos aren't interactive, so you can just sit back and watch the show. To stop a demo and get back to work, just press Escape.

1-2-3 Help

Help Topics   Print   Go Back

Using QuickDemos

Each of the Help topics listed below contains a QuickDemo. When you run a QuickDemo, 1-2-3 opens a sample file and shows you how to perform a particular task, using the data in the sample file. Most QuickDemos step you through a basic procedure; some QuickDemos introduce you to more complex tasks and concepts.

At the end of the QuickDemo, the sample file closes and you return to your workbook at the point you left off, with the Help window open, so you can perform the steps yourself.

To start a QuickDemo, just click the icon shown below whenever you see it in a Help topic.

QuickDemos in 1-2-3 Help
You can see QuickDemos of the tasks listed below.

Using the InfoBox
Using the InfoBox

Entering, editing, and calculating data
Filling a range using SmartFill
Filling a range with dates
Deleting data by dragging
Creating a cell comment
Summing a range automatically

Copying and moving data
Copying down to fill a range
Copying right to fill a range

1-2-3 offers hundreds of special built-in functions (called @*functions* and pronounced *at-funk-shuns*) that can do some outrageous calculations for you, and you don't even have to know what's going on behind the scenes. For example, most people faced with calculating the monthly payment for a car loan have no idea where to start. But 1-2-3 includes an @function that turns this process into child's play (parental guidance not required). 1-2-3 does the calculation work, giving you more time to go car shopping.

Here are a just a few examples of the types of worksheets you can develop in 1-2-3:

- ✔ **Budgets:** Develop simple household budgets, corporate department budgets, budgets for a complete company, or even a budget for an entire country (maybe I should call the president).

- ✔ **Financial projections:** Figure out how much money you're going to make or lose this year, using formulas that rely on various assumptions that you (or your boss) make. The slick Version Manager feature can turn this task into child's play — well, maybe adolescent's play.

- ✔ **Sales tracking:** Keep track of which salespeople are selling the most (and how much commission they receive) and which ones are falling down on the job (and when they should get their pink slips).

- ✔ **Loan amortization:** How much of that mortgage payment goes to interest (a great deal), and how much to principal (not much)? A spreadsheet can tell you the answer for every month of the loan's term.

- ✔ **Scientific information:** 1-2-3 offers dozens of very specialized built-in functions that only white-coated laboratory inhabitants understand.

- ✔ **Statistical stuff:** 1-2-3 provides many built-in functions for people who think in terms of standard deviations.

These examples just scratch the analytical surface. If you have a problem that involves numbers, chances are that 1-2-3 is the ideal tool to use — especially if you can't find a baseball bat.

Create killer charts

1-2-3 can take the numbers you put in a spreadsheet and transform them into a magnificent chart in just about any style you can imagine. And you won't believe how easy creating a chart is.

Here's what's great about charts: If the numbers in your spreadsheet change, 1-2-3 automatically updates the charts. And the best part is that you can literally waste hours of your company's time playing around with the charts to make them look just right. Even if your numbers aren't worth diddly-squat, you can still impress your boss (or your cat, depending on your proficiency level) with the quality of the chart. And that's what life is all about, right?

Figure 1-2 shows a modest example of a 1-2-3 chart.

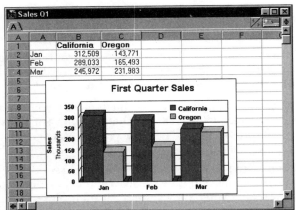

Figure 1-2:
1-2-3 enables you to transform dull numbers into more interesting charts.

Map your data geographically

If you deal with numbers that have a basis in geography — for example, if you track your company's sales by state or country — you'll get a charge out of the slick mapping feature provided by 1-2-3. Believe it or not, 1-2-3 can create an attractive map from a list of numbers with only a few mouse clicks from you. Rand McNally, look out!

Organize your lists

If numbers aren't your bag, you can also do some cool things with text. 1-2-3 has ready-made rows and columns, and you can make the columns as wide as you want — so the program is a natural choice for keeping track of items or lists (even better than a mere word processor).

Here are some popular lists that you can store in a 1-2-3 worksheet:

- ✔ Things to do today
- ✔ Things to avoid doing today
- ✔ Any of David Letterman's top-ten lists

> ✔ Logical flaws in *Gilligan's Island* (you may want to use a separate worksheet for each episode — otherwise, you'll quickly run out of room)

Lists can consist only of words (as in the preceding example) or of a combination of words and numbers. If you use numbers in your lists, you can even make formulas to add the numbers up or do other calculations. Here are some more lists that use numbers:

> ✔ Bills you can get by with not paying this month
>
> ✔ Itemized costs for fixing your wrecked car
>
> ✔ The amount of time the person in the next office spends goofing off each day

Take a look at Figure 1-3 for an example of a simple list.

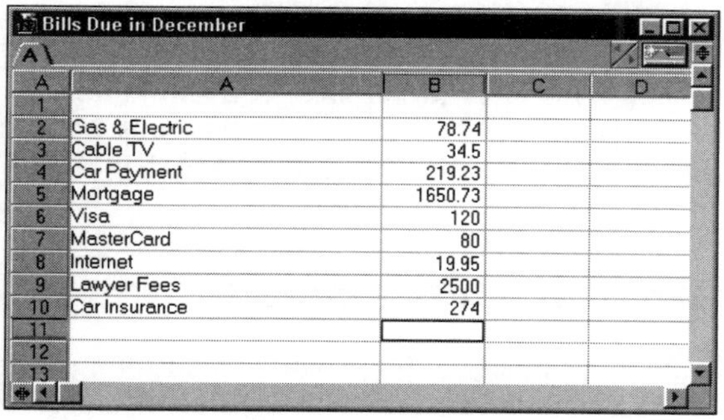

Figure 1-3: 1-2-3 is great for keeping track of lists.

	A	B	C	D
1				
2	Gas & Electric	78.74		
3	Cable TV	34.5		
4	Car Payment	219.23		
5	Mortgage	1650.73		
6	Visa	120		
7	MasterCard	80		
8	Internet	19.95		
9	Lawyer Fees	2500		
10	Car Insurance	274		
11				
12				
13				

Bills Due in December

Manage that data (zzzz . . .)

If the term *database management* conjures up images of boring, obsessively neat people whose socks always match their pocket protectors, you're right on track. Actually, a database is nothing more than an *organized* list. If you have gaggles of friends, you can keep track of them in a database, storing their names, addresses, phone numbers, and amount of money they owe you. By the way, you can easily transfer such information to your word processor and print out labels for your holiday cards.

Truth is, 1-2-3 is pretty good at helping you work with databases. You can sort the data, search for something in particular, display items that meet certain criteria, and do many other things. And you don't need to spend four years getting a Ph.D. in computer science.

Access other data

If you have to deal with a huge database — such as your corporate accounting system — that lives on a different computer, you can't load the whole shebang into 1-2-3 because you'll run out of memory. Fortunately (or perhaps unfortunately), you can still access such *external* databases from 1-2-3.

You can also transfer information across different programs using the Windows *Clipboard* (an area of memory that holds things that you cut or copy so you can paste them somewhere else). For example, if you want to put a table of numbers you've created in 1-2-3 into a report that you're writing, you can copy the table and paste it right into your word processor document. And you can even set things up so that, if the numbers change, the changes get transferred to your word processor document automatically. Technology is grand indeed, eh?

Do Internet stuff

1-2-3 is specially designed for Internet junkies. You can jump to the Internet without leaving the program, and you can even save your work in HTML (hypertext markup language) format — the language of the World Wide Web.

Automate actions with scripts

For hard-core spreadsheet junkies, 1-2-3 provides something called LotusScript. A *script* consists of a series of instructions that tell 1-2-3 what to do — kind of like a computer program (in fact, it *is* a computer program). Scripts can help you automate actions and take the drudgery out of repetitive spreadsheet tasks. You create scripts in one of two ways: Write them (difficult to do) or record them (easy to do).

Even novices can *record* scripts (using a process similar to a tape recorder). And you may need to *execute* a script that Melvin, the office computer nerd, wrote. Those with inquiring minds (and the nerd in all of us) can discover how to record and execute simple scripts within the very pages of this book.

Versions of 1-2-3 prior to 1-2-3 97 offered an automation feature called *macros.* Scripts you create using LotusScript are much more powerful and versatile. But don't worry if you're a 1-2-3 veteran; 1-2-3 can still execute macros developed with older versions of the product.

And into the great beyond . . .

1-2-3 can do other things that I can't even think of right now. It's a very versatile piece of software, and if you stick with it long enough, I guarantee that you can figure out some use that no one else has thought of. If you do, let me know, so I can borrow your idea and use it in the next edition of this book.

What Can't 1-2-3 Do?

Although 1-2-3 is sort of like a Swiss Army Knife, it's probably not the only software program you'll ever need. For example, 1-2-3 can work with small amounts of text and manipulate labels, but it's certainly no substitute for a real word-processing program. It offers some great chart features, but if you're really into creating cool computer graphics and images, many other products are available that excel in that area. And although you can do some simple project management, better project management packages are available. In other words, 1-2-3 is great, but owning it doesn't mean that you can lasso the moon.

Excursions into Versions

The latest version of 1-2-3 is labeled 1-2-3 Millennium Edition. To find out which release you have, just pay attention to the *splash screen* — the first screen you see when you start 1-2-3. Or you can choose Help⇨About 1-2-3 from the 1-2-3 menu bar.

If you're historically minded, you may enjoy a quick rundown of some of the more popular releases of 1-2-3 and how they differ. But this section isn't merely a history lesson. If you share your 1-2-3 files with other users, knowing which version they use is very important, because older versions can't always read the files produced by newer versions.

✔ **1-2-3 Release 1A:** The original release surfaced in 1983 and pretty much made Lotus what it is today. People bought PCs just so they could run this program. This product was designed for DOS, because it came out long before anyone even thought of Windows.

✔ **1-2-3 Release 2.***x:* The follow-up to Release 1A, Release 2 (for DOS) first appeared in 1984. This release had several new features, including the capability to use add-in programs to extend the power of the basic spreadsheet. Release 2 had several subreleases, and the last release was Release 2.4.

✔ **1-2-3 Release 3.***x:* Even more powerful than Release 2, this DOS release featured 3-D files, file linking, improved database access, and several other things.

✔ **1-2-3 Release 1.***x* **for Windows:** This version was the first Windows spreadsheet from Lotus. Many people, including myself, were rather disappointed because it left quite a bit to be desired when compared to other Windows spreadsheets. Still, many people bought this release.

✔ **1-2-3 Release 4.0 for Windows:** This one came out in June 1993. It has almost nothing in common with the preceding Windows version. By the way, Lotus skipped Release 2 and 3 for Windows, and went directly to Release 4 — probably to avoid confusion with the non-Windows versions (which are labeled Release 2 and 3).

✔ **1-2-3 Release 5.0 for Windows:** This version hit the streets in August 1994. It's very similar to Release 4, but has many new features tacked on.

✔ **1-2-3 97:** This release was the first 32-bit version of 1-2-3, and it requires a 32-bit operating system (Windows 95 or later, including Windows NT). Lotus did another major overhaul with this release, and the user interface differs significantly from the previous versions.

✔ **1-2-3 Millennium Edition:** The latest and greatest. This version closely resembles 1-2-3 97, but it includes several new features (which you can read all about in this book).

In addition to the versions that I list here, Lotus makes a ton of other versions of 1-2-3 for different computers, including Macintosh and several weird computers you probably haven't heard of. A whole slew of people have gotten rich consulting and training people to use 1-2-3, developing programs that work with 1-2-3, creating worksheet templates, publishing magazines, and even writing books about 1-2-3 (present author excepted).

So what's the deal with all these versions, and does it matter? The answer is that Lotus is an amazing success story, and the original release of 1-2-3 played a major role in the popularity of personal computers in the office. 1-2-3 Millennium Edition is the latest in a long line of great products, and you're doing yourself a favor — and maybe even making a significant career move — by understanding it. Are you beaming with pride?

Why the weird name?

Very few products have names that consist only of numbers (a bunch of car names are the only ones that come to mind). What were the folks at Lotus thinking when they came up with the name 1-2-3? Well, back in the old days of computing, software was typically very limited, and most programs did only one thing. But the people at Lotus who were developing a new spreadsheet wanted to give it powers far beyond those of existing spreadsheets. (Actually, their only real competitor at the time was VisiCalc, which was a rudimentary, yet very popular, spreadsheet.)

The Lotus people designed a product that offered

✔ Spreadsheet capabilities

✔ Graphing powers

✔ Database features

Because Spreadsheet-Graphing-Database is a bit unwieldy for a product name, they settled on 1-2-3 instead. A side benefit of choosing this name was that marketing types could say things like "It's as easy as 1-2-3" (even though it wasn't).

What's New in 1-2-3 Millennium Edition

If you're moving up from the previous version of 1-2-3, you may be interested in a quick overview of what's new and improved. Here's a list of some of the highlights:

✔ **More rows:** Previous versions of 1-2-3 were limited to 8,192 rows. Now, a worksheet has a whopping 65,536 rows.

✔ **Year 2000 support:** A new "sliding window" feature makes entering dates using 2-digit years easier — and ensures that the date falls into the proper century.

✔ **Ask the Expert:** If you ever get stumped (or should I say *when* you get stumped?), you can ask 1-2-3 for an answer. You can type your question in plain English (see Figure 1-4), and the Expert displays a number of help topics. In all likelihood, one of them has the answer you need.

✔ **New @functions:** 1-2-3 includes a slew of new functions that you can use in your formulas. In particular, engineers, financial wizards, and statisticians will be thankful.

✔ **Internet support:** For those of you who work in a wired office, 1-2-3 includes several new Internet features: improved HTML support, hyperlinks, and the capability to view a table from a Web page directly in your spreadsheet.

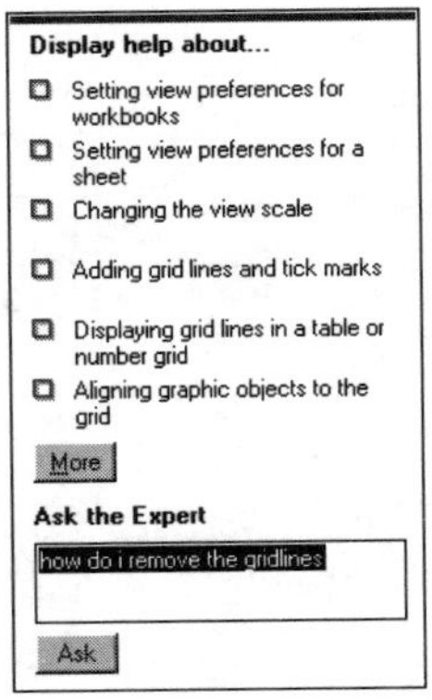

Display help about...

- ☐ Setting view preferences for workbooks
- ☐ Setting view preferences for a sheet
- ☐ Changing the view scale
- ☐ Adding grid lines and tick marks
- ☐ Displaying grid lines in a table or number grid
- ☐ Aligning graphic objects to the grid

More

Ask the Expert

how do i remove the gridlines

Ask

Figure 1-4:
Got a
question?
1-2-3
probably
has an
answer
for you.

✔ **Move or copy a worksheet:** Believe it or not, the previous version of 1-2-3 lacked this basic feature (the designers must have been napping). Fortunately, this omission has been fixed.

✔ **Copy column widths or row heights:** An exclusive! 1-2-3 is the only spreadsheet that enables you to do this.

✔ **SmartLabels:** Perform calculations without using formulas. Just enter a label such as SUM or AVERAGE, and 1-2-3 does the grunt work for you.

✔ **Improved graphic support:** 1-2-3 now enables you to import GIF and JPG graphic images — which are the most commonly used graphic file formats nowadays.

✔ **Better Excel file support:** If your colleagues use Microsoft Excel, you'll be pleased to know that 1-2-3 can read files produced by any version of Excel up to and including Excel 97.

Chapter 2
Jumping Right In (And Out)

• •

In This Chapter

▶ Making sure that you have 1-2-3 on your computer

▶ Starting 1-2-3

▶ Leaving 1-2-3 temporarily so you can do something else

▶ Quitting 1-2-3 — the right way and the wrong way

• •

*A*s with any software, you have to install 1-2-3 on your computer before you can use it. When you install software, you're simply copying files from floppy disks or CD-ROM to your hard disk in such a way that everything works when you start up the program. Back in the old days, you could run software directly from floppy disks. But those days are pretty much over, and virtually every program you get now must be installed on your hard disk.

Note: 1-2-3 has an installation option that enables you to run the software directly from the CD-ROM. This option is much slower, and you only want to use it if you don't have enough hard disk space to install the software.

After you install 1-2-3 on your computer, you can run the program, do all sorts of interesting things with it, and then exit the program after you finish. *Exiting a program* means to stop it from running. However, you don't have to exit a program in order to work on something else. While a program is running, you can put it aside temporarily and do other things (such as run other programs, jump to another program that's already running, delete files, throw in a load of laundry, and so on). I explain how to do all this stuff right here in Chapter 2.

Starting 1-2-3

Merely installing 1-2-3 on your computer won't make your life any easier. To benefit from 1-2-3, you need to run the program — otherwise, it just eats up space on your hard disk, and you've wasted several hundred of your company's dollars (or even worse, your own). In the following sections, I describe four easy ways to start 1-2-3.

Starting 1-2-3 from the Start button

Using the Windows Start button is one way of starting 1-2-3. Here's how:

1. **Click the Start button.**

   Most likely, this button lives in the lower-left corner of your screen, but it can be in the upper-left or upper-right corner. The Start button turns into a *menu* (a list of items), as shown in Figure 2-1.

2. **Click the item labeled Programs.**

   Yet another menu appears.

   Depending on how you installed 1-2-3, the Windows taskbar may display a tiny 1-2-3 icon. If so, click that icon to start 1-2-3, and skip the following steps.

3. **Locate the item labeled Lotus SmartSuite and click it.**

   You guessed it — yet another menu.

4. **Click Lotus 1-2-3.**

   1-2-3 starts.

Figure 2-1:
Starting
1-2-3 using
the Start
button.
(Your menu
items may
vary.)

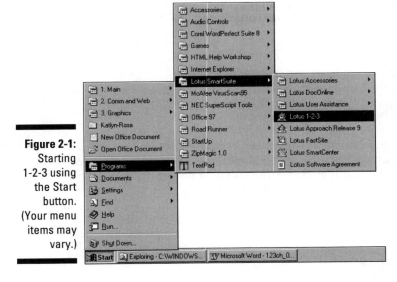

Starting 1-2-3 from the SmartCenter menu

Chances are, you acquired 1-2-3 as part of the Lotus SmartSuite — a collection of software that includes several other programs in addition to 1-2-3. If you have the full SmartSuite installed, Lotus SmartCenter is likely to start up automatically when you start Windows. If so, you can take advantage of another way to start 1-2-3:

1. **Click the bar labeled SmartSuite.**

   This bar is probably at the top of your screen, although it can also be at the bottom. Clicking the bar displays a menu.

2. **Click the icon labeled Lotus 1-2-3 (see Figure 2-2).**

   If you can't find that icon, click the colored tab labeled SmartSuite. 1-2-3 kicks into action.

Starting 1-2-3 from the taskbar

Depending on how your system is set up, you may have a 1-2-3 icon sitting right on your Windows taskbar (which is probably at the bottom of your screen). If such an icon exists, just click it to launch 1-2-3.

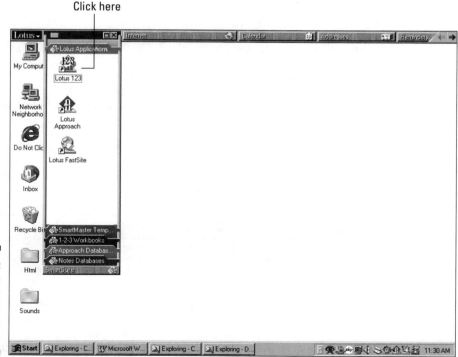

Figure 2-2:
Starting
1-2-3 from
the
SmartSuite
taskbar.

Starting 1-2-3 by double-clicking a workbook

You can start 1-2-3 by simply double-clicking a 1-2-3 workbook file. You can do this in a My Computer window or an Explorer window. 1-2-3 workbooks have a 123 extension.

The Screen Tour (It's the Law)

Federal Statute CB324.21.190 states that every computer book published in the United States must include a tour of the screen within its first 50 pages. I developed Figure 2-3 to satisfy this legal requirement. When you start 1-2-3 without opening an existing workbook, the screen shows a blank sheet just waiting to be used, abused, or misused.

Your screen may look different from Figure 2-3, depending on which type of display driver you've installed for Windows. The screen in Figure 2-3 is in 800 x 600 mode. You may have a display driver installed that has a different resolution. The other two common display resolutions are 640 x 480 and 1024 x 768. If you have an option, you're usually better off going with a higher resolution, because you can see more stuff on the screen. But make sure that your monitor can display high resolutions and that the text isn't too small for you to read.

If your screen doesn't look anything like Figure 2-3 (and you're sure that you're actually using 1-2-3), you probably have an older version of 1-2-3. The bad news: You're gonna have to upgrade to the latest version if you want to get anything out of this book (the upgrade cost is pretty inexpensive). The good news: The most recent version of 1-2-3 is light-years better (and much easier to use) than any previous version.

Like the human body, a spreadsheet is made up of various parts, some of which are definitely more interesting than others. Table 2-1 lists the parts of 1-2-3 that you eventually need to know. I discuss body parts (of 1-2-3, I mean) in more detail throughout the book.

Table 2-1	The More Popular 1-2-3 Body Parts
Screen Part	*Why It Exists*
Workbook window	Designed to hold your work in its many cells; each workbook has its own window
Title bar	Displays the name of the program you're running, as well as some messages from 1-2-3; for example, after you click a menu item or right-click a SmartIcon, the title bar displays a brief description of the function

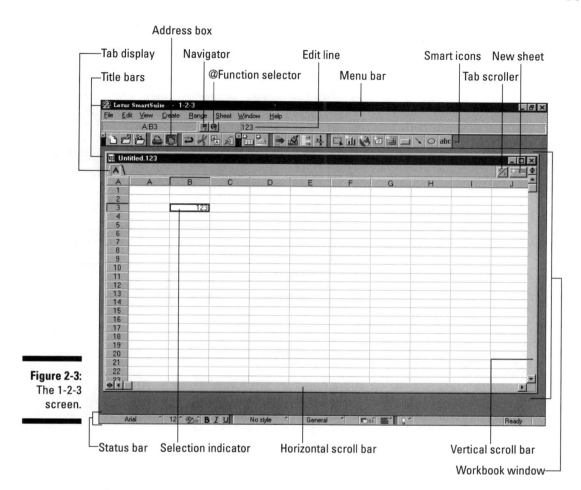

Figure 2-3:
The 1-2-3
screen.

Table 2-1 *(continued)*

Screen Part	Why It Exists
Address box	Shows the address of the active cell and also displays the contents of the current cell
Selection indicator	Displays the cell address of the active cell or the range selected
Navigator	Helps you move to specific cells (those with a name) or insert range names into a formula
@Function selector	Makes inserting an @Function into a formula easy
Edit line	Displays the contents of the active cell

(continued)

Table 2-1 *(continued)*

Screen Part	Why It Exists
Status bar	Tells you about the current selection and enables you to change the number format, type size, and other things
Menu bar	Displays the commands that you can choose to get 1-2-3 to work for you
SmartIcons	Little pictures that, when clicked, perform commands
Vertical scroll bar	Moves you up or down in a sheet when you click or drag here
Horizontal scroll bar	Moves you left or right in a sheet when you click or drag here
Tab display	Provides quick access to the additional sheets in your file (if you have any)
New sheet	Adds an additional sheet to your file
Tab scroller	Displays tabs not currently visible

Switching out of 1-2-3

When you start 1-2-3, any other programs that you may already have open continue to run. You can switch among the programs whenever you want to, and even display multiple programs on-screen at one time, as demonstrated in Figure 2-4.

Some useless terminology

What do you call the thing that you're working in 1-2-3? Well, the official name is a *workbook,* and a workbook is made up of at least one sheet (but no more than 256 sheets). Some people call a workbook a *file,* and others may call it a *document.* You may hear a sheet referred to as a worksheet. Some people call a sheet a spreadsheet, and others call a workbook a spreadsheet.

What's the bottom line? Don't worry about terminology. The important thing is to get your work done, so you can move on to other things. To keep things simple, I stick with the official terminology and call a 1-2-3 file a workbook. And I refer to individual sheets as sheets. Fair enough?

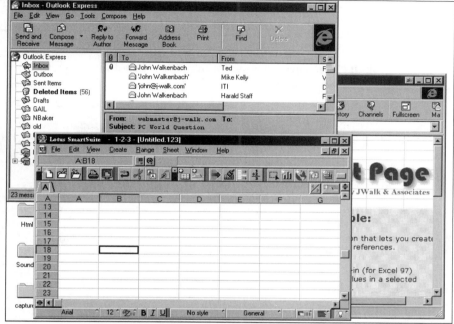

Figure 2-4:
One of the
benefits
to using
Windows is
that you
can run and
display
several
programs
at once.

Why would you want to run more than one program at a time? Most busy people tend to work on more than one project at once. Here are just a couple of examples:

✔ You're plugging away in your word processor (working on your resume) when your boss barges in and asks to see the latest sales figures. You don't have to exit your word-processing program before you fire up 1-2-3 to check the sales results (although you may want to minimize the window that contains your resume, so the boss doesn't see it).

✔ You've been working all day on a spreadsheet that's sure to revolution- ize the way your company calculates sales commissions. You're burned out and need a break. Click the Start menu and locate your favorite game. You can leave 1-2-3 running so that you can return to it after you finish playing your game.

Get into the habit of saving the file that you're currently working on before you jump to another program. You never know when another program may misbehave and cause your entire system to crash.

Use the following steps to activate other programs while you're using 1-2-3:

1. **Examine the Windows taskbar (probably at the bottom of your screen).**

2. **If the program you want to open is listed on the taskbar, click the icon to activate it — skip Step 3.**

   If the program you want isn't running, it won't be listed in the taskbar.

3. **To run the program, click the Start button, locate the program, and double-click it.**

   You may have to go through a few menus to find the right program.

4. **To return to 1-2-3, click its button on the taskbar.**

To switch to another running program without using your mouse, hold down the Alt key and then press Tab repeatedly until you see the icon for the program that you want to switch to (see Figure 2-5). After you find the right icon, release the Alt key to activate the application.

Figure 2-5:
To switch
quickly
between
running
applications,
press
Alt+Tab.

1-2-3 - [Untitled.123]

While 1-2-3 is running, you can use other programs without exiting your spreadsheet. Use the taskbar if the program is running. Use the Start button if the program isn't running.

Quitting 1-2-3

After starting 1-2-3, you can select an existing workbook to load or you can work on a blank workbook. The rest of this book shows you all the wonderful things you can do with worksheets, but you need to know one more thing first: the right and wrong way to quit 1-2-3.

The right way to quit

The safest (not to mention most civilized) way to quit 1-2-3 is to follow these steps:

1. **Choose File⇨Exit 1-2-3.**

   As I explain in this book's introduction, you perform the preceding command by clicking the word File on your menu. Figure 2-6 shows the pull-down menu that appears. From this menu, click Exit 1-2-3 to get out of 1-2-3.

2. **If you saved your work, 1-2-3 closes shop and sends you back to where you were before you started 1-2-3.**

   If you didn't save your work, 1-2-3 prompts you to save it first. Unless the stuff you've been working on is totally bogus or just for practice, you probably want to save it. I discuss all the ins and outs of saving your work in Chapter 8.

For a shortcut that saves you two to four seconds (depending on how fast you can type), get into the habit of pressing Alt+F4 to exit 1-2-3. In fact, the Alt+F4 shortcut works in just about all Windows programs.

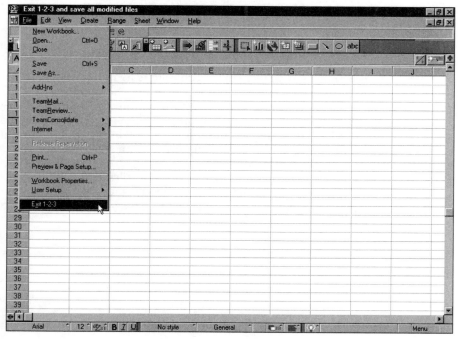

Figure 2-6:
Choose
File⇨Exit
1-2-3 to
quit 1-2-3.

Knowing when to quit

Many people like to keep 1-2-3 running all day long so that, when they need to use it, the program's only a mouse click away. Nothing is wrong with that method. However, if you tend to have many programs running at the same time, you may notice that things slow down. For example, switching to another program may take several seconds. Or operations that normally occur instantaneously suddenly happen in slow motion while your hard disk churns away. Sluggish system response is a good sign that you have too many programs running.

The number of programs that you can run at one time without experiencing sluggishness depends on two factors: the size of the program and how much memory your system has. If your system doesn't have much memory,

Windows makes up for it by using your hard disk — which is much slower than memory.

Because your computer, software, and tolerance for waiting are uniquely your own, you must decide for yourself when it's time to close some of your programs running in the background.

In addition, Windows tends to have a problem with what's known as system resources. Some programs eat up system resources and never return them. The only way to regain lost resources is to restart Windows. Therefore, restarting Windows periodically is a good idea — especially if you notice strange things happening.

The wrong way

One of the worst ways to exit a program is to simply turn off the computer. Even if you saved your work first, never use the power-switch method to exit 1-2-3. Why? Windows uses many other files that you don't even know about. If any of these files is not properly closed, you can potentially mess up your hard disk and scramble some information. Or you may end up with dozens of temporary files that merely take up space and do you no good.

So exit gracefully, as they say, by choosing File⇨Exit 1-2-3. Then you can turn off your computer and do what you normally do after you turn off your computer — head for the local pub, rehearse your couch-potato act in front of the TV, or get some Zs.

Chapter 3

Your Wish Is 1-2-3's Command

*T*o do useful things with 1-2-3, you have to issue commands — that is, give orders that tell 1-2-3 what to do. Of course, before you can get 1-2-3 to stand at attention, you have to know how to speak its language. The following features offer valid ways to give 1-2-3 your orders (ten-hut!):

✔ The menu system

✔ Dialog boxes that some commands display

✔ The floating InfoBox

✔ The seemingly endless supply of SmartIcons

✔ Buttons in the status bar

✔ Shortcut key combinations

✔ Function keys

✔ Formulas

✔ Scripts

In this chapter, I focus on menus, dialog boxes, and the InfoBox. I cover SmartIcons, status bar buttons, shortcut keys, and function keys in Chapter 15. Working with formulas is the topic of Chapter 5, and I briefly cover scripts in Chapter 18.

You can apply the same skills you use with the 1-2-3 menus and dialog boxes to other Windows programs; all these programs work in much the same way.

The 1-2-3 Classic menu

First came classic cars, then Coke Classic, and now you have the 1-2-3 Classic menu! This menu is for people who have mastered an old DOS version of 1-2-3 and are moving up to the vastly improved Windows version. The Classic menu, shown in the accompanying figure, appears after you press the slash key (/) in Ready mode.

If you're moving up from an older version of 1-2-3, you may find the Classic menu useful if you can't remember the actual 1-2-3 command. Use it if you must, but I strongly urge you not to get too dependent on it.

My advice: Forget that this menu exists. Compared to the normal 1-2-3 menu, the Classic menu is illogical, confusing, difficult to use, and it can't even deal with a mouse. I discuss the Classic menu here, so if you accidentally hit the slash key and see the menu, you at least know what it is. You can easily get rid of this menu by pressing Esc.

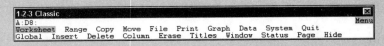

Perusing the Main Menu

When you're running 1-2-3, the main menu bar is always available at the top of the screen. The menu bar consists of a series of menu items, shown in Figure 3-1. When you click a menu item (such as File, Edit, and so on), the menu drops down a list of commands.

The menu items that are displayed at the top of your screen vary, depending on what type of information you have selected in your worksheet. For example, if you're working with a chart, the menu items differ from those that appear when you're doing normal spreadsheet work. Just remember that 1-2-3 always displays a menu system that's appropriate for what you're doing at the time.

Figure 3-1:
The main menu bar is located directly under 1-2-3's title bar.

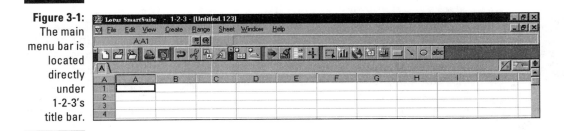

Using the main menu

Figure 3-2 shows the 1-2-3 main menu. If you've used other Windows programs, the 1-2-3 menu is probably no mystery to you. Here's how the menu works:

✔ As you move through the menu selections and their commands, 1-2-3 displays a brief description of the items in the title bar. This description helps you identify what the menu does.

✔ If you press F1 while working in a menu, 1-2-3 displays online help that tells you about the menu item or the command.

✔ When a command on a menu isn't appropriate for what you're doing, 1-2-3 *dims* the command (lightens the color). You can still see the command, but you can't select it.

✔ Menu commands that are followed by three dots (an *ellipsis*) display a dialog box after you select the command.

✔ Menu commands that have a shortcut key display the shortcut key combination on the pull-down menu. For example, the Cut command on the Edit menu displays Ctrl+X on the right side of the menu; therefore, pressing Ctrl+X accomplishes the same thing as choosing Edit⇨Cut.

✔ Some commands are followed by a small, right-pointing arrow. These commands, after being chosen, display yet another list of commands. This secondary command list is known as a *cascading menu,* but you can call it a *whatchamadoojie* and the effect is the same.

✔ The horizontal lines in the pull-down menus group the commands into logical groups; they have no great significance.

Mousing around

To access a menu item with your mouse, click that item. The menu drops down to display its commands. Then choose the command you need (see Figure 3-3). Things don't get much simpler than that.

Pecking the keyboard

If you prefer, you can also access the main menu by using the keyboard. The easiest way to choose a menu item is to use a key combination that combines the Alt key with the underlined letter in the menu item (called a *hotkey*).

For example, to access the View menu from the keyboard, press Alt+V (because the V in View is underlined, it's called the *hotkey*). The View commands drop down, just as if you clicked View with the mouse. Then you simply press another letter that corresponds to the underlined letter of the command that you want (no need to keep holding down the Alt key, but it doesn't hurt). Notice that the hotkey isn't always the *first* letter in the command.

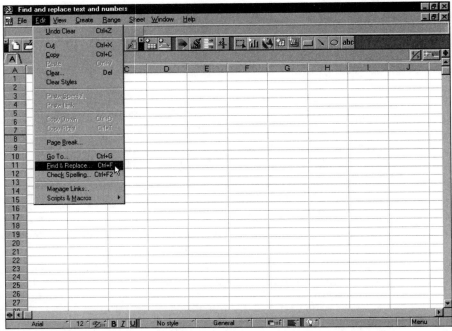

Figure 3-2:
A typical menu, pulled down to show its commands.

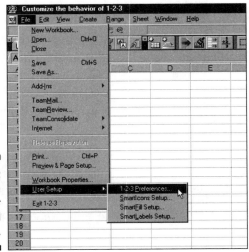

Figure 3-3:
Some menus offer additional choices.

Another way to access the menu with the keyboard is to press the Alt key by itself, which activates the menu bar but doesn't select a menu item. After you activate the menu bar, you can use the arrow keys to move among the menu items. After you get to the menu item you want, press Enter or the down arrow. You then can use the arrow keys to move to the command you want and press Enter to execute the command.

What menus are good for

The 1-2-3 menu system is very organized and complete. In fact, this system provides one of the best menus I've seen in *any* program (and I've seen many of them). Hopefully, you'll find the menus easy to work with. I discuss the specifics of the menus in other parts of this book. But if you want a general overview of what you can find under each menu item, check out Table 3-1.

Table 3-1	1-2-3 Menus
Menu	*What It's For*
File	Commands for working with files and printing
Edit	Commands for rearranging data in a sheet (copying, moving, inserting, deleting, and so on)
View	Commands that deal with how you look at (or view) your worksheet. These commands include zooming and splitting windows
Create	The place to go when you want to add something to a worksheet: a chart, a map, a drawing, and so on
Range*	Commands that enable you to work with ranges of cells — fill a range with data, sort a range, give meaningful names to a range, and do a great deal of advanced analytical stuff with the data in a range
Chart*	Commands for modifying a chart that you created (SmartIcons exist for many of these commands.)
Query*	Commands that enable you to manipulate the fields and records in a database and pick out the data that meets your criteria
Map*	Commands for customizing your maps
Sheet*	Commands for working with sheets in a workbook (delete them, hide them, unhide them, or create an outline from information on a sheet)
Web Table*	Commands for working with a table that you obtained from a Web page

(continued)

Table 3-1 *(continued)*	
Menu	*What It's For*
Window	Commands for arranging the windows neatly on-screen or jumping to a worksheet in another open file
Help	Commands for accessing 1-2-3's comprehensive online help system, finding out which version of the program you're using, and even starting an interactive tutorial lesson to help you discover more about specific topics

*These menus appear only in the correct context.

Other Types of Menus

Besides the main menu, 1-2-3 offers two other types of menus: shortcut menus and control menus.

Shortcut menus

Unlike the main menu, a shortcut menu (sometimes called a *quick menu*) isn't visible unless you select an item (such as a cell, a range, or a chart) and press the right mouse button. When you right-click a selected item, a shortcut menu pops up wherever the mouse pointer is, enabling you to conveniently choose a command from the list. The commands on the shortcut menu vary, depending on which item you select. A shortcut menu always contains the most common commands that you can execute with the selection you've made. (It's almost as if 1-2-3 can read your mind — but it can't, so don't worry.)

Figure 3-4 shows a shortcut menu that appears when you right-click after selecting a range of cells.

Control menus

As you work with Windows programs, you encounter yet another menu: the Control menu. Every Windows program (including 1-2-3) offers a Control menu that you use to control various aspects of the program. You access the Control menu by clicking the icon in the upper-left corner of an application's title bar.

The Control menu, shown in Figure 3-5, enables you to do such things as minimize the window (make it an icon), maximize the window (make it fill the screen), or close the application.

Figure 3-4:
A context-
sensitive
shortcut
menu
appears
when you
right-click
after
making a
selection.

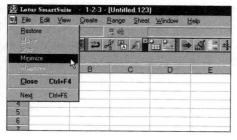

Figure 3-5:
The 1-2-3
Control
menu is like
the Control
menu found
in other
Windows
programs.

And to confuse things even more, the windows within an application usually provide their own Control menus. Because every 1-2-3 worksheet is actually a separate window, each workbook window has its own Control menu.

If you want to know more about this stuff (or more about the wonderful world of Microsoft Windows), pick up a copy of *Windows 95 For Dummies,* 2nd Edition, by Andy Rathbone (IDG Books Worldwide, Inc.).

A Meaningful Dialog

Menu commands tell 1-2-3 what you want to do. But dialog boxes go a step further and enable you to tell the program *exactly* what you want to do. All menu commands that end with three dots (officially known as an ellipsis) lead to a dialog box. A dialog box is, essentially, a convenient way for you to make your wishes known to the program.

To understand how a dialog box works, picture yourself in your favorite restaurant: After you arrive, you look at the menu and give your order to the waiter. The waiter looks down at you and asks you to choose between soup or salad, baked potatoes or french fries, and beer or wine. Using a dialog box is like responding to the waiter's questions. In other words, you use a dialog box to clarify your order to 1-2-3. And a benefit of using the dialog box is that you don't have to leave a tip for 1-2-3.

Because dialog boxes appear in almost every Windows application, you need to understand these animals as best as you can. Figure 3-6 shows a typical 1-2-3 dialog box, the one that appears after you choose Create⇨ Sheet.

Figure 3-6:
One of the
many 1-2-3
dialog
boxes.

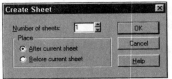

The anatomy of a dialog box

All dialog boxes in 1-2-3 have the following characteristics in common:

- ✔ **A title bar at the top:** The title bar tells you the name of the dialog box (which is usually the command that you selected to get there).

- ✔ **An OK button:** Click OK after you finish using the dialog box and you want 1-2-3 to carry out your orders. Sometimes — just to keep you on your toes — this button is labeled Done. You can usually just press Enter instead of clicking the OK button.

- ✔ **A Cancel button:** Click the Cancel button if you find yourself in a dialog box that you didn't want to get into. Even if you make changes in the dialog box, clicking the Cancel button eliminates all the changes, as if you never opened the dialog box in the first place. You can also press Escape to cancel a dialog box.

- ✔ **A Help button:** Click this button to find out how to use the dialog box.

- ✔ **An "X" button in the upper-right corner:** Clicking this button cancels the dialog box. This action is the same as clicking the Cancel button.

- ✔ **One or more controls:** Dialog box controls include such things as buttons, list boxes, and check boxes. You use the dialog box controls to indicate your choices.

Occasionally, a dialog box pops up and covers up what you want to see on-screen. You can move the dialog box by clicking and dragging its title bar.

Mousing through dialog boxes

Dialog boxes were invented with mouse users in mind, so it's not surprising that most people prefer to use the mouse for most of their dialog box action.

Generally, you click the control that you want in order to activate it. After you activate the control, you can make your selection — the exact technique varies with the specific control, but the controls do work pretty much as you expect them to work. In other words, the process is very intuitive.

To check or uncheck a check box, click that box. To select an option in an option button, click that button. To select an option from a drop-down list box, click the arrow and make your choice from the list by clicking. My best advice to you is to start clicking and see what happens. You'll get the hang of it in no time. But save any work you've started before you go clicking away, just in case your mouse goes rabid!

If you prefer the keyboard

Although most people like to use the mouse in a dialog box, other people find that the keyboard is actually faster, because they don't have to move their hands from the keyboard. The truth is, working with dialog boxes is more efficient after you get the hang of using the keyboard.

Table 3-2 lists some useful keys and key combinations that are active when you work with a dialog box from the keyboard.

Table 3-2	Keyboard Combinations to Use with Dialog Boxes
Key Combination	*What It Does*
Alt+*hotkey*	Selects the control of the hotkey (underlined letter) that you press
Tab	Moves forward and activates the next control
Shift+Tab	Moves backward and activates the preceding control
Spacebar	Checks or unchecks an option button or check box
Alt+↑ or Alt+↓	Opens and closes a drop-down list box
Arrow keys (↑, ↓, →, ←)	Moves within a group of controls (such as option buttons)

(continued)

Table 3-2 *(continued)*

Key Combination	What It Does
End	Selects the last item in a list box or drop-down list box
Home	Selects the first item in a list box or drop-down list box
PgUp or PgDn	Moves to the top or bottom item in the list of items currently visible in a drop-down list box or list box and selects the item
Enter	Completes the command and closes the dialog box (just like clicking the OK button)
Esc	Closes the dialog box without completing the command (just like clicking the Cancel button)

Introducing the InfoBox

The InfoBox is a special type of dialog box. InfoBoxes provide handy one-stop-shopping spots for practically anything you want to do with a particular object. Getting on friendly terms with the InfoBox is definitely in your best interest. Figure 3-7 shows the Range InfoBox.

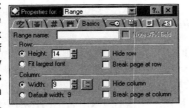

Figure 3-7: The Range InfoBox (just one of many InfoBoxes available in 1-2-3).

It changes!

The InfoBox is like a chameleon; it changes its looks frequently. In fact, the InfoBox changes itself automatically whenever you select something. If you select a range of cells, the InfoBox displays items for working with ranges. If you select a chart, the InfoBox displays items for chart work. If you select a map . . . well, you get the picture.

If the InfoBox is not visible, use one of the following methods to summon it:

✔ Press Alt+Enter.

✔ Click the Change xxxx Properties SmartIcon.

✔ Right-click and select xxxx Properties from the shortcut menu (the exact shortcut menu item depends on what's selected).

✔ Choose a menu command. The command you choose varies, depending on which item is currently selected. If you select a range, the command is Range⇨Range Properties. If you're working with a chart, the command is Chart⇨Chart Properties.

In some cases, you can change the InfoBox yourself by selecting an item from the drop-down list in the title bar of the InfoBox. Figure 3-8 shows how a drop-down list looks when you're working with a chart.

Figure 3-8:
When you're working with a chart, the drop-down list displays all the chart's parts.

To get rid of the InfoBox, click the X button in its title bar.

If you find that the InfoBox takes up too much of your screen real estate (but you don't want to get rid of it completely), you can roll it up kind of like a window shade. To reduce the size of the InfoBox, just double-click its title bar. Doing so makes the InfoBox less intrusive but still readily available (see Figure 3-9). To bring it back to its normal size, double-click the title bar again, or click one of the tabs.

Click a tab, any tab

The InfoBox is made up of a series of notebook-like tabs. The number of tabs varies with the particular InfoBox. Click a tab and you get a new set of controls. Generally, the controls in a particular tab are all pretty much related.

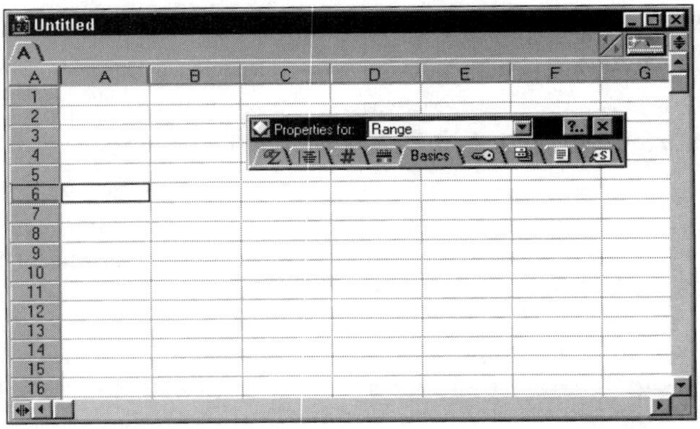

Figure 3-9:
Double-
clicking the
title bar of
the InfoBox
makes the
InfoBox
take up less
space.

The important thing to remember is that the InfoBox always works with the element that you selected: a cell, a range, part of a chart, a drawing object, and so on. You can tell what's selected by looking at the title bar of the InfoBox.

The InfoBox can remain visible while you go about your business. In fact, this characteristic is what makes the InfoBox so useful. When you're working with something in 1-2-3, the InfoBox is very handy. If you want to do something with your selection, chances are you can perform the task by using the InfoBox (you just have to figure out which tab to click!).

Getting InfoBox help

No doubt about it, even experienced users can become overwhelmed by all the tabs in an InfoBox, and the icons aren't always very recognizable. If you want to find out what a particular tab is good for, just move the mouse pointer over the tab and leave the pointer there for about a second. 1-2-3 pops up a yellow balloon that describes what you can do with the tab. Figure 3-10 shows an example.

You may have noticed that the InfoBox has a little question mark icon in its title bar. Clicking this icon displays a help screen that describes the current tab.

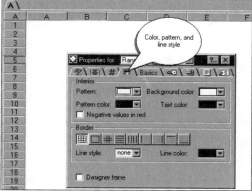

Figure 3-10:
Moving the
mouse
pointer over
a tab tells
you what
the tab
does.

All about settings

After you make a selection in the worksheet, you use the InfoBox to make changes to it. The InfoBox is smart enough to recognize the current formatting of what is selected. For example, suppose that you select a range of cells that have bold formatting. Then you open the Range InfoBox and click the tab labeled Font, attribute and color. Notice that the Attributes part of the InfoBox has a check mark next to Bold. This process works for all parts of the InfoBox. In fact, being able to view the current settings for your selection can be quite handy.

But sometimes the settings in your selected range are not the same for all the cells in the range. For example, some cells in your selection may be bold while others are not. Or the selection may consist of cells that use different fonts or colors. In this case, the Range InfoBox doesn't show any setting for the mixed attribute. However, you can make your change in the InfoBox so that all the selected cells take on that new attribute.

Part II
Getting Busy

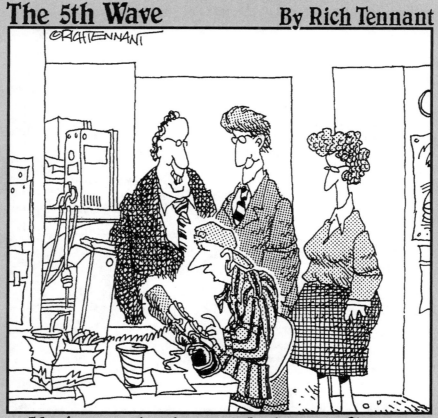

"Kevin here heads our Windows software development team. Right now he's working on a spreadsheet program that's sort of a combination Lotus 1-2-3, - FrankenWolf."

In this part . . .

The chapters in this part get down to the nitty-gritty. I describe how to enter data into cells and how to create formulas that make your spreadsheet spring to life. You also find out how to use built-in 1-2-3 functions to make your formulas even more useful. Finally, I discuss the various methods for changing things around (we all change our minds occasionally, right?).

Chapter 4

Filling Those Cells with Numbers, Text, and Other Stuff

- -

In This Chapter

▶ Keeping your cool when faced with a blank sheet

▶ Moving from cell to cell (a common pastime among restless prisoners)

▶ Putting numbers and text into cells

▶ Removing information from a cell

▶ Reviewing lots of marginally useful terminology that you can read once
and then forget

- -

*Y*ou already know that this book is designed to cut to the chase and
protect you from lots of the gory details that get in the way of your
becoming adequately proficient in 1-2-3. Unfortunately, you just can't
overlook some things.

This chapter provides enough information to make you feel relatively safe
about going off on your own to make something out of the vast wasteland
called a blank sheet. I've crammed a great deal of information in here, so
don't feel bad if you can't digest it all in one sitting.

Rows, Columns, Cells, and Sheets

A sheet is made up of a bunch of *cells*. (Refer to an unabridged computer
dictionary for the definition of the technical term *bunch*.) Each cell is the
intersection of a row and a column. Rows are numbered 1, 2, 3, and so on, up
to 65,536. Columns are labeled A, B, C, and so on.

Previous versions of 1-2-3 were limited to 8,192 rows. 1-2-3 Millennium
Edition provides you with eight times as many rows. Gee, thanks Lotus!

Each sheet contains 256 columns, but because the English alphabet stops at the letter Z, a team of Lotus experts was formed to determine how to label spreadsheet columns after you run out of letters. The experts arrived at an ingenious solution: Use two letters. After column Z comes column AA, which is followed by AB, AC, and so on. After AZ comes BA, BB, BC, and so on. If you follow this train of thought to its logical conclusion, you discover that the 256th column is actually column IV.

Every workbook can also have more sheets stacked behind the first one, kind of like pages in a notebook. In fact, you can add as many as 255 more sheets behind the first one, each exactly the same size as the first one.

So how may cells are in a sheet? If your math is rusty, allow me to fire up 1-2-3 and do the calculation for you: 65,536 rows times 256 columns times 256 sheets equals 4,294,967,296 cells — that's billion, with a B. If you need more cells than this, you're reading the wrong book.

One or two of you may be curious about why 1-2-3 uses such odd numbers. Why not 250 columns instead of 256? Why not an even 70,000 rows instead of 65,536? Why not 200 potential sheets? Good questions. The use of these strange numbers is a by-product of the binary system rearing its ugly head. Computers rely heavily on the binary system (you know, the geeky number system with only 0s and 1s in it). Here's where those odd numbers come from: 256 is 2 to the 8th power, and can be represented using exactly eight binary digits; 65,536 is 2 to the 16th power, and can be represented with 16 binary digits. Using these nice binary numbers actually optimizes the way things are stored within 1-2-3. I bet you're sorry you asked.

Gimme your address

With four and some odd billion cells in a sheet, the normal person may have trouble keeping track of them. Actually, it's not all that hard, because each cell has its own address (but not its own zip code).

The address of a cell is made up of three things: its sheet letter (optional), its column letter, and its row number. The sheet letter has a colon after it, but the column letter and row number are stuck together with no space in between. Therefore, the upper-left cell is known as cell A:A1. The last cell, way down at the bottom of the fifth sheet (sheet E) and in the last column, has an address of E:IV65536.

If your workbook consists of only a single sheet (which is how they all start out), you don't have to be concerned with sheet letters. In fact, cell addresses don't even use the sheet letter when you have only a single sheet. I discuss everything you need to know about working with files containing multiple sheets in Chapter 10.

By the way, you use cell addresses in formulas, which I cover in the next chapter. As you may have already noticed, cell addresses can quickly turn into a bowl of alphabet soup. To combat this problem, 1-2-3 enables you to give meaningful names to the sheets in a workbook. For example, you can name the first sheet Income, and the second sheet Expenses. Then, if you want to refer to the upper-left cell on the second sheet, you can use a reference such as Expenses:A1. Much simpler, eh?

To change a sheet letter into a more meaningful name, just double-click the sheet tab (which has a default name such as A, B, or C), type in the new name, and press Enter. You can use spaces in your sheet names, but the total number of characters can't exceed 15.

You can often omit the sheet letter part of a cell address. If you don't include it, 1-2-3 uses the current sheet. For example, if you're working on the second sheet, you can refer to the upper-left cell on that sheet as A1 rather than B:A1. But, if you're on the second sheet and need to refer to the upper-left cell on the first sheet, you must use the full A:A1 reference (which makes sense).

Point the way

Take a look at the sheet in Figure 4-1. Notice that one of the cells has a darker outline than the others. That rectangular outline is known as the *cell pointer*. This cell in which the cell pointer is located is called the *active cell* (or sometimes, the *current cell*). In this case, the active cell is cell C4. (I'm leaving off the sheet-letter part of the cell address, because this file has only one sheet.) The edit line also tells you which cell is active. When you move the cell pointer around, the active cell changes — just like you would expect.

Move it along

To do anything useful, you need to select a particular cell. You select a cell by moving the cell pointer, which makes whichever cell you choose the active cell. So how do you move the cell pointer? Simple — use a mouse or your keyboard.

Mousing around

When you move your mouse around, notice how the little mouse arrow (also known as the *mouse pointer*) moves on the screen. When the pointer is over one of the cells, click the left mouse button. The outline around the cell becomes thicker, and this cell magically transforms into the active cell.

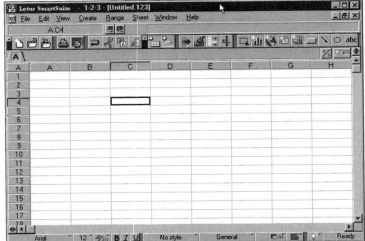

Figure 4-1:
The active
cell has a
darker
outline, and
its address
appears
directly to
the left in
the edit line.

Mouse freaks can also use the scroll bars to see other cells. You have two scroll bars: the vertical one and the horizontal one. To move down one full screen in a sheet, click toward the bottom of the vertical scroll bar. To move up a screen, click toward the top of the vertical scroll bar. To move one screen to the right, click the right side of the horizontal scroll bar. To move one screen to the left, click the left side of the horizontal scroll bar. You can also drag the little button that appears on the scroll bar to scroll the sheet either up or across. This scroll bar stuff is actually easier to do than it is to describe, so play around with clicking and dragging the scroll bars until you get the hang of it.

The scroll bars don't actually change the active cell — they just scroll the sheet. To change the active cell, you have to click a cell after you use the scroll bars.

You can activate another sheet by clicking the appropriate tab at the top of the screen.

Tapping the keyboard

Because you have to remove your hand from the keyboard to use your mouse, you may find that using the keyboard is more efficient for moving around a sheet. (I do, and I'm an expert.) Use the cursor-movement keys ($\uparrow$, $\downarrow$, $\leftarrow$, $\rightarrow$).

If the arrow keys spit out numbers when you press them, instead of moving you to the next cell, press the key labeled Num Lock. Most keyboards have a little light that tells you the status of the Num Lock key (either on or off). If your Num Lock light is on, the numeric keypad produces numbers. If the Num Lock light is off, the numeric keypad produces cursor movements. It's as easy as that.

The arrow keys move the cell pointer one cell at a time in the direction of the arrow. When you hold down one of these keys, the cell pointer zips along until you let go. Here are some better methods for moving the cell pointer long distances:

- Press PgUp to move the cell pointer up one full screen.
- Press PgDn to move the cell pointer down one full screen.
- Press Ctrl+→ to move one screen to the right.
- Press Ctrl+← to move one screen to the left.
- Press Ctrl+PgUp to move to the next sheet in the workbook (if you have one).
- Press Ctrl+PgDn to move to the preceding sheet (if you have one).

Moving by one screen gives you different results, depending on how large the sheet window is. For example, if you make the sheet window very small (say, five rows high), PgDn only moves you down five rows. If the sheet window shows 20 rows, PgDn moves you down 20 rows. So, depending on the size of the window, you may have to bang away incessantly on these keys to get to where you want to go.

At some point in your spreadsheeting life, you may find yourself lost deep in the bowels of a workbook and trying to get back home (back to cell A:A1). To take the express route, press Ctrl+Home and you instantly find yourself safe and sound back in cell A1 of the first sheet. To quickly jump to cell A1 of the current sheet, press Home.

If, for some unknown reason, you need to move the cell pointer to some off-the-wall cell address such as A:FE459, you can bang away on the cursor control keys all day and still not find your way there. Or you can use a shortcut: Press the F5 key on your keyboard. 1-2-3 displays a Go To dialog box. Type A:FE459 (or whatever obscure cell address you want to get to) and click OK. Voilà! You're there. This shortcut is magic, and nobody else knows about it. Let's keep it our little secret, okay?

When you first start out with 1-2-3, you may have trouble remembering all the specific navigation options. Fortunately for you, I've put together a handy summary of keyboard movements in Table 4-1. As you become more familiar with 1-2-3, you discover the keyboard movements you enjoy using, or you may decide to use them all, depending on what you're doing.

Table 4-1	Navigation Options	
Movement	*Keyboard*	*Mouse*
One cell up	↑	Click the cell
One cell down	↓	Click the cell
One cell left	←	Click the cell
One cell right	→	Click the cell
One screen down	PgDn	Click the bottom of the vertical scroll bar
One screen up	PgUp	Click the top of the vertical scroll bar
One screen left	Ctrl+←	Click left of the horizontal scroll bar
One screen right	Ctrl+→	Click right of the horizontal scroll bar
Next sheet	Ctrl+PgUp	Click sheet tab
Preceding sheet	Ctrl+PgDn	Click sheet tab
A long distance	F5, type address	Drag scroll bar button

Ready, Set, Type

A lot of good knowing how to move the cell pointer to any cell in the sheet does you when all you have is an empty sheet, right? Face it, blank sheets just don't cut it in the business world. In all likelihood, your boss is going to want information in the cells of your sheet. The next section details how the information goes into those cells.

Minding your modes

If you're really observant, you may have noticed a single word (probably Ready) in the bottom of your screen, on the right corner of the status bar (see Figure 4-2). This space is the *mode indicator*. When you open a new worksheet, 1-2-3 is in Ready mode, meaning that the program is ready for you to perform a task, such as move to another cell (as I describe in the previous section) or put information into a cell (as I describe in the following sections).

1-2-3 has several other modes, and the current mode always appears on the right side of the status bar. For the record, Table 4-2 shows a complete list of the 1-2-3 modes.

Figure 4-2:
The mode
indicator
appears
in the
status bar.

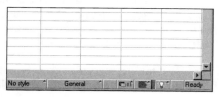

Table 4-2	The Many Modes of 1-2-3
Mode	*What It Means*
Edit	You're in the process of editing a cell.
Error	1-2-3 is displaying an error message.
Label	You're entering text into a cell.
Menu	You're choosing a menu command or selecting options in a dialog box.
Point	You're selecting a range of cells while working in a dialog box or while entering a formula.
Ready	1-2-3 is ready for you to enter information into cells or choose a command.
Value	You're entering a number into a cell.
Wait	1-2-3 is busy doing something, such as saving a file.

Filling your cells

A sheet cell can hold any one of the following four types of information:

- **A value:** You don't have to stray any farther than this chapter to discover how to enter values — known to you and me as *numbers*.

- **A label:** This chapter also shows you how to enter labels, which you may recognize as normal words or text.

- **A formula:** In Chapter 5, I show you how to use formulas to do miraculous things (like adding and averaging) to the contents of other cells.

- **Nothing:** Zip, nada, zilch, nil. Cells can be completely empty, void of all content (like some political speeches I can think of). Leave cells empty when you don't have anything to put in them or when you want to have some space between cells that do have information in them. By default (that is, unless you do something about it) all cells contain nothing.

Cells containing formulas look as though they contain either a number or a label, because cells display the results of formulas, not the formulas themselves. If you want to see the formula itself, move the cell pointer to that cell, and the formula appears in the edit line at the top of the screen.

Figure 4-3 shows a sheet with numbers, labels, formulas, and blank cells. Notice that you can't see the formulas themselves, only their results.

	A	B	C	D	E	F	G
1	Sales by State						
2							
3		Missouri	24590				
4		Illinois	32882				
5		Kansas	14900				
6							
7		Total	72372				
8		Average	24124				

Figure 4-3: A sheet, showing examples of numbers, labels, formula results, and (yes) even blank cells.

Numbers, labels, and formulas are the only things you can put *into* sheet cells. However, a sheet can also hold charts, maps, pictures, and drawings. These items aren't in cells; they kind of float on top of cells, and you can move them around and resize them independently of the cells.

Numbers versus labels

Why the distinction between numbers and labels? When do you need to use numbers, and when do you need labels? Do you really need formulas at all? And does the refrigerator light really go out when you close the door?

You use numbers when you work with a subject that uses quantities or values. If you make a sheet to keep track of your gambling losses, for example, you may enter a number for the amount you lose on each gambling excursion. A nice fact about numbers is that you can refer to them in your formulas. For example,

you can enter a formula that adds up a bunch of numbers and displays the total in a separate cell (but for your gambling loss sheet, you may not want to know the total damage).

Labels, on the other hand, are more useful for describing what the numbers are and for adding titles to your work. In your gambling loss sheet, you can put the following labels next to your numbers: Reno blackjack table, Santa Anita Racetrack, and so on. You can also use words to make a simple list without getting any numbers involved.

Entering a number

Throughout the recent course of history, spreadsheets have acquired a reputation for being good to use with numbers. Therefore, it's only fitting that you get your feet wet by finding out how to enter a number into a cell.

Before you put anything into a cell, make sure that you're in Ready mode (see "Minding your modes," earlier in this chapter). For example, when you open a drop-down menu, 1-2-3 is in Menu mode, so you can't enter data into a cell.

When you're ready to enter a number (and 1-2-3 is Ready too), you have the following two choices for entering the numbers into the cells:

- ✔ You can use the number keys along the top of your keyboard (not the keys with Fs on them, but the keys with punctuation characters above the numbers).
- ✔ If your Num Lock light is on, you can use the keys on the numeric keypad to input numbers.

To enter a number into a cell in your spreadsheet, follow these steps:

1. **Move to the cell in which you want to enter a number.**

   Use any of the sheet navigation methods I describe in Table 4-1 to get to the desired cell. You know you're there when the cell you want becomes active (that is, the border around that cell is darker than the others).

2. **Type a number of your choice.**

   Notice that the mode changes from Ready to Value. 1-2-3 is pretty smart. As soon as you type the first number, 1-2-3 realizes that you're entering a value into a cell.

3. **Press Enter to make the number stick in the cell.**

   Take a peek at the mode indicator: 1-2-3 is back in Ready mode — just waiting for more numbers.

Entering text

Spreadsheets are boring enough as they are, but just think how much worse they could be if they held *only* numbers. Fortunately, 1-2-3 can cope with text *(labels)* as well as with numbers *(values)*. The steps for entering text into a cell are similar to the steps for entering a number:

1. **Move to the cell you want and type a word or letters.**

   1-2-3 reads your mind and changes the mode indicator to Label.

2. **Press Enter.**

   A label can consist of more than one word, so feel free to use the spacebar.

What do you call the non-numeric information that you enter into a cell? The 1-2-3 manual refers to non-numeric cell entries as labels. Some people call this stuff *text*. Others call it *words*. You may catch me using the term *string*. The bottom line? It doesn't matter what you call it. Just remember that a difference exists between numbers and whatever you call that non-numeric stuff that goes into a cell.

Fitting a big entry into a small cell

A cell can hold as many as 511 characters of text, yet the default column size is only about nine characters wide. Sometimes, you may want to put more than nine characters of text into a cell without adjusting the column width. For example, what if you want to type "Bills I Need to Pay This Month" into a cell, but you don't want to make the column any wider?

When you type a long entry such as this one into a cell, the text appears to spill over into the cells to the right of the active cell. Actually, the text is contained all in the one cell. Because the cells next door are empty, 1-2-3 borrows their space to display the spillover from the active cell.

Watch out for spaces!

Entering numbers into cells is pretty straightforward, but you have to watch out for one thing: Don't include any spaces in your numbers. If a number has a space in it (either before the number or in the middle of the number), 1-2-3 considers it to be a *label*. And, in the program's mind, a label has a value of zero.

For example, if you accidentally hit the spacebar before entering a value into a cell, the cell looks as though it holds a number, but it really doesn't. Similarly, if you enter a number followed by a space and a percentage sign, the cell looks as though it holds a percentage — but it really holds a zero.

The real problem rears its head when you use such an erroneous value in a formula (which I cover in Chapter 5). For example, you may enter a formula to add a range of numbers. If the range includes a value with a space in it, the formula displays an erroneous answer.

So what happens if you move the cell pointer one column to the left and type something else, such as "Car Loan Payment " into this cell? Because the cell to the right is occupado, 1-2-3 can't borrow its space to display the spillover from the cell. Therefore, the program appears to shorten its display for this cell (see Figure 4-4). Don't worry, all the text is still in there — it just doesn't show up on the screen.

The solution to the "failure to spillover problem" is to make the entire column wider. A quick way to widen a column is to drag it. Click the column border to the right of the column letter and drag the border until it's the width you want. I discuss other ways to adjust the width of columns in Chapter 5.

Figure 4-4:
Lengthy text
(in cell B6)
appears to
be cut off if
the cell to
the right
isn't empty.

| Untitled.123 |
| A\ |
	A	B	C	D	E
1					
2					
3					
4					
5		Bills I Need to Pay This Month			
6		Car Loan Pa	249.65		
7					
8					
9					
10					
11					

Another way to handle lengthy text in a cell is to make the text wrap onto more than one line. The option to wrap text resides in the Alignment tab of the Range InfoBox. See Chapter 12 for details.

1-2-3 Millennium Edition has a new feature called SmartFill that can help you with some types of data entry. For example, if you need to enter the days of the week, just type the first day into a cell. Then, move the mouse pointer to the bottom or right edge of the cell. When the mouse pointer displays four arrows, click and drag. 1-2-3 fills in the subsequent days of the week. This technique also works with month names. Even better, you can create your own SmartFill lists by using the File⇨User Setup⇨SmartFill Setup command.

Changing the way the Enter key works

Most people tend to press Enter to signal the end of their numbers and labels. Depending on how your system is set up, pressing Enter either moves the cell pointer to the next cell below, or it does nothing at all; the cell pointer stays put.

If you want to change what happens when you press Enter, do the following:

1. **Choose File⇨User Setup⇨1-2-3 Preferences.**

2. **In the 1-2-3 Preferences dialog box, click the Classic Keys tab.**

3. **Click one of the two options at the top.**

   The first option keeps the cell pointer in the cell when you press Enter; the second option makes the cell pointer move down to the next cell.

You can also use any of the arrow keys in place of Enter. Using the arrow keys has a dual effect: The label or numbers stick in the cell, and the cell pointer moves in the direction of the arrow key. If you're entering a series of numbers in a row, you can use the right-arrow key instead of Enter. Doing so enters the value in the cell and automatically moves to the next cell in the row.

Dressing Up Your Entries

Appearances aren't everything, but they can make your spreadsheet a great deal more effective. If you care about how the numbers and text that you enter into the cells look, check out the following sections.

Making numbers look right

After you start entering numbers into cells, you may not be happy with how the numbers look. If you have a very long number, 1-2-3 automatically displays it using scientific notation (you may see something like 1.45E+011). You may want other numbers to show up with commas in them. If you're tracking dollar amounts, you may want all numbers to have two digits to the right of the decimal point. And speaking of money, accountants usually like to see dollars signs tacked on to their numbers. And what if you work with percentages? The answer, my friend, is formatting.

Take a look at the numbers in Figure 4-5. The numbers in the first column are plain old numbers, and the numbers in the second column are formatted. Which numbers look better to you?

Formatting affects only how the numbers look; formatting doesn't change the actual number in any way. In Figure 4-5, the cells in each row hold exactly the same value. The only difference in the numbers is the way they look (one group of numbers is formatted and the other is not).

Figure 4-5:
The
difference
between
plain and
formatted
numbers.

	Plain Numbers	Formatted Numbers	Number Format Used
2	9782.54	$9,782.54	Currency, two decimals
3	1098223	1,098,223	Comma, no decimals
4	0.359	35.90%	Percent, two decimals
5	0.359	36%	Percent, no decimals
6	89800980983	8.98E+010	Scientific, two decimals

Using the Range InfoBox to format numbers

Most of the time, you format numbers to make them look the way you want.
You can format numbers by doing the following:

1. **Move the cell pointer to the cell that has the number you want
   to format.**

   You also can select a range of cells that you want to have the same
   formatting.

2. **Bring up the Range InfoBox if it's not already on-screen.**

   Do so by right-clicking the mouse and then choosing Range Properties
   from the shortcut menu. Or press Alt+Enter.

   The Range InfoBox has nine tabs.

3. **In the Range InfoBox, click the tab with the number sign (#).**

   The InfoBox now resembles Figure 4-6.

Figure 4-6:
The
Number
Format tab
in the
Range
InfoBox is
where you
specify the
numeric
format you
want.

4. Select a category from the list labeled Category, and then select a format from the list labeled Current format.

Watch the selected cell or range to see what your number looks like as you select various formats. For most numeric formats, you also can indicate how many decimal places to use.

After you format a number, you're not stuck with it. You can keep applying different numeric formats until you get the one you like.

You can even format empty cells. Then, if you ever decide to put a number in the cell, the number appears in the format that you gave it when the cell was empty.

Using the status bar to format numbers

You may find using a status bar button to format numbers easier than using the Range InfoBox. The default numeric format is General, which appears on the status bar. General number format is your basic plain-Jane format: no commas, no dollar signs, no percent signs, and as many decimal places as you enter. If the number is too big, 1-2-3 automatically displays it in scientific notation.

To use the status bar to format numbers, start by selecting a cell or range. Then click the word General in the status bar. A list of numeric formats pops up, as shown in Figure 4-7.

Click the name of the format you want. You can control the number of decimal places by clicking the button directly to the right of the numeric format button on the status bar. The only disadvantage to this method is that it doesn't give you the complete list of number formats. In most cases, however, you find exactly what you need.

Formatting numbers automatically

1-2-3 is smart enough to recognize some symbols contained in numbers and to format the cell for you automatically. More specifically, you can enter the following characters along with your numbers, and 1-2-3 formats the cell accordingly:

- Dollar sign ($)
- Comma (,)
- E (used for scientific notation)
- Percent sign (%)

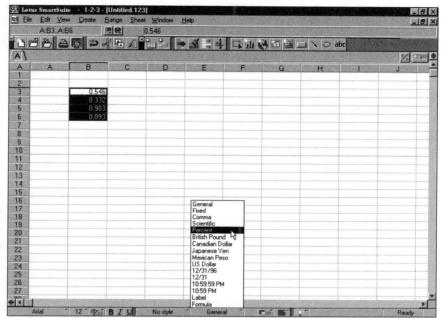

Figure 4-7:
Using the
status bar is
a quick way
to format
numbers.

Aligning text and numbers

Normally, when you enter text into a cell, 1-2-3 aligns that text to the left in
the cell. When you enter a number, the program aligns it to the right in the
cell. You're not stuck with this alignment, however. You easily can change
how numbers and labels are aligned within cells. Figure 4-8 illustrates
several alignment choices you can make with labels and numbers by using
the Alignment tab in the Range InfoBox.

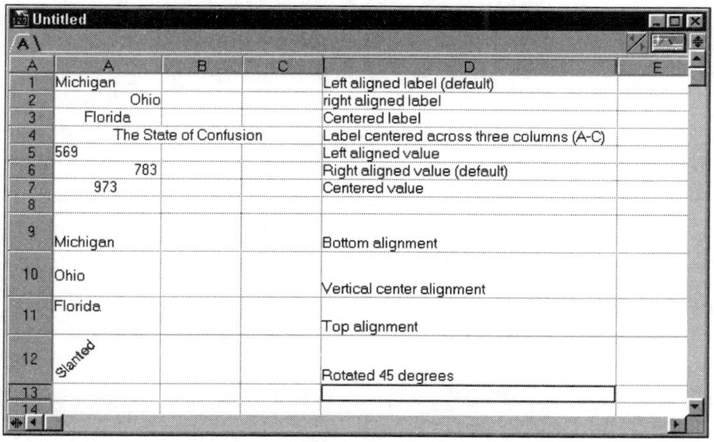

Figure 4-8:
Different
types of
alignment
for text and
numbers.

The easiest way to change the alignment is to use the status bar button designed expressly for this purpose. Start by selecting the cells you want to align. Click the alignment button and a graphic list of alignment options appears (see Figure 4-9). Click one of these options and the selected cell or cells take on that alignment.

After you enter text into a cell, 1-2-3 adds a new character to the beginning of the cell. This character, which is visible only when you're in Edit mode, is called a *label prefix*.

Normally, when you enter text, 1-2-3 adds a single quotation mark (') at the beginning of your text. This symbol makes the contents of the cell left-aligned — the default. Actually, you can put your own label prefix at the beginning of a label to change how cell contents are aligned. Table 4-3 lists the label prefixes you can use. (By the way, you definitely can forget the term *label prefix* as soon as you finish with this chapter.)

Table 4-3	Label Prefixes and What They Do	
Label Prefix	*English Translation*	*How the Label Is Displayed*
'	Single quote	Left aligned in the cell
"	Double quote	Right aligned in the cell
^	Caret	Centered in the cell

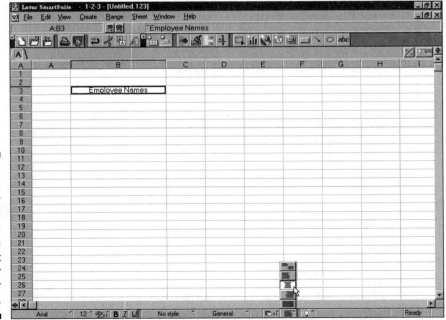

Figure 4-9:
Clicking the status bar button gives you some alignment options for text or numbers.

Changing Your Work

The time will come when you realize that you've entered something incorrectly into a cell. (Although this has never happened to me personally, I have heard stories about people making such mistakes.)

Suppose that you typed the following label into a cell: An Analisys of 1998 Investments. Your boss, a former grade school spelling bee runner-up, points out the misspelled word. To smooth your employer's ruffled feathers, you have the following two choices (three, if you include taking spelling lessons from your boss):

- ✔ Move the cell pointer back to the offensive cell and reenter the entire label.
- ✔ Edit the cell.

For all you major-league bad spellers out there, 1-2-3 provides a built-in spelling checker, which you can invoke by choosing Edit➪Check Spelling. This feature works just like the spell checker that you (probably) use in your word processor. But, like all computerized spelling checkers, it can't tell you whether a properly spelled word is used incorrectly in a sentence. For example, the spelling checker doesn't warn you if you enter United Snakes of America into a cell, because *snakes* is a legitimate word.

Overwriting a cell

To replace the information that a cell already contains, move the cell pointer to the cell and enter the new information. The new stuff replaces the old stuff. You can replace a number with a number, a label with a number, a number with a label, and so on.

Editing a cell

If you need to make only a minor change to what's in a cell, you can save a few seconds by editing the cell rather than reentering the information. Use the following steps:

1. Move the cell pointer to the cell you want to change.

2. **Press the F2 key or double-click the cell.**

   The contents of the cell also appear up on the edit line, but the editing occurs within the cell itself. Notice that the mode indicator reads Edit, a sure sign that you are, in fact, editing a cell.

3. **Using the editing keys (which I describe in the next section), type new characters, delete unwanted characters, or replace existing characters to make the cell correct.**

   The flashing vertical bar thingamajig that indicates where you are in the cell you're editing is known by the provocative term *insertion point*. (After you finish with this chapter, you can safely forget the official name for this item.)

4. **Press Enter.**

When you're editing a cell, 1-2-3 goes into a state of suspended animation. In other words, when 1-2-3 is in Edit mode, you can't do anything with the menus or SmartIcons.

The editing keys

While you're in Edit mode, a few keys come in mighty handy to speed up the editing process. If you're interested, check out Table 4-4. If not, you'll waste a great deal of time reentering data.

Table 4-4	Handy Keys to Use While Editing a Cell (Press F2 First)
Key	*What It Does*
Backspace	Erases the character to the left of the insertion point
Left arrow	Moves the insertion point by one character to the left (and doesn't erase anything)
Right arrow	Moves the insertion point by one character to the right (and doesn't erase anything)
Del	Erases the character to the right of the insertion point
Esc	Leaves the cell just as it was before you started this escapade (Press if you screw up royally and want to start over.)

Use these keys to move around in the cell, to erase unwanted characters, and to insert new characters. When the cell contents looks right, press Enter (or any of the arrow keys).

Insert or overwrite?

When you edit a cell, inserting new characters causes the current contents to shift to the right. But you can change this process by pressing the INS key while you edit. The characters that you type now *overwrite* (replace) those that get in the way.

Why would you ever want to overwrite characters? Overwriting is a minor timesaver, because it prevents you from having to erase a character and then type a new one. In overwrite mode, you can add a good character and get rid of a bad one with a single keystroke.

Nuking a cell completely

You know how to change the contents of a cell, but what if you want to wipe it completely off the face of the earth and convert it to a blank cell? Easy! Move the cell pointer to the undesired cell, press Del, and kiss it good-bye. Any formatting that you applied to the cell remains there — only the cell's contents go away.

Another way to go about clearing a cell is to choose Edit⇨Clear. This method is a bit more versatile, because it gives you the option (by popping up a small dialog box shown in Figure 4-10) of clearing only certain parts of the cell:

Figure 4-10:
The Clear dialog box gives you many options when you clear a cell.

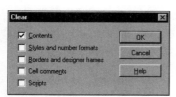

✔ Contents (that's the information that you entered into the cell)

✔ Styles and number format (any formatting that you applied to the cell)

✔ Borders (lines that you draw around the cell)

✔ Cell comments (notes to yourself that are attached to the cell)

✔ Scripts (programs that are attached to the cell)

You can select as many of these options as you want. Say, for example, that you've gone overboard and applied far too many formatting options and fancy borders to a range. Your boss tells you that your sheet looks terrible. You can use the Clear dialog box to quickly delete the formatting and borders, but leave the values and text intact.

Never erase a cell by pressing the spacebar. Although this technique appears to get rid of the cell contents, pressing the spacebar actually inserts an invisible space character (preceded by an apostrophe) into the cell. This invisible character can cause serious spreadsheet problems that are very difficult to diagnose. Take my word for it — pressing the spacebar to erase a cell is a no-no.

Chapter 5

Formulas: Not Just for Babies Anymore

This is it — the chapter that makes trudging through all the basics of 1-2-3 worthwhile. This is the chapter that shows you how to bring your worksheets to life. This is the chapter that gives you the skills to actually do something useful with 1-2-3. For this, my friend, is the chapter about formulas. (Can't you just hear the chorus swelling in the background?)

When you're able to navigate a spreadsheet like a pro, enter numbers and text into cells, and save all your fine work, you're ready for the next logical step toward earning your degree in 1-2-3 — creating formulas.

Formulas Defined

A worksheet without formulas is like the fake food you see displayed in the window of a Chinese restaurant — it looks pretty good on the surface, but it doesn't do a whole lot for you. In fact, without formulas, you may as well be using a plain old word-processing program. But because you're using a powerful spreadsheet program instead, I recommend that you get turned on to formulas as soon as possible.

After you enter a number or a label into a cell, 1-2-3 simply displays the number or the text in the cell. You also can enter a formula into a cell, but the difference is that a *formula* does some type of calculation and displays the result in the cell. You can still see the formula itself in the contents box in the edit line when you move the cell pointer to the cell containing the formula.

1-2-3 requires certain formulas to begin with a plus sign (+). To keep things simple and consistent, I recommend that you begin *all* formulas with a plus sign. Or, if you prefer, you can begin formulas with an equal sign (=).

Simple formulas use only numbers and operators and don't use any cell addresses. For example, if you enter the formula +100+45 into any cell, you find that 1-2-3 displays the answer (which, by the way, is 145). Figure 5-1 proves that I'm not lying. Cell B2 has this simple formula in it, but the cell itself shows the result of the calculation that the formula performs. The actual formula appears in the contents box of the edit line.

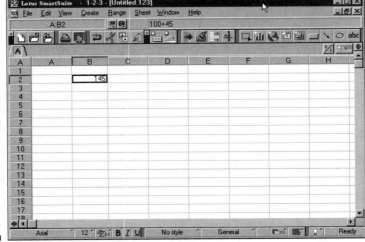

Figure 5-1:
A formula displays its results in the cell. To see the actual formula, look in the edit line.

But formulas are most useful when they use cell addresses rather than actual values. Allow me to demonstrate. Take a look at Figure 5-2, which shows a worksheet with labels in column A and numbers in column B. Although cell B5 appears to contain an ordinary number, it actually contains a formula. What you're seeing displayed in the worksheet is the formula's *answer* (or its result). Because the active cell happens to be cell B5, the content of this cell (the *formula*) appears in the contents box of the edit line. Here it is again:

```
+B1+B2+B3+B4
```

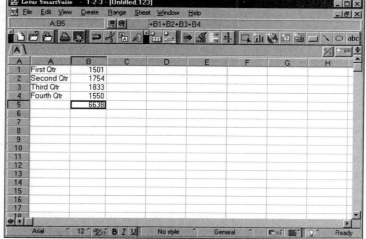

Figure 5-2:
A bunch of
numbers?
No way,
José. Cell
B5 has a
formula in it.

What this formula is saying, in plain English, is, "Hey 1-2-3, take the number in cell B1 and add it to the number in B2. Then add the number in B3 to the total. And while you're at it, add the number in B4 to that total. Now, display the final answer in my cell. Thanks, dude."

You may think that typing **+B1+B2+B3+B4** is a rather lengthy way to get the sum of these numbers. But you have to admit that doing so is much easier than typing out the instructions in complete words.

Actually, a much easier way exists to get the sum of a bunch of cells, but that's the topic for another chapter. *Hint:* It involves @functions, which I discuss in Chapter 6.

Hello, Operator?

The preceding section shows how a formula can use the plus sign to add values. As you may expect, you can use other mathematical *operators* to perform even more amazing feats. For example, you can subtract values using the minus sign and multiply values using an asterisk (not the letter X, as you may expect). And you can't overlook the ever-popular division operation, which uses a slash (/). Finally, people with a penchant for large numbers may be interested in the exponential operator (^), which raises a number to a power.

Table 5-1 shows some examples of formulas using these operators.

Table 5-1	Some Sample Formulas That Use Various Operators
Formula	**What It Does**
+A1*23.5	Multiplies the value in cell A1 by 23.5
+A1-A3	Subtracts the value in A3 from the value in A1
+A4/A3	Divides A4 by A3
+A3^3	Raises A3 to the third power (equivalent to +A3*A3*A3)
+(A1+A2)/A3	Adds A1 to A2 and then divides the answer by A3

Remember that a cell address can include a sheet letter. To refer to the
upper-left cell on the second sheet, use B:A1. The cell references in Table 5-1
don't include a sheet letter because they refer to cells on the same sheet. If
your formula refers to a cell in a different sheet, you need to use the sheet
letters to clarify which cell you want to use, like this:

```
+B:A1*C:A1
```

This particular formula multiplies the upper-left cell on sheet B by the
upper-left cell on sheet C.

Using parentheses in formulas

You may notice that the last entry in Table 5-1 introduces something new —
parentheses. You can use parentheses to tell 1-2-3 the order in which you
want the calculations to occur. Why is this step necessary? Consider the
same formula without any parentheses:

```
+A1+A2/A3
```

Written this way, the formula is rather ambiguous. Do you want to add A1 to
A2 and divide the result by A3? Or do you want to divide A2 by A3 *and then*
add A1 to that result? Does it matter? Yep. Read on to find out why.

A formula with two answers

Just for the sake of argument, assume that column A contains three cells,
each with a value. The values are as follows:

```
A1:        4
A2:        10
A3:        2
```

Take another look at this now-familiar formula:

```
+A1+A2/A3
```

If you forget about cell addresses and use the real numbers, the formula looks like this:

```
4+10/2
```

Add 4 to 10, and you get 14. Divide 14 by 2, and you get 7. That's the answer, right? Well, you can also look at it in this way: Divide 10 by 2, and you get 5. Add the 4 to this 5, and you get 9. Hmmm. This formula can produce an answer of either 7 or 9, depending on the order in which you do the operations. Computers, like some people, can't handle ambiguity well (see Figure 5-3 for proof). Therefore, you need to be very specific at times.

Figure 5-3:
Visual proof that a formula can produce different results by changing the order of the calculations.

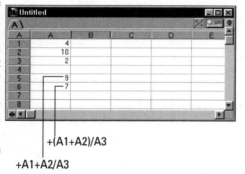

+(A1+A2)/A3

+A1+A2/A3

The result of a formula may depend on the order in which the arithmetic operations are performed. You can control the order in which the calculations occur by using parentheses.

How 1-2-3 copes with ambiguity

So what happens if you leave out the parentheses? Does 1-2-3 go into an endless loop trying to resolve the ambiguity? Not quite. Some built-in rules determine how the program handles these types of ambiguities. These rules are called *order of precedence* (a term that you can safely forget — understanding the concept is what's important).

For example, multiplication has higher precedence than addition; therefore +2+3*4 produces an answer of 14, not 20. In other words, when 1-2-3 doesn't find any parentheses to guide it, the program first does the multiplication (3*4) and then performs the addition (2+12).

Table 5-2 lists some of the world's most popular mathematical operators, along with a number that indicates the precedence level. Operations with lower-precedence numbers are performed first, and those with equal precedence are performed from left to right.

Table 5-2	Some Commonly Used Mathematical Operators and Their Precedence	
Operator	**Description**	**Precedence**
^	Exponentiation	1
*	Multiplication	2
/	Division	2
+	Addition	3
–	Subtraction	3

If a formula doesn't contain any overriding parentheses, 1-2-3 always performs the exponentiation (^) operator first; then it performs multiplication and division, and finally it performs addition and subtraction.

The thing about formulas

Here's the thing about formulas: They always look more complicated than they really are because most people are used to seeing things that hold some inherent meaning. A cell address such as +F13 is meaningless. Face it, formulas would be much less intimidating if you could write

```
+(current - previous)/previous
```

rather than

```
+(C12-B12)/B12
```

The fact is, you *can* write formulas that use meaningful names. As I explain in Chapter 6, you can give a name to a cell, to a range, and even to a complete worksheet.

No comment

Sometimes, you may find including a note to yourself (or to others) useful in explaining what's going on in a formula. That clever trickery you came up with last March may totally baffle you by July. You can add a comment to a

The nesting instinct

Frankly, I've been using spreadsheets since the Reagan administration, and I confess that I can never remember how this precedence business works (and I just don't trust it, for some reason). Therefore, I tend to use more parentheses than are necessary — which isn't bad, because parentheses leave no doubt as to how a formula is calculated. However, you can easily get confused when parentheses are nested several levels deep.

Consider the following formula:

```
+(((A1+B1)*2)-((C1+D1)*2))/4
```

Notice that the number of left parentheses is exactly equal to the number of right parentheses. When this isn't the case, 1-2-3 gets upset and does not accept the formula. When you press Enter, 1-2-3 evaluates a formula starting in the innermost set of parentheses and working its way out. Whatever is most deeply nested (that is, within the most parentheses) gets first attention, and 1-2-3 uses the result of that part of the formula to evaluate the remaining parts.

In the preceding formula, two sets of parentheses exist at the deepest level: (A1+B1) and (C1+D1). 1-2-3 first finds these two answers and then evaluates the next level. Again, two sets of parentheses exist at the next level. In this case, the program uses the answers from the preceding level and multiplies them each by 2. At the next level up, the program subtracts the second answer from the first. At the top level, it divides the preceding answer by four. This final answer is the one that shows up in the cell.

This, of course, all happens in the blink of an eye (actually, quite a bit faster than that). The point I'm trying to make is that using more parentheses than you really need can actually help you make sense of gobbledygook formulas such as the preceding one.

cell by using the Range InfoBox — the dialog box that enables you to do practically anything with a selected cell or range. More specifically, follow these steps to add a comment to a cell:

1. **Select the formula cell.**
2. **Press Alt+Enter to bring up the Range InfoBox.**

   (Skip this step if the Range InfoBox is already displayed.)
3. **In the Range InfoBox, click the tab labeled Cell comment.**

   Cell comment is the second tab from the right.
4. **Enter the comment in the box.**

Figure 5-4 shows what entering a comment looks like in real life.

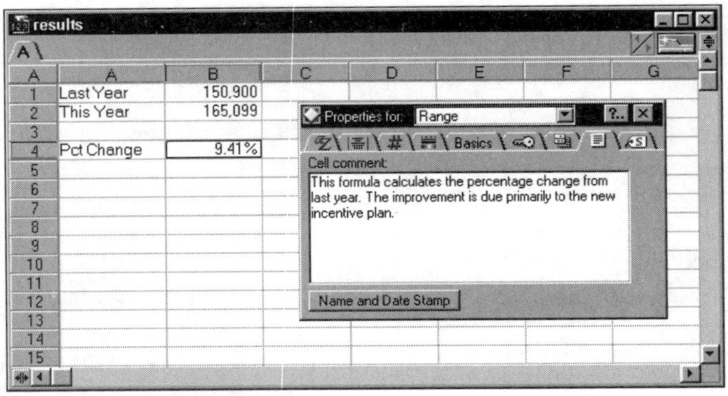

Figure 5-4:
Adding a
comment to
a cell.

A cell with a comment attached displays a small red dot in the upper-left corner. To read the comment, make sure that the Range InfoBox is displayed (and the Cell comment tab is selected) and then activate the cell containing the comment.

You can add a comment to any cell, not just a cell that contains a formula.

Entering Formulas into Cells

One way to enter a formula is to type it into a cell. You can enter any of the formulas in this chapter by typing them exactly as they appear. Include all the cell addresses, worksheet letters (if necessary), mathematical operators, parentheses, actual values, and whatever else is required.

But the easiest way to enter a formula is to *point* to the cells and let 1-2-3 help you build the formula. When you're entering a formula, 1-2-3 offers a slick alternative to typing the actual cell references. The typing method can be very tedious (and prone to errors). This alternative method is called *pointing* (see Figure 5-5).

Here are the general steps required to construct a formula by pointing to the cell references:

1. **Use the arrow keys to point to the cell that you want to contain a formula.**

2. **Press + or = to tell 1-2-3 that a formula is on its way.**

   Notice that the mode indicator in the status bar now reads `Point`. Also notice that the formula is being created in the cell before your very eyes.

When a formula is not a formula

You use a plus sign (or an equal sign) to signal the beginning of a formula. But what if you want to enter text that begins with a plus sign or an equal sign? For example, say your company is developing a new steak sauce named +A1 Steak Sauce. If you try to enter that product name into a cell, you are greeted with ERR; 1-2-3 thinks the name is a formula and can't make any sense out of it.

Before you rush out and change the name of the product, here's the solution: Precede the product name with a label prefix: either an apostrophe ('), a quote ("), or a caret (^). The label prefix you use determines the alignment in the cell (I discuss label prefixes in Chapter 4). Every cell that begins with a label prefix is considered to be text — even if the text looks like a formula.

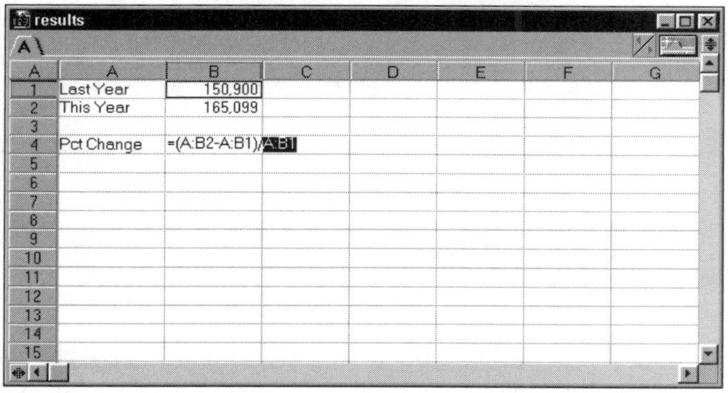

Figure 5-5:
Building a formula by pointing (or, letting 1-2-3 do the dirty work).

3. **Move the cell pointer to the first cell you want to reference in the formula you're building.**

   For example, if you're building a formula that adds the values in cells B1 through B3 (that is, +B1+B2+B3), move the cell pointer to B1.

4. **Enter an operator such as +, –, *, or /.**

   The cell pointer jumps back to the cell where you're building the formula.

5. **Use the arrow keys to move the cell pointer to the next cell.**

   More stuff is added to the formula.

6. **Repeat Steps 3 through 5 until the formula is complete.**

7. **Press Enter to finish.**

   1-2-3 evaluates the formula, and the cell shows the formula's result, not the formula itself. (The actual formula appears in the edit line.)

To ERR is human — and very common

Don't be alarmed if, upon entering a formula into a cell, you're greeted with an ERR message instead of a friendlier result. These messages are actually quite common, even among experienced users. In a nutshell, ERR means that you made a boo-boo, such as the following:

✔ You typed a cell reference that doesn't exist (such as +ZA1).

✔ You're trying to do something impossible, such as calculate the square root of a negative number or divide by zero. These particular mathematical operations are illegal in most countries and often result in a severe fine or imprisonment.

✔ You tried to use a named cell or range and that name doesn't exist.

✔ Your formula is trying to use a cell that is returning ERR. If the formula uses a cell that is returning ERR, the formula also returns ERR. This phenomenon is known as the *ripple effect*, because a single ERR can ripple through an entire worksheet.

Usually, if you examine the formula that's returning ERR, you can figure out the problem; look for unusual cell references or undefined range names. You can then edit the cell to correct the problem, and the formula returns a better result.

Pointing is only useful to automatically enter a cell reference. You still need to manually enter the operators, parentheses, and values used in the formula.

Using this pointing technique means that you never have to be concerned with the actual cell address — just point to the cells you want, and 1-2-3 takes care of the repulsive details. This technique also cuts down on errors. After all, you can easily make a typing mistake when you enter a formula manually (or womanually) — and you may not even discover the mistake until your boss asks you how 12+9 could possibly equal 197.

When you're pointing to create a formula, you're not limited to pointing to cells on the current worksheet (assuming that you have more than one sheet in your file). If you press Ctrl+PgUp while you're pointing to a cell, 1-2-3 transports you to the next sheet. Pressing Ctrl+PgDn sends you to the preceding sheet. In either case, after you get to the new worksheet, you can move the cell pointer to the cell you want to refer to in the formula. And, of course, you can press Ctrl+PgUp and Ctrl+PgDn any number of times until you get to the right worksheet.

Relative and Absolute References

To really understand how formulas work, you ought to know something about relative and absolute references. This topic can be rather confusing, but it's important stuff. So bear with me, okay?

It's all relative

When you put a formula into a cell, you can copy that formula to other cells. In fact, copying formulas is one of the most common things that spreadsheet users do. I tell you all about copying in Chapter 7; for now, just understand that you can enter a formula once and then copy it so that the same formula works on other ranges. For example, if you have six columns of numbers, you can put a formula below the first column to add the preceding numbers. Then you can copy that formula to the five cells to the right to add the other columns.

In the previous sections of this chapter, all the cell references I use in formulas are *relative*. If you copy a formula with relative references, the copies of the formula change. For example, assume that cell A3 contains the following formula:

```
+A1+A2
```

If you copy this formula to the cell next door (B3), the formula in cell B3 reads:

```
+B1+B2
```

In other words, copying the formula changes the cells in a *relative manner*. No matter where you copy the formula, it always computes the sum of the two cells directly above it. This adjustment is pretty nifty, and most of the time it's exactly what you want to happen.

By default, all cell references are relative.

Absolutely absolute

What if you want the copy of the formula to return exactly the same result as the cell it was copied from? In this case, you need to specify *absolute* cell references. Here's a formula with absolute cell references:

```
+$B$1+$C$1
```

Behind the scenes

If you're like me, you may be curious about what goes on behind the scenes when you enter a formula into a cell. If you've ever wondered what a computer thinks about, here it is.

When you start entering a formula into a cell, 1-2-3 goes through the following "thought" process:

1. **Okay, this person is entering a formula.**

   The entry isn't just a number or a label, so this person must know something about 1-2-3 (little does the computer know, right?).

2. **Is this person using Point mode?**

   If so, I need to show the cell addresses as this user points to them and stick them in the formula. (Sheesh, I have to do all the work.)

3. **This person just pressed Enter.**

That means the formula is finished.

4. **I'll just check this formula to make sure that it follows all my rules.**

   If it doesn't, I'll beep and make this person feel foolish.

5. **Looks okay to me.**

   Now I'll calculate the results using the values in the specified cells.

6. **Now I'll finish up by displaying the answer in the cell.**

1-2-3 continues thinking as you do your work. Every time you put a value into a cell or create a new formula, the program checks every single formula on the worksheet to see whether it needs to be recalculated based on your new input. But this all happens so quickly that you usually don't even realize it.

I warned you that this reference stuff can get ugly. Using a dollar sign before the column part and before the row part of a cell reference tells 1-2-3 that the cell reference is absolute — that the cell reference always refers to those specific cells, even if you copy the formula.

So why would you want to use absolute references, anyway? The best way to understand the need for absolute references is to go through an example. Figure 5-6 shows a worksheet designed to calculate the sales tax on several purchase prices. The sales tax rate is in cell B1. Column A displays labels, column B shows amounts, and column C contains formulas that calculate the sales tax on the amounts in column B.

The formula in cell C4 is

```
+B4*$B$1
```

The first cell reference (B4) is a normal relative cell reference, but the second part of the formula ($B$1) is an absolute reference. When you copy this formula down the column, the first part of the formula changes to reflect the price in the cell to the left of it, but the copied formula *always* refers to cell B1 — which is just what you want. For example, the formula, when copied to cell C5, reads

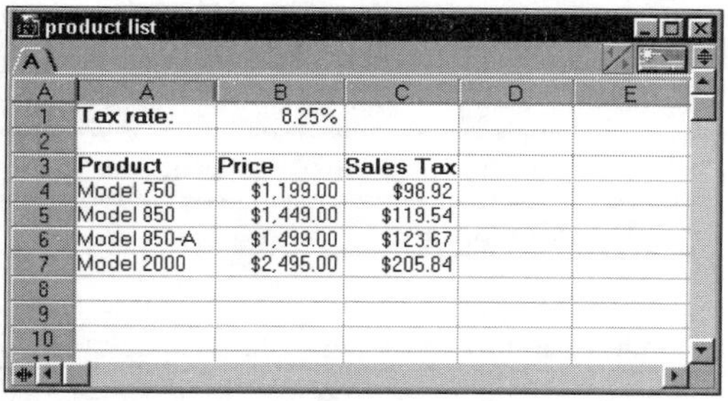

Figure 5-6:
An example
of when to
use
absolute
references.

	A	B	C	D	E
1	Tax rate:	8.25%			
2					
3	Product	Price	Sales Tax		
4	Model 750	$1,199.00	$98.92		
5	Model 850	$1,449.00	$119.54		
6	Model 850-A	$1,499.00	$123.67		
7	Model 2000	$2,495.00	$205.84		
8					
9					
10					

```
+B5*$B$1
```

If you use a relative reference (B1) rather than the absolute reference
($B$1), the copied formula is

```
+B5*B2
```

This formula returns the wrong answer, because the sales tax rate isn't in
cell B2. If this explanation doesn't make sense, read it again until it does.
Believe me, this stuff is important.

By the way, I cover copying formulas in Chapter 7.

. . . And it gets even uglier: Mixing absolute and relative references

If you think you understand the difference between relative and absolute
cell references, let me throw some more information at you. Cell references
can also be *mixed.* That is, one part can be relative and the other can be
absolute. Here's an example of a mixed cell reference:

```
+A$1
```

In this case, the column part of the cell reference is relative, but the row
part is absolute because it's preceded by a dollar sign. What happens when
you copy a formula that includes a mixed cell reference like this? Copying a
formula with this particular mixed reference always results in a reference to
row 1, because that part of the formula is absolute. The column part
changes in a relative manner.

When you start dealing with cell references on different worksheets, you can
also get involved with absolute and relative worksheet references. This
transition works very logically, and if you understand relative and absolute
references, you should have no trouble extending the concept to include
sheet letters.

To help clarify things (or muddy the waters completely), Table 5-3 shows all possible types of cell references.

Table 5-3	Types of Cell References
Example Reference	*Type of Reference*
A:A1	All relative
A:$A1	Sheet and row relative, column absolute
A:A$1	Sheet and column relative, row absolute
A:$A$1	Sheet relative, row and column absolute
$A:A1	Sheet absolute, row and column relative
$A:$A1	Sheet and column absolute, row relative
$A:A$1	Sheet and row absolute, column relative
$A:$A$1	All absolute

When you're editing a cell, press F4 to cycle through all the possible absolute/relative combinations of the cell reference that you're editing (the one with the edit cursor on it). This process saves lots of wear and tear on your dollar sign key.

Where Are the Formulas?

When you're looking at a worksheet, you can't easily tell which cells contain formulas and which cells contain other information. If you scroll around the worksheet, you can look at the contents box. If the active cell contains a formula, you see the formula in the contents box.

1-2-3 provides a feature — formula markers — that makes seeing which cells contain formulas easy. This feature is an option. Normally, displaying formula markers is turned off. To turn on the display of formula markers:

1. **Choose View⇨Set View Preferences.**

   1-2-3 displays its Workbook Properties dialog box.

2. **Click the View tab.**

3. **Place a check mark next to the Formula markers option and click OK.**

After you perform these steps, every cell containing a formula displays a small dot in its lower-left corner.

External cell references

A cell reference can actually be even more complex than what's described in this chapter. In addition to a worksheet letter, a column letter, and a row number, a reference can also include a filename. Here's an example of a formula that uses cells stored in two different workbooks:

+(<<BUDGETA.123>>A:A1)+(<<BUDGETB.123>>B:A1)

To refer to a cell in another workbook, precede the normal cell reference with a filename enclosed in double angle brackets. You can get 1-2-3 to create this reference automatically by pointing to a cell in the other worksheet as you're building a formula.

Chances are, you won't be using this feature much, if at all. But if you ever run across a formula with all those strange angle brackets in it, you'll know that the formula is using cells from a different workbook. This type of cell reference is known as an *external cell reference*.

Controlling Recalculation

As you know, a formula displays a different result if you change the values in any of the cells that the formula uses. Normally, 1-2-3 automatically performs this recalculation. Whenever you change anything in a worksheet, 1-2-3 quickly scans all the formulas and checks to see whether any of them need to be updated to show a new answer.

Some people, however, create very large worksheets that contain hundreds or even thousands of formulas. In such a case, 1-2-3 continues to scan each formula every time you make a change in the worksheet and makes the appropriate recalculations. But, because scanning thousands of formulas takes a while — even for a computer — you'll notice that you often have to wait for 1-2-3 to do its scanning. The net result is that your computer slows down, and it may even take some time for what you type to show up on the screen (a delayed reaction).

The solution is to tell 1-2-3 that *you* want to control when it does its recalculation. In other words, you want to turn off automatic recalculation and set manual recalculation. Here's how:

1. **Choose File⇨User Setup⇨1-2-3 Preferences.**

    1-2-3 displays its 1-2-3 Preferences dialog box.

2. **Click the Recalculation tab.**

    The dialog box looks similar to the one shown in Figure 5-7.

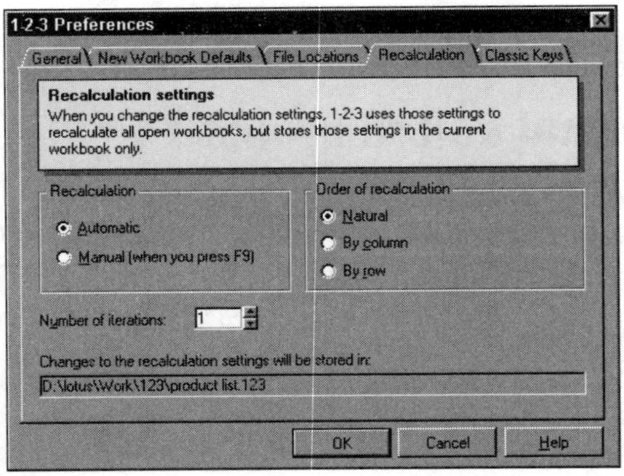

Figure 5-7:
Here's
where you
tell 1-2-3
that you
want to
control
when the
worksheet is
calculated.

1-2-3 Preferences

General \ New Workbook Defaults \ File Locations \ Recalculation \ Classic Keys

Recalculation settings
When you change the recalculation settings, 1-2-3 uses those settings to recalculate all open workbooks, but stores those settings in the current workbook only.

Recalculation
- ○ Automatic
- ○ Manual (when you press F9)

Order of recalculation
- ● Natural
- ○ By column
- ○ By row

Number of iterations: 1

Changes to the recalculation settings will be stored in:

D:\lotus\Work\123\product list.123

[OK] [Cancel] [Help]

---

3. Select the Manual option button and then click OK.

To switch back to automatic recalculation, use the same steps, but select the Automatic option button.

If you do choose to use manual recalculation, you have to remember to recalculate yourself by pressing the F9 key. 1-2-3 reminds you when a recalculation is needed by displaying Calc in the status bar at the bottom of the screen. If the Calc indicator is showing, you know that you can't always trust that what's displayed on the screen (or on paper) is really accurate. After you press F9, the worksheet is recalculated and the Calc indicator disappears.

Other Types of Formulas

This chapter focuses mainly on arithmetic formulas — formulas that deal with numbers and values. Two other types of formulas exist that you may run across:

✔ **Text formulas:** These formulas work with text that you put in cells, and you can do some clever things. For example, you can create a formula such as:

```
+"Hello"&" there"
```

This formula uses the ampersand (&) operator to join two strings of text — sort of like adding them together. This formula, when evaluated by 1-2-3, displays **Hello there** in the cell.

✔ **Logical formulas:** These formulas return either True (1) or False (0). Here's an example of a logical formula:

```
+A1=B1
```

This formula returns 1 (for True) if the contents of cell A1 are the same as the contents of cell B1. Otherwise, the formula returns 0 (for False). Most people really don't have much of a need for logical formulas, so this book more or less ignores them.

If you want to see some fairly useful formulas at work, check out Chapter 24.

Chapter 6
Creating Functional Formulas

· ·

In This Chapter

▶ Solutions for simple formulas that just can't cut the mustard

▶ An overview of @functions — who, what, why, when, where, and how

▶ Pointing skills that deal with ranges of cells

▶ @functions that just may come in handy some day

▶ An introduction to the delightful (and useful) concept of named ranges

· ·

Formulas are great — and if you don't believe me, check out Chapter 5. But, as the saying goes, "You ain't seen nothin' yet." This chapter tells you how to coax even more power from formulas by using some of the built-in functions that 1-2-3 provides for your analytical pleasure.

@Functions @Work

Sooner or later — probably later — you'll discover that your formulas need something more than the capability to refer to cell addresses and to use numbers, awesome as that is. There's gotta be more, right? You betcha.

The developers of 1-2-3, realizing that number crunchers such as yourself may actually want to do something useful with their spreadsheets, included more than 300 @functions (338, by my count) to help you out.

Okay, what's an @function?

Think of an *@function* as a shortcut for telling 1-2-3 to perform some type of operation. For example, an @function called @AVG computes the average of a range of numbers. This function saves you the trouble of adding up the numbers in the range and then dividing by the number of elements in the list. Another example is the @PMT function, which produces the monthly payment on a loan. (You need only to supply the loan amount, the interest rate, and the length of the loan.)

So what's with the *at* sign?

The *at* sign (@) is weird — I admit it. But the built-in functions in 1-2-3 are called @functions (pronounced *at funk shuns*). The at sign (@) is used to distinguish these functions from other information that you may type into a cell.

The reason for the name is mainly historical (and slightly hysterical). You see, the original version of 1-2-3 was developed a long time ago — before spreadsheet designers realized that they didn't really need to use such an arcane character to distinguish functions from other things. However, people got used to

using the at signs, so Lotus keeps them. Don't worry, getting used to this weirdness doesn't take long. And besides, you can easily spot the at sign in an @function stuck in a long formula.

This chapter doesn't cover most of the @functions, because they are beyond the scope of this book. Others are just plain worthless, frequently called *@dysfunctions*. However, you can rest assured knowing that 1-2-3's online help describes every single @function in painful detail.

Using the @functions is like having your own personal calculator built into your own personal computer. The calculating capabilities of the @functions are well beyond those of you or me. As a matter of fact, most @functions enable you to perform some feat that can't be done in any other way. @SQRT, for example, returns the square root of a number. (Try to do that without using an @function!)

A functional example

I start with an example so that you can see how to use @functions. The worksheet in Figure 6-1 contains a range of numbers that you need to add up to get a total, and you want the total to appear in cell B15. If you knew nothing about @functions, you would use the following formula:

```
+B1+B2+B3+B4+B5+B6+B7+B8+B9+B10+B11+B12+B13+B14
```

This formula certainly gets the job done, but a much easier and quicker way to create a formula is by using (you guessed it) an @function. In this case, the @SUM function does the trick just fine. Instead of typing the preceding unwieldy formula, type the following @function into cell B15 (or any cell for that matter):

```
@SUM(B1..B14)
```

In this case, the formula consists of nothing more than a single @function. The stuff in the parentheses is called the @function's *arguments* (more about the arguments later in this chapter). This @SUM function contains just one argument: a range of cells.

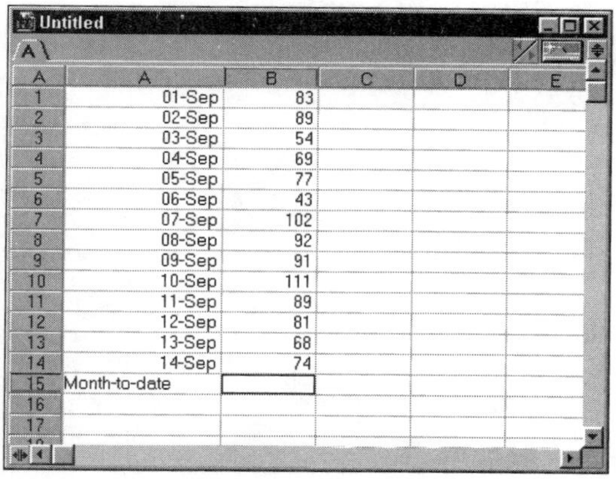

Figure 6-1:
An
@function
enables
you to
determine
the sum of
all these
numbers.

You may have already discovered the SmartIcon in Figure 6-2 that automatically adds up cells. Clicking this icon specifies a range to total in the current cell by using the @SUM function. The icon examines your worksheet, figures out what you're trying to add, and does the work for you. Now, if Lotus could only come up with a SmartIcon that makes the coffee in the morning. . . .

Figure 6-2:
This
SmartIcon
creates a
formula
automatically
by using the
@SUM
function.

In an ongoing effort to reduce the amount of work you must do, 1-2-3 provides yet another way to get an @SUM formula. When you type the word **Total** into a cell, 1-2-3 quickly scans your worksheet and determines whether you're about to add up some values. If the next column contains numbers, 1-2-3 goes ahead and enters the appropriate @SUM formula for you — and keeps looking in other columns (see Figure 6-3).

In addition to recognizing the word **Total**, 1-2-3 Millennium Edition recognizes some additional so-called SmartLabels: Average, Max, Min, Subtotal, and others. And if those SmartLabels weren't enough, you can even create your own SmartLabels. To do so, choose File⇨User Setup⇨SmartLabels Setup. You get a dialog box that lists all the existing SmartLabels. Click the Help button for details on creating your own.

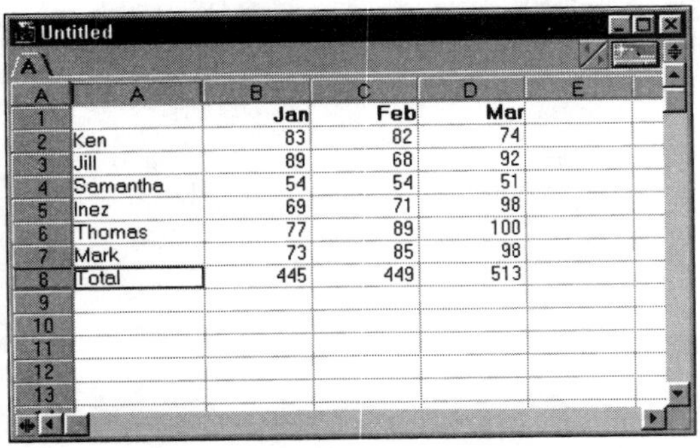

Figure 6-3:
Typing the
word Total
into cell A8
causes 1-2-3
to enter
@SUM
formulas
into cells
B8, C8,
and D8.

	A	B	C	D	E
1		Jan	Feb	Mar	
2	Ken	83	82	74	
3	Jill	89	68	92	
4	Samantha	54	54	51	
5	Inez	69	71	98	
6	Thomas	77	89	100	
7	Mark	73	85	98	
8	Total	445	449	513	

SmartLabels are not all that smart. For example, a SmartLabel can be upper- or lowercase, but it must appear by itself in the cell. For example, typing Total Sales into a cell doesn't trigger this automatic behavior.

Understanding cells and ranges

A cell is a cell, but a group of contiguous (consecutive) cells is a *range*. For example, the cells A1 through A10 are a range. You can specify a range of cells in a formula by using the following format:

```
FirstCell..LastCell
```

FirstCell and *LastCell* each represents a normal cell address. A *range reference* is simply two cell addresses separated by two periods (for example, A1..A12). The reason for using two periods goes back to the way the original 1-2-3 was set up — another strange practice that you just have to live with.

The following examples of range references give you an idea of how to interpret them:

Range Reference	*Explanation*
A1..A12	12 cells, beginning in cell A1 and extending to and including cell A12
A1..Z1	26 cells, beginning in cell A1 and extending across to and including cell Z1
A1..B12	24 cells, beginning in cell A1, going down to cell A12; and also including cell B1, going down to cell B12 (In other words, this range consists of 2 columns and 12 rows)

1-2-3 also can deal with a group of cells that is not contiguous. A group of noncontiguous cells is called a *collection*. You can refer to a collection by using a comma to separate the noncontiguous ranges or cell references that make up the collection. For example, to refer to cell A1 and the range C1..G1, the collection appears as follows:

```
A1,C1..G1
```

You normally use a collection when you select cells before you issue a command to act on the cells. Also, you can often use a collection as an argument to an @function that's expecting a range of cells. (To find out about arguments, see the upcoming section "Having an argument.")

Adding sheets to cell references

If the reference in your @function happens to extend across multiple sheets (or if you're referring to cells on a different sheet), you have to tack on a sheet reference so that 1-2-3 knows which sheets to use. You precede the range reference with a sheet letter and a colon, as illustrated in the following examples:

Sheet and Range Reference	*Explanation*
A:A1..A:A12	A range of 12 cells, all on sheet A, starting in cell A1 and going to cell A12
A:A1..C:A12	A three-dimensional range of 36 cells, beginning in cell A1 of sheet A and extending to cell A12 on sheet C. In other words, this reference consists of the following ranges: cells A:A1 through A:A12, B:A1 through B:A12, and C:A1 through C:A12.

Using @Functions

This section provides the details you need for using @functions in your formulas.

Having an argument

The information that an @function uses to perform its magic is called its *arguments*. Arguments are always enclosed in parentheses, directly following the @function name. You should remember the following information about @function arguments:

✔ Some @functions need more than one argument. In such cases, the arguments are separated with a comma.

✔ Some @functions need a single cell for an argument, and others need a range reference.

✔ Some @functions need numbers for arguments, and others need text.

✔ You usually can use a normal number or text in place of a cell reference.

✔ You can also use a range name as an argument for a range reference, or a cell name as an argument for a cell reference.

The following examples illustrate how the different arguments work in the @SUM function:

@SUM Function	Explanation
@SUM(A1..A12)	Adds the numbers in the range A1..A12
@SUM(A1)	Displays the number in cell A1 (Not a terribly useful formula, but it is valid.)
@SUM(A1,A2,A3,A4)	Adds the numbers in cells A1, A2, A3, and A4; you can do this calculation more efficiently by using @SUM(A1..A4)
@SUM(1,2,3,4)	Adds the numbers 1, 2, 3, and 4 and displays the result (which is 10)
@SUM(A1..A12)/2	Adds the numbers in the range A1..A12 and then divides the result by 2
@SUM(A:A1..C:A12)	Adds the numbers in the three-dimensional range, starting in cell A1 on sheet A and extending through cell A12 on sheet C (the third sheet)

Entering @functions two ways

Just as you can build a formula either by typing it directly into a cell or by pointing to the cells that you want to include in the formula (see Chapter 5), you use the same two processes for entering @functions into your cells.

The direct approach

Entering an @function directly involves, well, entering an @function directly. In other words, if you want to calculate the average of the numbers in the range A1..C12 and have the answer appear in cell A13, put the following @function into cell A13:

```
@AVG(A1..C12)
```

By the way, you can type the @function in uppercase, lowercase, or mixed case. The case doesn't matter at all, because 1-2-3 always converts the letters to uppercase.

The pointing method

Sometimes, pointing out the cell or range (called an argument) may be faster than typing it — and it's usually more accurate. To point out a range for an @function's argument, do the following:

1. **Move the cell pointer to the cell that will hold the formula.**

2. **Type @, followed by the @function's name, and then an open parenthesis.**

   For example, if you're entering an @SUM formula, type

   @SUM(

3. **Use the arrow keys to move to the first cell of the range that will be the function's argument.**

4. **Press the period key.**

   Pressing the period key makes the first cell "stick" so that you can point to the last cell in the range (this action is also known as *anchoring* the cell).

5. **Use the arrow keys to move to the last cell in the range.**

6. **Type a closing parenthesis.**

7. **Press Enter to insert the formula.**

Rather than go through all the preceding steps with your keyboard, you can simply click and drag the mouse over the range after you type the @function's name and an opening parenthesis. As you drag the range, 1-2-3 displays the selected range in the cell. After you finish, type the closing parenthesis and press Enter.

Editing @functions

It should come as no surprise that you can edit formulas that contain @functions. You edit @functions just as you edit any other cell. First, you do one of the following:

✔ Press F2.

✔ Click the edit line with your mouse.

✔ Double-click the cell.

Then you can use the normal editing keys (arrow keys, Backspace, Delete) to change the formula. After you get the formula right, press Enter. I discuss basic cell editing in Chapter 4.

Insert @function here, insert @function here!

With more than 300 of these suckers to choose from, how can you possibly remember the names and correct spellings of all the @functions? Well, chances are you may only use a small percentage of the @functions, but you can get a complete list when the need arises.

When you're entering a formula and need an @function, you can just click the @ icon on the edit line. (Officially, this icon is known as the *@Function Selector.*) Clicking this icon drops down the list shown in Figure 6-4. The actual list varies, and you can customize this list so it displays the @functions that you use most often (see "Enhancing the @Function Selector list," later in this chapter).

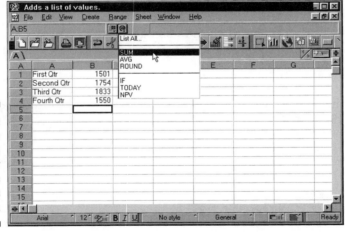

Figure 6-4: Clicking the @Function Selector icon drops down this list.

The first entry in this drop-down list is always List All. If you select List All, you get the dialog box shown in Figure 6-5.

The first step is to select an @function category from the drop-down list named Category. (I describe these categories later in this section.) When you choose a category, the @functions list box shows all the @functions in that particular category. If you select the All @Functions category, the list box shows every @function. In other words, your scope isn't narrowed.

Figure 6-5:
The
@Function
List dialog
box is the
place to be
when you
need to
insert an
@function.

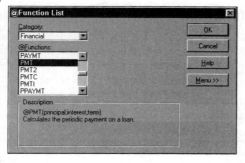

After you select a category, scroll through the list of @functions in that category and select the one you want by clicking it. Then click OK. 1-2-3 inserts the chosen @function into your formula — and also includes "dummy" arguments for you. These placeholders tell you how many arguments an @function needs and also give you an idea about what each argument should be.

After you insert an @function, notice that the first dummy argument is selected, or highlighted (see Figure 6-6). This highlighting lets you type the argument, point to the argument, or select a named cell or range from the Navigator icon (which is directly to the left of the @Function Selector icon). You always need to substitute actual cell or range references for the dummy arguments. If you fail to replace the dummy arguments with real arguments, the formula returns ERR.

While the @Function List dialog box is displayed, you have quick and easy access to 1-2-3's online help. Just select an @function from the list and click the Help button (or press F1). You'll find out more than you ever wanted to know about that particular @function.

Figure 6-6:
When you
insert an
@function,
1-2-3
provides
you with
placeholders
for the
arguments.

	A	B	C	D	E	F
1	Loan Amount	125,000				
2	Interest Rate	8.5%				
3	Term (months)	360				
4						
5	Monthly Payment	@PMT(principal,interest,term)				
6						
7						
8						
9						
10						
11						
12						
13						
14						
15						

Using @function categories

To help you avoid @function overload (a common malady among spreadsheet users), the 1-2-3 developers placed each @function into a particular category. These categories make narrowing your search easier when you need an @function but you don't know its name. Table 6-1 shows the @function categories.

Table 6-1	@Function Categories
Category	**What It Does**
Calendar	Calculates values that deal with dates and times
Database	Performs queries and calculations in database tables
Engineering	Performs engineering calculations and other advanced mathematical operations (plastic pocket protector not required)
Financial	Deals with investments, annuities, securities, depreciation, cash flows, and loans
Information	Returns information about cells, ranges, the operating system, and some 1-2-3 tools
Logical	Calculates the results of logical or conditional formulas
Lookup	Gets the contents of a cell in a table, based on some other information
Mathematical	Performs mathematical operations and trigonometric calculations
Statistical	Performs calculations on lists of values
Text	Provides information about text in cells and performs other operations on text

Enhancing the @Function Selector list

If you find that you use a particular @function on a regular basis, you may want to set things up so the @function appears in the @Function Selector list — the list that appears when you click the @ symbol in the edit line. To add a new @function to this list:

1. **Click the @ symbol in the edit line.**

2. **Select List All to display the @Function List dialog box.**

3. **Select the @function from the @Functions list.**

4. **Click the Menu>> button.**

5. Click the >> button to add the selected @function to the list.

6. Click OK to close the @Function List dialog box.

After you perform these steps, your new @function appears in the list when you click the @ symbol. You can add as many new @functions as you like.

Numerical @Function Examples

In previous sections of this chapter, I tell you about the @SUM function — which is, by far, the most commonly used @function. I also mention the ever popular @AVG function (which works just like @SUM, except it returns the average of the cells in its argument). Because you're probably yearning for more, I won't keep you in suspense any longer. Keep reading for details on some more useful @functions.

@MAX

Suppose that you start a worksheet with the monthly sales figures for all the salespeople in your organization. The worksheet may look something like Figure 6-7. You want to know the maximum sales amount for the month so you can use this information to motivate the other salespeople. You can scan through the numbers and try to figure out which number is the highest, or you can use the @MAX function. Just type the following formula into the cell where you want to display the maximum sales figure:

```
@MAX(B2..B20)
```

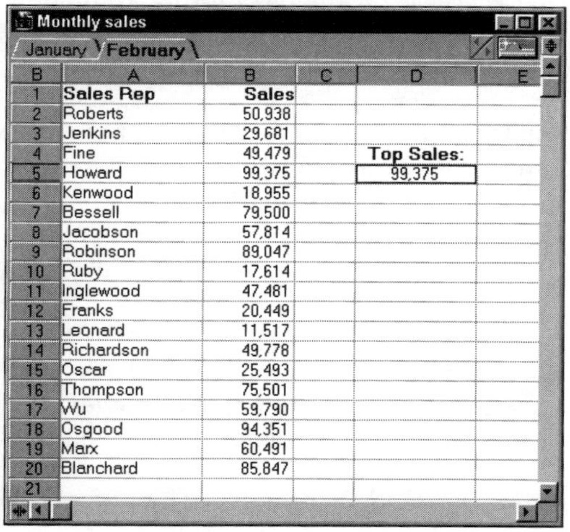

Figure 6-7:
The @MAX function can tell you the largest sales figure.

	A	B	C	D	E
1	Sales Rep	Sales			
2	Roberts	50,938			
3	Jenkins	29,681			
4	Fine	49,479		Top Sales:	
5	Howard	99,375		99,375	
6	Kenwood	18,955			
7	Bessell	79,500			
8	Jacobson	57,814			
9	Robinson	89,047			
10	Ruby	17,614			
11	Inglewood	47,481			
12	Franks	20,449			
13	Leonard	11,517			
14	Richardson	49,778			
15	Oscar	25,493			
16	Thompson	75,501			
17	Wu	59,790			
18	Osgood	94,351			
19	Marx	60,491			
20	Blanchard	85,847			
21					

Monthly sales — January / February

In some cases, you may prefer to use an entire column as the argument. This arrangement is particularly useful if you plan to add new data to the worksheet. For the preceding example, you can use the following formula, which returns the maximum value in column B, regardless of the number of entries in the column.

```
@MAX(B1..B65536)
```

@MIN

If you need to locate the lowest sales volume in the list, you can use the following @MIN function, which works like the @MAX function but displays the lowest sales figure:

```
@MIN(B2..B20)
```

@SQRT

The @SQRT function is a shortened version of the term *square root*. The square root of a number is the number that, when multiplied by itself, gives you the original number. For example, 4 is the square root of 16 because $4 \times 4 = 16$.

You can calculate the square root of the value in cell A1 by entering the following formula in any cell:

```
@SQRT(A1)
```

If cell A1 contains the value 225, the formula returns 15. @SQRT is an example of an @function that requires a single cell for its argument — perfectly logical, because calculating the square root of an entire range and putting the result in one cell doesn't make sense.

On this planet, calculating the square root of a negative number is illegal. Because 1-2-3 is a law-abiding citizen, it dutifully returns ERR if you try to do so.

@ROUND

The @ROUND function rounds off its argument and displays the result. If cell A1 contains 12.67, you can round it off to the nearest integer and display the result (13) in cell B1 by entering the following formula in cell B1:

```
@ROUND(A1,0)
```

Does this formula look different from what you expected? To produce the correct result in your worksheet, this function needs two arguments. The first argument tells the program which cell you want to round off; the second argument tells 1-2-3 how many decimal places to round the number to. In this case, the second argument is 0, which tells the program to round off the number in cell A1 to no decimal places.

To round off the number to the first decimal place, 12.7, you change the formula to look like the following example:

```
@ROUND(A1,1)
```

Using the @ROUND function is not the same as changing the number format to display a different number of decimal places. Formatting only affects the way a number looks. A formula that uses the @ROUND function returns the actual rounded value.

Date and Time @Function Examples

The @functions that deal with dates and times get their information from your computer's internal clock. Make sure that your computer's clock is set properly or these functions may return the wrong dates and times. You can correct your computer's clock by using the Windows Control Panel.

By default, 1-2-3 doesn't recognize all date-formatted entries as dates. However, you can change the defaults (see the nearby sidebar, "How about a date?"). Table 6-2 shows samples of common date formats, along with 1-2-3's interpretation of the entry.

Table 6-2	Entering Dates into Cells
Entered into a Cell	*1-2-3's Interpretation*
6-1-98	Incorrectly interprets entry as a formula
6-1-1998	Incorrectly interprets entry as a formula
1-Jun	June 1, of the current year
1-Jun-98	June 1, 1998
6/1/98	June 1, 1998
6/1/1998	June 1, 1998
Jun-98	June 1, 1998
6-1/98	Incorrectly interprets entry as a formula

(continued)

Table 6-2 *(continued)*	
Entered into a Cell	*1-2-3's Interpretation*
June 1, 1998	Incorrectly interprets entry as a label
June 1	Incorrectly interprets entry as a label
6/1	Incorrectly interprets entry as a formula
6-1	Incorrectly interprets entry as a formula

If you plan to use dates in formulas, make sure that the date you enter is actually recognized as a date; otherwise, your formulas produce incorrect results.

@DATE

You can either enter a date into a cell using one of the accepted formats listed in Table 6-2, or you can use the @DATE function. The @DATE function argument contains three parts: a year, a month, and a day. To enter December 25, 1998, into a cell, use the following formula:

```
@DATE(98,12,25)
```

1-2-3 displays the number 36154 — its special date number for the specific date that you entered. To make the date number show up as a date, use the Number Format tab of the Range InfoBox (press Alt+Enter if the Range InfoBox is not displayed). Just specify one of the date format options. Or you can use the numeric formatting button in the status bar.

@TODAY

This function doesn't need an argument. It simply returns the date number that corresponds to the current date stored in the computer's clock. For example, if you enter @TODAY into a cell on September 1, 1998, the function returns 36039 — the date number that corresponds to that date. If you save the file and load it again the next day, the function returns 36040. In other words, @TODAY always returns the current date.

What about this Year 2000 thing?

A hot topic lately concerns the year 2000. As you've probably heard, some software isn't programmed to handle 4-digit years. Therefore, at the stroke of midnight on December 31, 1999, all heck will break loose as computers across the world make incorrect calculations. The seriousness of this issue remains to be seen, but it's a good idea to be mindful of this type of thing when working with 1-2-3.

Before 1-2-3 Millennium Edition, all 2-digit dates were interpreted to be in the 20th century — between 1900 and 1999. The latest edition of 1-2-3 introduces a new date-related concept known as a "sliding window." The sliding window defines a window of 100 years around the current year (determined by the system date on your computer). When you enter a year using only two digits, 1-2-3 compares the two digits you entered with the years that fall within this 100-year window.

By default, 1-2-3 uses an 80/20 rule for this sliding window — the window begins 80 years before and ends 19 years after the current year. If the current year is 1998, a window spanning 100 years includes the years 1918 to 2017. So any 2-digit year you enter from 18 to 98 equals years from 1918 to 1998. Any 2-digit year you enter from 01 to 17 equals years from 2001 to 2017. If you want to enter a date before 1918 or after 2017, you must enter all four digits for the year. It may sound a bit confusing, but it's really not.

If you want to ignore this whole sliding window thing, choose File⇨User Setup⇨1-2-3 Preferences and click the General tab. Change the option in the Dates section (see the accompanying figure).

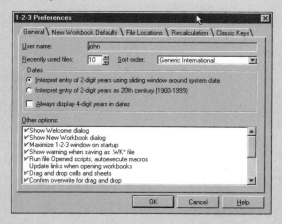

How about a date?

If you want 1-2-3 to be able to recognize a different style of entering dates, you have to make a few adjustments. For example, assume that you like to enter dates in a format like *January 1, 1998*. This entry consists of the month name spelled out, the date, a comma, and a four-digit year. Normally, 1-2-3 interprets such an entry as a label. In order to force 1-2-3 to recognize this date format as an actual date, do the following:

1. **Choose Range⇨Range Properties.**

   1-2-3 displays its Range InfoBox.

2. **Click the Number Format tab.**

3. **Click the Date category.**

4. **Scroll down the list of formats until you find one that looks like the format you want.**

5. **Place a check mark next to the check box labeled Show in frequently used list.**

After completing these steps, you can enter a date in a format such as March 3, 1998.

@TIME

Like the @DATE function, the @TIME function argument has three parts: an hour, a minute, and a second. To enter 5:30 p.m. into a cell, use the following formula:

```
@TIME(17,30,0)
```

Why the number 17? Remember that in 24-hour time, 5:00 p.m. is 5 hours past 12:00 noon, so that you add 12 + 5 to get 17 hours. The formula represents 17 hours, 30 minutes, and 0 seconds into the day, or 5:30 p.m. If you enter this @TIME function into a cell, 1-2-3 displays .7292824074. To see this number as readable time, use the Number Format tab of the Range InfoBox and choose one of the time formats provided.

Using @Functions in Formulas

The example formulas I present in previous sections of this chapter consist of only single @functions. You can, however, combine @functions in formulas. Take a look at the following formula, for example:

```
@SUM(A1..A10)+@SUM(C1..C10)
```

Here, the formula takes the sum of the numbers in the range A1..A10 and adds the result to the sum of the numbers in range C1..C10. Another way of

You got the time?

1-2-3 not only deals with dates but also handles time, by extending the date number concept to include decimal values. As you know, the date number 36154 corresponds to December 25, 1998. By adding a decimal point to the number, you also can work with times during that day. For example, 36154.5 corresponds to 12:00 noon (halfway through Christmas day, 1998); 36154.1 corresponds to 2:24 a.m. (one-tenth of the way through the day).

Because a day has 86,400 seconds, one second works out to be .000011574074074 in this serial number format. One minute, on the other hand, equates to .0006944444. And one hour is .041666667. Therefore, to express 1:00 a.m. on December 25, 1998, you enter 36154.041666667 into a cell. If all these numbers have your head reeling, don't fret. Using the @TIME function makes the whole process relatively painless.

looking at the formula is that it's taking the sum of the range A1..C10, but skipping the range B1..B10. Therefore, the following formula produces the same result:

```
@SUM(A1..C10)-@SUM(B1..B10)
```

Yet another way to get the same result (without using any mathematical operators) is to use two arguments for the @SUM function:

```
@SUM(A1..A10,C1..C10)
```

You can also work with dates and times in a formula. Suppose that you want to know the number of days between August 3, 1998, and July 16, 1998. Use the following formula to get the desired results:

```
@DATE(98,8,3)-@DATE(98,7,16)
```

In this case, putting the date formulas in separate cells (such as A1 and A2) and then using a simpler formula (such as +A1 – A2) to do the subtraction may be better. By putting the date formulas in separate cells, you can easily change the dates without having to mess with a more complex formula. In other words, you are making the spreadsheet more general — a good idea to keep in mind.

@functions inside of @functions

The fact is, you can create some very complex formulas by using @functions. You can even use @functions as arguments for other @functions, a concept known as *nested @functions* (a topic that's for the birds).

Figure 6-8, for example, displays values in column B and formulas in column C. The formula in cell C2 is @ROUND(B2,0), which rounds the value in cell B2 to zero decimal places. Rows 3 – 5 in column C each have similar formulas that round the values in their corresponding column B cells. Row 6 contains @SUM formulas to compute the total of the cells above.

	A	B	C	D	E	F
1		Value	Rounded			
2		14.58	15.00			
3		23.78	24.00			
4		45.02	45.00			
5		60.03	60.00			
6	Sum	143.41	144.00			
7						
8	Rounded Sum	143.00				

@ROUND(@SUM(B2..B5),0)

Figure 6-8: An example of a nested @function.

Cell B8 contains a nested @function:

```
@ROUND(@SUM(B2..B5),0)
```

How can you interpret this complex formula? 1-2-3 tackles the formula as follows: First, it evaluates the @SUM function and stores the answer in its memory. Then the program uses this answer as the first argument for the @ROUND function and combines the answer with the second argument for the @ROUND function (which is 0). The program then displays the final answer in cell B8.

Rounding off the sum of the values doesn't produce the same result as summing the rounded off values. If you don't believe me, examine Figure 6-8 again and notice that the result in cell C6 isn't the same as the result in cell B8.

Testing conditions

One of the more useful @functions is the @IF function. This @function essentially allows your formulas to make decisions based on values in your worksheet. Giving decision-making power to 1-2-3 can result in some very powerful worksheets.

The @IF function requires the following three arguments:

- ✔ A condition to test
- ✔ What to display if the condition is true
- ✔ What to display if the condition is false

The following example tests whether the number in cell A1 is positive or negative:

```
@IF(A1>0,"Positive","Negative or zero")
```

Notice that the three arguments are separated by commas. The first argument is the condition, which, in this case, asks whether the number in cell A1 is greater than zero. If the number is greater than zero, the formula displays the second argument (the word *Positive*); if the number is zero or less than zero, the formula displays the third argument (the words *Negative or zero*).

Suppose that you want to know specifically whether the number in a cell is positive, negative, or zero (three responses — an added twist to the same concept). Now you need to use a nested @IF function to produce the desired result. Before you read the explanation, try to figure out the following formula on your own to see how it works:

```
@IF(A1>0,"Positive",@IF(A1<0,"Negative","Zero"))
```

1-2-3 first tests to see whether the number in cell A1 is greater than zero. If so, the program responds with the word Positive and is done with the formula. If the value of cell A1 is not greater than zero, the program goes to the third part of the first @IF argument and discovers another @IF function there, which it proceeds to evaluate. This second (nested) @IF function checks to see whether the value of cell A1 is less than zero. If so, the program responds with the word Negative. If not, the program responds with the final choice of Zero.

If you understand how the nested @IF function works, congratulations! You're well on your way to being a more-than-adequate 1-2-3 user.

What Shall We Name It?

Naming cells and ranges may not be absolutely necessary for your well-being, but you may find that doing so makes your spreadsheeting life easier — and also makes your formulas much more readable. You can give a meaningful name to any cell or range (I discuss this process in the upcoming section "Naming cells and ranges"). After doing so, you can use that name wherever you normally use a cell or range reference.

A named cell example

Assume that your worksheet has a cell (for example, F2) that contains the number of employees in your company. Further assume that another cell (say, M1) has a value that represents the total salary paid to all employees in your company. To calculate the average salary, you use this formula:

```
+M1/F2
```

That formula is perfectly fine, but wouldn't you prefer to use this formula instead:

```
+TOTAL_SALARY/EMPLOYEE_COUNT
```

As you probably surmise by now, 1-2-3 lets you provide meaningful names to cells and ranges. Naming cells and ranges offers two advantages:

- ✔ Anyone who looks at the formula gets a pretty good idea of what it does.
- ✔ You reduce the chance of making an error.

A named range example

You can name single cells, or give a name to an entire range. For example, if range G1..G12 is named EXPENSES, you can write the following formula that adds the expenses in the entire range, using the name of the range alone:

```
@SUM(EXPENSES)
```

The formula @SUM(G1..G12) also requests the sum of the range but doesn't indicate what the formula is adding. Not only does using the name of the range simplify your formula, but the name also makes the formula clear to anyone who sees it.

Naming cells and ranges

Naming a cell or range is easy. Just follow these steps:

1. Move the cell pointer to the cell you want to name.

   If you want to name a range, select the entire range.

2. Choose Range⇨Name.

1-2-3 pops up the dialog box shown in Figure 6-9.

Figure 6-9:
The Name
dialog box,
where you
give a name
to a cell or
range.

3. Type the name for the cell or range in the Name box and click OK.

Keep the following information in mind as you go about naming cells and ranges:

✔ 1-2-3 always converts names to uppercase.

✔ Names can be up to 15 characters long, and you can't use math operators or spaces. Also, avoid creating names that look like cell addresses. For example, 1-2-3 may confuse a range named *ab1* with cell AB1.

✔ If you already have one or more names in your worksheet, 1-2-3 displays a list of these names in the Name dialog box. By choosing a name from this list, you can see the cell or range the name refers to in the Range box.

✔ You can name a bunch of single cells that have labels next to them, and you can name them all with a single command. Use the Range⇨Name command and click the Use Labels button. In the list box below the button, tell 1-2-3 where the labels are in relation to the cells that you want to name.

✔ You can quickly move the cell pointer to a named range by using the Range Selector icon in the edit line. Clicking the Range Selector icon displays a list of all named ranges, similar to the one in Figure 6-9. Select the range you want, and you're there in a flash.

Chapter 7

Making Changes to Your Work (And Living to Tell about It)

In This Chapter

▶ Cutting and pasting cells and ranges

▶ Copying cells and ranges of cells (or, how to make many from one)

▶ Changing column widths to avoid the asterisks problem

▶ Making rows taller

▶ Inserting and deleting rows and columns

▶ Turning horizontal data into vertical data — and vice versa

▶ Using Find & Replace to make lots of changes with little effort

▶ Sorting a range of data — and all kinds of options you have

*I*f you're like most people, you spend a large part of your spreadsheeting time changing things that you've already done. This is perfectly normal, and it's not a sign of an indecisive personality disorder. (I don't think so, anyway. On second thought, it may be. Well, then again, I'm not sure.) Anyway, you'll soon discover that when you start making changes to a worksheet, taking something that used to work and somehow messing it up so that it doesn't work anymore is far too easy.

Therefore, understanding what goes on behind the scenes when you set out to change something in your worksheet is in your best interest. This rule especially applies to copying, cutting, and pasting cells and ranges — particularly when they contain formulas. That's why this chapter has more than its share of Warning icons.

How Do I Change You? Let Me Count the Ways

What kinds of changes can you make to a worksheet? Here are some examples:

- ✔ You spend five minutes creating a killer formula that does magic with a column of numbers. You have 20 more columns that need the same formula applied to them. What to do? Copy the formula so that it works for the other ranges of cells.

- ✔ You have a nice table of numbers, but you fell asleep on the keyboard and put the table about 50 rows below where it should be. So you need to move it up to a more reasonable location in the worksheet. This procedure is known as *cutting and pasting*.

- ✔ You're just about ready to turn in your department budget when you realize that you forgot to enter a budget item (Pet Neutering) that should go right between the categories Outboard Motor Repair and Quilting Supplies. You need to insert a new row to make room for it.

- ✔ Your boss informs you that you can no longer budget for office mud baths. Eventually, regardless of the resentment you feel, you must zap the entire Mud Bath row in your budget worksheet.

- ✔ You have a great worksheet, but the numbers are all crammed together and difficult to read. You want to widen some of the columns.

- ✔ You have a bunch of labels entered in a column — and you realize that you should've put them in a row. You need to transpose these labels, and you don't feel like typing them all again.

- ✔ Marketing informs you that it changed the name of one of your company's products from Sugar Munchies to Health Munchies. Your worksheet has dozens of labels with this product's name in it, and you need to change every occurrence of *Sugar* to *Health*. You can do so manually — or let 1-2-3 do it for you with its find and replace capability.

- ✔ You spend two hours entering all your sales figures in alphabetical order by sales rep name. Then your boss informs you that the figures need to be in descending order by sales amount. Unless you like to redo your work, you need to sort this range of cells.

The preceding list describes just some of the changes that people make to their worksheets. The rest of this chapter tells you how to make these types of changes — without destroying what you've already done and causing more work for yourself.

Undo: Your built-in safety net

When you start making changes to a worksheet, remember that you can reverse the effects of most things that you do by choosing Edit⇨Undo (or pressing Ctrl+Z) immediately after you make the change. But you have to issue this command before you do *anything* else. Therefore, getting into the habit of examining what you did before you move on to something else is a good idea.

To make sure that the Undo feature is enabled, choose File⇨User Setup⇨1-2-3 Preferences to bring up the 1-2-3 Preferences dialog box. Click the General tab and make sure that the Undo check book is checked; otherwise, the Edit⇨Undo command isn't available.

When you're performing major surgery on a workbook (which sometimes requires lots of patience), making a backup copy of your file is also good. That way, if the surgery isn't successful, you can always revert to the previous version.

Cutting and Pasting (Without Using Glue)

When you enter something into a cell, that information isn't stuck there for life. You can cut it and paste it anywhere else on the worksheet — or even paste it to a different worksheet or workbook. In other words, if you want to move something from one place to another, you cut it and then paste it.

Say you enter a list of numbers into a worksheet column and then discover that you forgot to leave space for a heading. You *could* insert a new row and stick the heading in the new row. But if you have other information in the first row, inserting a new row would mess it up. Therefore, the easiest solution is to move the list of numbers down one row — cut it and then paste it. Another reason to move things around in a worksheet is simply to better organize your information. We all change our minds occasionally, right?

How cutting and pasting works

If you're going to use Windows software, you have to understand the concept of *cutting and pasting,* and that involves getting to know the infamous Windows Clipboard. (See the sidebar "More about the Windows Clipboard" for additional information on this Clipboard business.) When you tell 1-2-3 to cut, it takes whatever is selected at the time (a cell or a range), removes it from the worksheet, and puts a copy of it on the Clipboard. Then, when you tell 1-2-3 to paste, it takes what's in the Clipboard and pastes it to your current selection (usually a different cell or a range). After you understand this concept, you should have no problems moving stuff around.

When you paste a cell or range and the area that you're pasting to already contains something, 1-2-3 overwrites the cells with the pasted information — without warning. So, if you have some important stuff on your worksheet, be careful when moving things around.

When you're dealing with the Windows Clipboard, you can save yourself lots of time by getting into the habit of using shortcut keys or SmartIcons instead of menus. The shortcut keys and SmartIcons for cutting, pasting, and copying are

Edit⇨Cut	Ctrl+X	
Edit⇨Paste	Ctrl+V	
Edit⇨Copy	Ctrl+C	

Throughout this chapter, I talk about the Edit⇨Cut, Edit⇨Paste, and Edit⇨Copy commands. A faster way to access these commands is by right-clicking after you make a selection. Doing so brings up a shortcut menu on which you can choose Cut, Paste, or Copy.

More about the Windows Clipboard

As this chapter so eloquently describes, cutting and pasting within 1-2-3 uses something called the Windows Clipboard. Basically, this Clipboard is an area of your computer's memory that's sort of a temporary holding spot. So, when you cut or copy a cell or a range, 1-2-3 puts the information on the Clipboard. When you paste something to a cell or range, 1-2-3 takes whatever happens to be in the Clipboard and pastes it wherever you want it to go.

The Clipboard can hold only one thing at a time. So, if you copy a cell or range to the Clipboard, that information replaces what's already there (if anything). The Clipboard is pretty versatile, and it can hold all sorts of information — the contents of a single cell, a range of cells, an entire chart, or part of a graph.

The nice thing about the Clipboard, though, is that all Windows programs have access to it. Thus, you can copy a range of cells from 1-2-3 and then paste them into your Windows word processing program. The Clipboard works as the intermediary. Although you can't paste all types of information that can be stored on the Clipboard into every application, the Clipboard is pretty adaptable — and after you get used to it in one application, you can use it in virtually all Windows applications.

Cutting and pasting a cell

Here's how to move the contents of a cell from one place to another:

1. **Start by moving the cell pointer to the cell that you want to move.**

 2. **Choose Edit⇨Cut (or press Ctrl+X or click the Cut SmartIcon).**

   1-2-3 removes the contents of the cell and places them on the Windows Clipboard. Notice the message in the title bar: `Select destination and press ENTER or choose Edit Paste.`

3. **Move to the new location where you want to paste the contents of the cell.**

 4. **Press Enter (or choose Edit⇨Paste or press Ctrl+V or click the Paste SmartIcon).**

   1-2-3 puts the contents of the Clipboard in the selected cell.

Clearly, cutting and pasting the contents of a single cell is no great time-saver — unless the cell contains a long label or a formula. If you just have a value or a short label, simply deleting it and retyping it somewhere else may be easier.

Cutting and pasting a range

The real value of cutting and pasting becomes apparent when you start dealing with ranges of cells. Moving a range of cells is very similar to moving one cell. Select the entire range you want to move and then choose Edit⇨Cut (or press Ctrl+X) to remove the range and put in on the Clipboard. Next, move the cell pointer to the new location (you need to select only the upper-left cell in the new range — not the entire range). Press Enter, and 1-2-3 retrieves the information from the Clipboard and puts it in the new location you specified.

You can relocate dozens, hundreds, or even thousands of cells using the cut-and-paste method.

Cutting and pasting formulas

You can move cells that contain formulas just like you move other cells. So, if you cut and paste a cell that has a formula such as +A1+A2, the formula continues to refer to those same cells no matter where you move it. This result is almost always what you want, because you generally don't want to change the formula itself — just relocate it.

Moving cells that contain formulas doesn't change the cell references in the formulas.

The E-Z way to move things

Now that you know how to use the Clipboard to cut and paste information, you may be interested in another, easier way to move cells or ranges. This method is really easy and quite intuitive: Simply select the cell or range that you want to move, drag it to where you want to put it, and then drop it in place. This method works best when the place you're moving to isn't too far away.

The only thing you have to remember when you want to drag something is that the mouse pointer must look like a hand before you can drag a cell or range. To get the mouse pointer to turn into a hand, just move it to one of the edges of the selection. When the pointer turns into a hand, click and hold down the left mouse button. The hand closes, and the cell or range has a dark outline around it. You can then drag your selection to its new location. When you release the mouse button, the cell or range appears in its new location, and you're done. Figure 7-1 shows what this pointer looks like before you click (open hand) and after you click (closed hand).

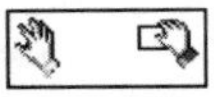

Figure 7-1:
The mouse pointer, before and while dragging a selection.

When you're dragging a cell or range, you don't drag the actual selection. Rather, you drag an outline of the selection.

You can also use the drag-and-drop method to move a cell or range to a different workbook. But to do so, you must have both workbooks visible. You may need to do a bit of window rearranging before you begin moving.

If drag-and-drop isn't working, you probably have this feature disabled. To enable drag-and-drop, choose File⇨User Setup⇨1-2-3 Preferences. Click the General tab in the 1-2-3 Preferences dialog box, and make sure that the Drag-and-drop cells and sheets option is checked.

Copy-Catting

One of the most common spreadsheet operations is copying. You have three options when you want to copy something:

- ✔ Copy a single cell to another cell.
- ✔ Copy a single cell to a range of cells.
- ✔ Copy a whole range of cells to another area.

The most obvious reason to copy a cell or a range of cells is so you don't have to type in the information again. Copying is also useful for duplicating a formula so that the formula works on other ranges. When you copy a formula, 1-2-3 does some interesting things, as I explain in the next section.

How copying works

As you may expect, copying is similar to moving — and both operations use the Clipboard. The difference, however, is that 1-2-3 leaves the copied cell or range contents intact when it puts them on the Clipboard. When you make a copy of a cell or range, the original cell or range remains the same — you're simply making a replica of it and sticking it somewhere else. Think of it like this: Moving information consists of *cutting* and pasting; making a copy of information consists of *copying* and pasting.

Just as with cutting and pasting, when you copy something and the area that you're copying to already contains something, 1-2-3 overwrites the cells with the new copied information — without notice. So, if you have some important stuff on your worksheet, be careful when copying.

Copying a cell to a cell

Here's how to copy the contents of one cell to another cell:

1. **Move the cell pointer to the cell you want to copy.**

2. **Choose Edit⇨Copy (or press Ctrl+C or click the Copy SmartIcon).**

   1-2-3 makes a copy of the cell contents and stores it on the Windows Clipboard. The contents of the cell remain intact. Notice that a message appears in the title bar: Select destination and press ENTER or choose Edit Paste.

3. **Move the cell pointer to the cell where you want to place the copy.**

4. **Press Enter (or choose Edit⇨Paste or press Ctrl+V or click the Paste SmartIcon — so many options, so little time!).**

   1-2-3 retrieves the contents of the Clipboard and inserts them into the cell. Mission accomplished.

   The cell you specified in Step 3 now contains the same information as the original cell.

Copying a cell to a range

Copying a single cell to a range of cells works exactly the same as copying to a single cell. You start by selecting the cell you want to copy and then choosing Edit⇨Copy (or one of the alternate methods). Then you select a *range* of cells and choose Edit⇨Paste (or one of the alternate methods). After you do so, the single cell you originally copied to the Clipboard is duplicated in every cell in the range you selected.

Figure 7-2 shows what happens when you copy a single cell to a range of cells.

Figure 7-2:
Copying a
single cell
to a range
puts the
contents of
the cell into
every cell in
the range.

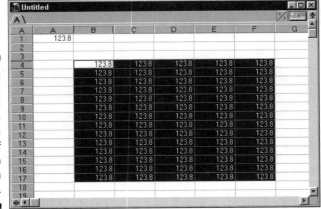

Copying a range to a range

Copying a range of cells to another range is very similar to the other copy operations I describe in this chapter. Select the range to be copied and choose Edit⇨Copy. Then move the cell pointer to the new location and choose Edit⇨Paste. You need only select the upper-left cell before you do the pasting (you don't have to select the entire range).

Figure 7-3 shows a range of cells that has been copied to another range.

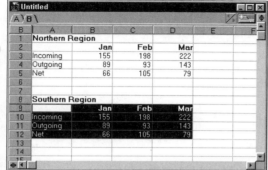

Figure 7-3: Copying an entire range duplicates that range somewhere else.

Copying formulas

Copying formulas works exactly like copying anything else. In other words, you can copy a single formula to another cell, copy a single formula to a range of cells, or copy a range of formulas to another range of cells.

When you copy a formula, something special happens: All the cell references in the formula get adjusted. Assume for a minute that cell A3 has the formula +A1+A2. When you copy this formula to cell B3, the formula reads +B1+B2. In other words, the cell references get changed to refer to the same relative cells in their new position.

"Wait a minute," you say. "If I make a copy of a formula, the copy should be exact, right? Copying a cell that contains +A1+A2 should produce +A1+A2 in the cell that it gets copied to." Well, if you think about it, you usually never want to make an exact copy of a formula. Rather, you want the copied formula to refer to a different set of cells. And that's exactly what 1-2-3 does — automatically.

Figure 7-4 shows what happens when you copy the formula in cell B5 to the range C5..D5.

An exception to this fact is an absolute cell reference, which I discuss in Chapter 5. An absolute cell reference uses dollar signs (for example, +$C$9) to indicate that you don't want the cell reference to change when it's copied.

When you copy a formula (using copy-and-paste), the cell references are adjusted automatically — unless you use absolute cell references. When you *move* a formula (using cut-and-paste), the cell references are never adjusted.

Figure 7-4:
When you copy a formula, 1-2-3 automatically adjusts the cell's references so that the copied formula works as it should in its new home.

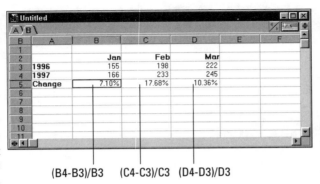

(B4-B3)/B3   (C4-C3)/C3   (D4-D3)/D3

If, for some bizarre reason that I won't even try to guess, you ever want to make a copy of a formula *without* adjusting the cell references, you need to take a few extra steps. First, convert the formula to a label (the easiest way to do so is to edit the formula and insert an apostrophe as the first character). Then copy the new label and paste it wherever you want. Finally, remove the apostrophe from both the original and the copy.

Drag-and-drop copying

If you read the previous section that covers moving cells or ranges by copying and pasting, you know that you can also move things using a simple drag-and-drop procedure. 1-2-3 extends this feature and enables you to *copy* cells or ranges using drag-and-drop.

This procedure has a minor limitation. You can copy a single cell to another location, or copy a range of cells to another location — but you *cannot* copy a single cell to a range. You have to use the normal copy and paste procedure to do that.

To copy by using drag-and-drop:

1. **Select the cell or range to be copied.**

2. **Move the mouse pointer to an edge of the selection until the mouse pointer turns into a hand.**

3. **Hold down the Ctrl key while you press the left mouse button.**

    The hand closes, and it also has a plus sign (+) on it.

4. Drag the selection to where you want to copy it to and release the mouse button.

1-2-3 places a copy of your original selection in the new location.

If drag-and-drop copying isn't working, this feature is probably disabled. To enable drag-and-drop, choose File⇨User Setup⇨1-2-3 Preferences. Click the General tab in the 1-2-3 Preferences dialog box and make sure that the Drag-and-drop cells and sheets option is checked.

Shortcut keys for copying

When you're copying a cell or range to an adjacent range, 1-2-3 has two handy shortcut keys. Before you use these keys, select the cell or range that you're copying *and* the adjacent range that you're copying to. Then you can use one of these key combinations:

- **Ctrl+D:** Copy the selection down.
- **Ctrl+T:** Copy the selection to the right.

Adjusting Column Widths

When you start working on a new worksheet, all the 256 columns are the same width: Nine characters. You can make any or all of these columns wider or narrower to accommodate the information you enter. You can't adjust the width of individual cells. When you change a column width, the entire column changes.

The preceding paragraph states that a standard column is nine characters wide. Actually, this number is rather arbitrary, because the number of characters that display in a so-called 9-character cell depends on the actual characters used, the type size, the font, and whether the characters are in bold. So adjust column widths based on what you see on-screen, not on the number of characters in the cells.

I can think of three reasons to adjust column widths:

- To make long numbers display properly. Numbers that are too wide to fit in a column show up as a series of asterisks, like this: *********.
- To make the worksheet look better by spacing things out or moving them closer together.
- To make long labels display properly. Text that is too wide has a truncated display if the cell to the right is occupied.

Figure 7-5 shows a worksheet that has several different columns widths to accommodate various entries.

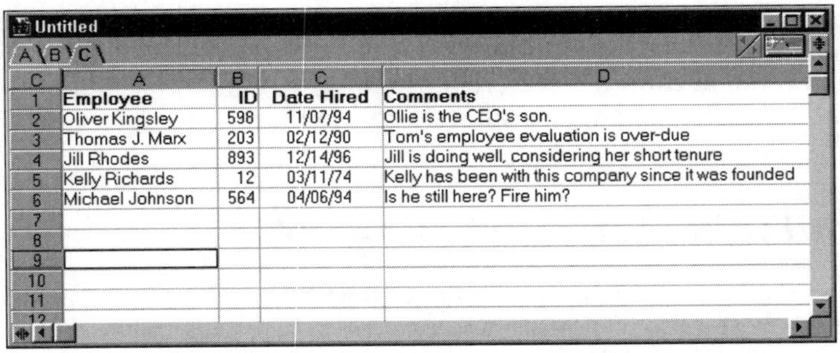

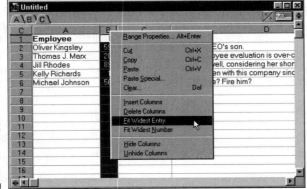

Figure 7-5:
You can adjust the widths of columns to handle practically anything you can put in a cell.

Adjusting column widths automatically

Here's how to let 1-2-3 change the width of one or more columns:

1. **Select the entire column or columns you want to adjust.**

   You select a column by clicking in the top border that shows the column letters. To select nonadjacent columns, hold down Ctrl while you click on the column letters.

2. **Right-click on the mouse.**

   1-2-3 displays the shortcut menu shown in Figure 7-6.

Figure 7-6:
This shortcut menu enables you to adjust column widths automatically.

3. Click either Fit Widest Entry or Fit Widest Number.

If you click the Fit Widest Entry menu option, each column in the selection is made just wide enough to handle the widest entry in the column (text and numbers).

If you choose the Fit Widest Number menu option, each column in the selection is made just wide enough to handle the widest numeric entry (text is ignored). This feature is useful if the column has a long label as a header for a bunch of numbers. Normally, you want to make the column wide enough to display the numbers — but not wide enough to fit the long label.

Another way to make a column just wide enough to display the widest cell entry (including both text and numbers) is to simply double-click the right border of the column (in the column letter area). If you like, you can pre-select multiple columns to auto-adjust more than one column with one double-click.

Using the InfoBox to adjust columns

You can make some column-width adjustments using the Basics tab of the Range InfoBox. If the Range InfoBox isn't displayed, press Alt+Enter.

When you use the InfoBox, you can select either entire columns or just cells. You have the following options (see Figure 7-7):

 ✔ Enter a value to set the width in terms of number of characters.

 ✔ Click Default width to return the columns to the default width.

 ✔ Click the icon (located to the right of the Width option) to adjust the columns to fit the widest character.

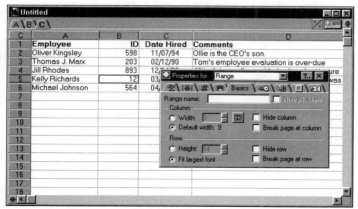

Figure 7-7:
The Basics tab of the Range InfoBox enables you to adjust column widths.

What a drag

Yet another way to change a column's width is to drag the column border. You have to grab the right column border, directly to the right of the column's letter. When you move the mouse pointer to the column border, the mouse pointer changes shape to let you know that you can drag. Drag the border to the right to make the column wider or to the left to make it narrower. As you drag the mouse, a little box pops up and tells you how many characters wide the column is.

To change the widths of several columns by dragging, first select the complete columns that you want to change. Do so by clicking and dragging across the column letters. Then drag the border of any of the selected columns to change the widths of all of them.

Changing Row Heights

You can also change the height of rows. Most of the time, you'll be satisfied with the fact that 1-2-3 handles this step automatically. For example, if you make a cell's font larger, 1-2-3 automatically increases the row height to handle the bigger font. But you can also increase the row heights yourself to adjust vertical spacing.

If you want to have the appearance of *double spacing,* increasing row heights is a better approach than inserting blank rows.

Figure 7-8 shows a worksheet with several different row heights.

Figure 7-8: You can adjust the height of individual rows to space things out vertically.

	A	B	C	D	E
1	California	982			
2	Oregon	432			
3	Washington	733			
4	**Total West Coast**	**2,147**			
5					
	Missouri	344			
6	Illinois	542			
7	Kansas	239			
8	**Total Midwest**	**5,419**			
9					
	New York	872			
10	New Jersey	744			
11	Massachusetts	322			
12	Rhode Island	75			
13	**Total East Coast**	**12,851**			
14					

To change the height of a row automatically, select the entire row and then right-click. In the shortcut menu, choose Fit Largest Font.

Another way to change row heights is to drag the row border with your mouse — just like you do when adjusting a column width. Click the bottom border and drag it down to make the row taller or drag it up to make it shorter.

Erasing Cells and Ranges

Getting rid of the contents of a cell — or a whole range of cells — is easy. This process is known as erasing, deleting, wiping out, nuking, killing, annihilating, zapping, and all sorts of other terms that aren't suitable for all family members. Regardless of what you call it, after you do it, the information is gone.

Okay, so the section on cutting and pasting, earlier in this chapter, reveals that choosing Edit⇨Cut gets rid of the contents of cells and ranges and puts the information on the Clipboard. But a faster and more efficient way to zap a cell's contents is to press the Del key.

Still another way to erase a cell or a range is to choose Edit⇨Clear. Start by selecting the offending cell or range and then issuing the command. You get a dialog box that enables you to select exactly what you want to clear.

Why do three ways exist to zap a cell or range? The difference is that Edit⇨Clear (or Del) doesn't put the erased information on the Clipboard (Edit⇨Cut does). So, if you want something to remain on the Clipboard (so that you can paste it later), you can choose Edit⇨Clear (or press Del) to erase cells without affecting the Clipboard.

Adding New Rows and Columns

Discovering that you need to insert something between two other cells is not at all uncommon. You may have a list of products and prices and then realize that you left one out. One approach is to move part of the range down one row to make room for the new entry. A faster method is to simply insert a new row.

Actually, the number of rows and columns always remains the same (65,536 rows and 256 columns). But you can scoot everything down, causing the last row in the worksheet to disappear and making room for your forgotten stuff.

Inserting a new column moves everything over to the right, and the last column in the worksheet disappears. If the last column has something in it, you can't insert a new column. The same goes for rows. If the last row in your worksheet isn't empty, you can't insert a new row.

Adding new rows

Here's how to add a new row to your worksheet:

1. **Select the complete row that's just below the row that you want to insert.**

   To do so, click the row number.

2. **Choose Range⇨Insert Rows (or right-click and choose Insert Rows from the shortcut menu).**

   1-2-3 pushes all the rows down and gives you a new blank row.

If you want to add more than one row, simply start by selecting more than one row. For example, to add 5 rows below row 10, select rows 10 through 14 before you choose Range⇨Insert Rows. In other words, the row or rows that you select before choosing Range⇨Insert Rows become blank rows after you execute the command.

Adding new columns

Adding one or more columns works just like adding rows. The only difference is that you start by selecting one or more columns. Then choose Range⇨Insert Columns (or right-click and choose Insert Columns on the shortcut menu). 1-2-3 inserts the new columns.

A word of caution

This warning may sound pretty dumb, but you need to remember that deleting a row or column does just that — it deletes an entire row or column. Lots of users tend to focus on just one part of their spreadsheet, and forget that other parts are out of view. They go about inserting and deleting rows and columns and are then surprised to discover that another area of their worksheet is all messed up. So let that be a warning.

Actually, if your worksheet has several different, separate parts, you may be better off using separate sheets for the various parts (use the New Sheet button to add new sheets). That way, things you do on one worksheet don't affect the other worksheets in the file. See Chapter 10 for more details on using these 3-D multisheet workbooks.

Hiding things

1-2-3 enables you to hide individual cells, ranges, or complete columns and rows. When something is hidden, it's still in the worksheet and can be referred to in formulas — it just doesn't appear on screen. Hiding is often handy when you're printing and you don't want particular information to be printed. Simply hide the unwanted information and commence printing.

To hide a cell or range, use the Security tab of the Range InfoBox. Make your selection and click the Hide cell contents check box. To unhide hidden cells, use the same procedure, but remove the check mark from the Hide cell contents check box.

To hide a row or column, use the Basics tab of the Range InfoBox. Make your selection and use the Hide column or Hide row check box.

Getting Rid of Rows and Columns

Because you can add rows and columns, you ought to be able to take them away, right? 1-2-3 enables you to remove as many rows and columns as you like. However, the total number of rows and columns always remains the same. If you remove a row, for example, all the other rows move up one slot and 1-2-3 inserts another row at the bottom. The comparable thing happens when you remove a column.

If you discover that you don't need the information in a row or column, you can get rid of it quickly by deleting the entire row or column. This alternative is much faster than deleting the range and then moving everything else around to fill up the gap.

Be careful when removing rows and columns. If they contain cells that you use in any of your formulas, the formulas are messed up in a major way and no longer return the correct answer.

Eliminating rows

To get rid of a row, select the entire row and then choose Range⇨Delete Rows. To delete more than one row, simply extend the row selection before you issue the command. The Delete Rows command also appears on the shortcut menu when you right-click after selecting one or more rows.

Deleting columns

Getting rid of entire columns works the same way as deleting rows — except that you start out by selecting the column or columns that you want to zap. Then choose Range➪Delete Columns to do the deed. And, of course, this command is also on the shortcut menu that appears when you right-click after selecting one or more columns.

Transposing Rows and Columns

Transposing a range means changing its orientation. If you have numbers in three columns, you can transpose them so that they appear in three rows — and vice versa.

You transpose rows and columns if you discover that information in the worksheet is in the wrong orientation: Vertical when it should be horizontal, or horizontal when it should be vertical. Figure 7-9 shows a range of cells before and after being reoriented.

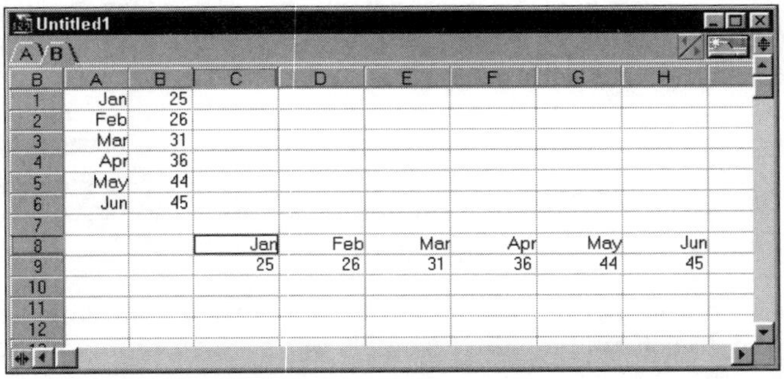

Figure 7-9:
Transposing
a range
changes its
orientation.

To transpose rows and columns, follow these steps:

1. **Select the range to be transposed and then choose Range➪Transpose.**

   1-2-3 displays the dialog box shown in Figure 7-10. The upper range box displays the range you selected. In the lower range box, you need to specify the upper-left cell of the range that you want to transpose it to.

2. **Click the diagonal arrow button in the lower range box and select the upper-left cell.**

   Or you can just enter the cell address directly.

3. **Click OK to close the dialog box.**

   1-2-3 copies the original range to the new area — but transposed.

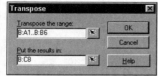

Figure 7-10:
The
Transpose
dialog box.

The 1-2-3 Range⊃Transpose command has a serious flaw. If the range to be transposed contains any formulas, the formulas are converted to values in the transposed range. In other words, the transposed range is essentially a dead (but transposed) version of the original range. This problem has always existed and I would have bet good money that it would have been fixed in the latest version. But I would have lost the bet.

Finding and Replacing — Where Art Thou, Text String?

Every word processor I've ever seen has a pretty sophisticated find-and-replace feature. You can instruct your software to find a particular text pattern (or *string*) and replace it with something else. You can do this automatically or have the software stop and tell you each time it finds the string. 1-2-3 isn't a word processor, but it, too, has this feature — which is great for making large-scale changes to a worksheet. This feature works with text, numbers, and formulas.

Fortunately, using this powerful tool is very straightforward. Here's the general procedure for using find and replace:

1. Choose Edit⊃Find & Replace (or press Ctrl+F).

You get the dialog box shown in Figure 7-11.

Figure 7-11:
The Find
and
Replace
dialog box.

2. Enter the text you're looking for in the Find box, and enter the text you want to replace it with in the Replace with box.

3. Use the Look in drop-down list to identify the scope of your search.

You can search all workbooks, the current workbook, the current sheet, or the selected range.

You also have the option of replacing text in labels, formulas, or numbers. You can select any or all of these.

4. Specify how you want the matching to take place.

If Case is checked, 1-2-3 matches text only if it matches in terms of upper- and lowercase.

5. Click the Find button to search for the first match.

1-2-3 goes to work looking for the string. Click Replace to replace the text. Or click Replace All to automatically replace everything without having to verify each occurrence.

Sorting Rows

Rearranging a range of cells such that the order of the rows gets changed (in an orderly manner) is called *sorting*. You may want to sort rows for a number of reasons. You may have entered data haphazardly and need to print it out in some order. Or you may want to sort your data to make finding a particular item easier. Or you want to see how a group of numbers looks in terms of rank orders. Or you may want to change the order before charting the numbers. And so on, and so on.

Let 1-2-3 do the sorting!

The following steps demonstrate how to sort a range of data. To see these steps in action, take a look at Figure 7-12, which shows a range of unsorted data. Following these steps, you can sort this range alphabetically by name. And when more than one row has the same name, you can sort by category. In other words, these steps show you how to use two sort keys.

1. Select the entire range to be sorted.

The range can consist of any number of columns and any number of rows. In Figure 7-12, that range is A1..C20.

2. Choose Range⇨Sort.

1-2-3 displays the Sort dialog box, shown in Figure 7-13.

	A	B	C
1	Name	Category	Amount
2	Bob	Hotel	$129.32
3	Jill	Food	$11.43
4	Frank	Transportation	$189.32
5	Bob	Food	$32.93
6	Bob	Miscellaneous	$5.65
7	Bob	Transportation	$11.87
8	Frank	Hotel	$109.32
9	Jill	Food	$32.89
10	Frank	Miscellaneous	$19.33
11	Frank	Miscellaneous	$7.00
12	Jill	Supplies	$79.88
13	Frank	Hotel	$145.32
14	Frank	Food	$32.90
15	Jill	Food	$45.73
16	Frank	Entertainment	$123.76
17	Jill	Transportation	$45.32
18	Jill	Hotel	$189.30
19	Bob	Transportation	$15.00
20	Bob	Miscellaneous	$22.32

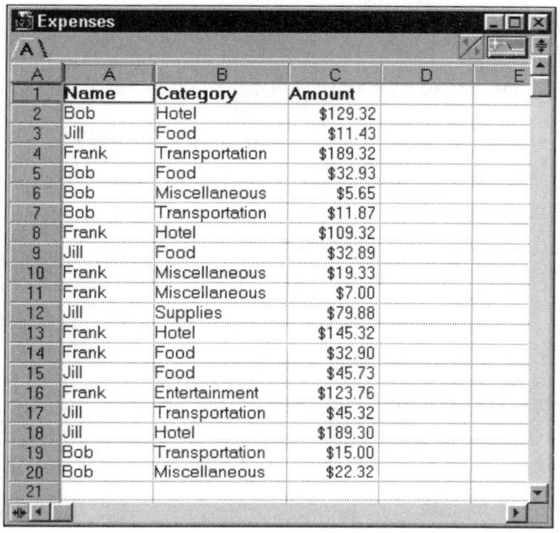

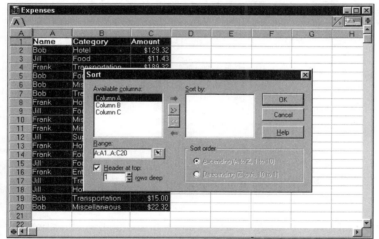

Figure 7-12: Unsorted data that you want to sort alphabetically by name.

Figure 7-13: The Sort dialog box.

3. Specify which column to sort on.

Because names are in column A, click Column A in the Available columns list and drag it to the Sort by list. (You can click the >> button instead of dragging.)

4. Specify the second sort key (to sort by category within each name).

Because the categories are in column B, click Column B in the Available columns list and drag it to the Sort by list under Column A. (You can click the >> button instead of dragging.)

5. **If the range that you originally selected includes one or more header rows, make sure that you check the option labeled Header at top and indicate the number of header rows.**

   When Header at top is checked, 1-2-3 ignores the header row (or rows) when sorting — which is what you want.

6. **Click OK to do the sorting.**

   1-2-3 goes to work, and your data is now sorted per your instructions (see Figure 7-14).

	A	B	C	D
1	**Name**	**Category**	**Amount**	
2	Bob	Food	$32.93	
3	Bob	Hotel	$129.32	
4	Bob	Miscellaneous	$5.65	
5	Bob	Miscellaneous	$22.32	
6	Bob	Transportation	$11.87	
7	Bob	Transportation	$15.00	
8	Frank	Entertainment	$123.76	
9	Frank	Food	$32.90	
10	Frank	Hotel	$145.32	
11	Frank	Hotel	$109.32	
12	Frank	Miscellaneous	$7.00	
13	Frank	Miscellaneous	$19.33	
14	Frank	Transportation	$189.32	
15	Jill	Food	$11.43	
16	Jill	Food	$45.73	
17	Jill	Food	$32.89	
18	Jill	Hotel	$189.30	
19	Jill	Supplies	$79.88	
20	Jill	Transportation	$45.32	
21				

Figure 7-14: The sorted data.

You can also specify the sort order for each sort key. In the Sort dialog box, click the Ascending or Descending option after selecting a sort key in the Sort by box.

Normally, 1-2-3 considers letters to be "greater than" numbers when it sorts. In other words, if the entries in your sort key column contain both values and labels, 1-2-3 puts the values before the labels when you sort in ascending order. If you want to change this rule so that sorting places labels before numbers, choose File⇨User Setup⇨1-2-3 Preferences. Click the General tab and make your change in the Sorting section.

What to watch out for when sorting

Screwing up when sorting is one of the most common mistakes people make with spreadsheets. And the leading cause of screwing up when sorting is failing to select the entire range as the sort range.

For example, suppose you have a range that consists of three columns: Name, Age, and Salary. If you want to sort the range in alphabetical order using Name as the sort key, selecting the data in *all three columns* is critically important when you specify the sort range. If you only select the column with the names, only the names get sorted. This means that everyone now has a different age and salary (some people will be happy about that; others, not so happy). In other words, the data is royally messed up, all the work you put into entering this information is for naught, you lose your job, the house goes on the auction block, and your dog hates you.

Be on the safe side and save your worksheet before you sort any data. That way, if you mess up (and Edit⇨Undo can't come to the rescue) you can always go back to the old file and start again.

The moral: Make sure that you select the range, the whole range, and nothing but the range.

Part III
Saving, Printing, and Creating New Sheets

The 5th Wave   By Rich Tennant

WELL, OBVIOUSLY ONE OF THE CELLS IN THE NAVIGATIONAL SPREADSHEET IS CORRUPT!

In this part . . .

Part III consists of three chapters. The first chapter describes everything you need to know about files — opening them, saving them, and making sure that you don't lose them. The second chapter in this part focuses on printing; find out how to ensure that your printed output looks good and contains no surprises. The final chapter in this part deals with using multisheet workbooks — a technique that can simplify your life quite a bit.

Chapter 8

Fiddling with Files

• •

• •

*I*f you work with computers, sooner or later, you're going to lose some work and be mighty upset. No denying it; it happens to everybody. After you exhaust your supply of curse words, you have to bite the bullet and repeat the work you've already done.

You can do several things to minimize the heartbreak of data loss. But if you like to live on the edge and don't mind wasting time redoing hours of work that disappeared down the toilet, feel free to skip this chapter.

Files and Windows

1-2-3, like most Windows programs, enables you to work with more than one file at a time — something you can fully appreciate if you've ever used any of the old DOS versions of 1-2-3 Release 2.*x*. Working with multiple files means that you don't have to close one project to work on another one. If you tend to juggle a bunch of tasks at once (which is fairly common in the offices where I've worked), you'll enjoy this capability.

When a file is loaded into 1-2-3, it's referred to as a *workbook*. Every workbook that's open appears in its own window, and the workbook's filename appears in the title bar. You can move the windows, resize them, compare their data, and perform many other tasks. Only one window can be active at a time. The others just lurk in the background waiting for their turn to be useful. Figure 8-1 shows several workbooks, each in a separate window, arranged nicely on-screen. This way, you can see what's in them and jump around among them.

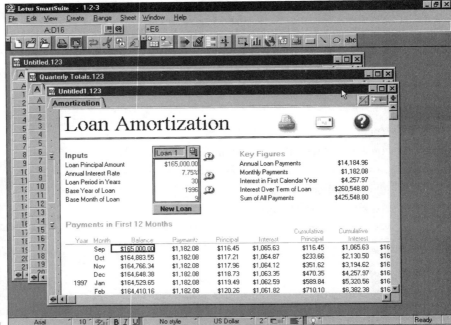

Figure 8-1:
1-2-3
enables you
to work with
as many
files as
you need,
each in a
separate
window.

Notice that the title bar of the active window is a different color. You need to remember one more thing: Every workbook can also have more than one sheet (like additional pages). Even if a workbook has extra sheets, the workbook is still contained in its own window. You use the tabs to move to different sheets within a file.

Workbook windows can be maximized to fill up the entire 1-2-3 workspace or turned into a small title bar (minimized). If a worksheet window isn't maximized or minimized, you can move it around and resize it within the 1-2-3 workspace. Only one window at a time can be the active window. The active window is the one your cursor is currently in; the active window is on top of the stack of windows and has a different color title bar.

If you want to work on a different workbook, you need to activate that workbook's window. You can do so in any of three ways (take your pick):

- If the window that you want to get to is showing, you can just click that window with your mouse, and it miraculously appears at the top of the stack.

- You can keep pressing Ctrl+F6 to cycle through all the windows until the one you want appears.

✔ You can choose the Window menu. Doing so drops down a list of commands. At the bottom of the list, you see a list of all the windows you have open. Select the window you want to activate, and you're off to the races.

To minimize (or *iconize*) a workbook window, click the minimize button in the upper-right corner of the window's title bar. Double-click the title bar of a minimized window to restore it to its previous size. To maximize a window, click the maximize button in the title bar. If a window is maximized, you can restore it to its former size by clicking the restore button. To close a window, click its close button (the X). If the file was not saved, 1-2-3 prompts you to save it.

Figure 8-2 shows where these buttons are located.

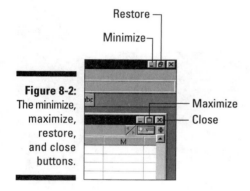

Figure 8-2:
The minimize,
maximize,
restore,
and close
buttons.

Restore
Minimize

Maximize
Close

If you have several workbook windows open, the screen can become a bit cluttered, and some windows may be hidden behind others. 1-2-3 provides three commands to clean things up:

✔ The Window➪Tile Left-Right command arranges all the windows left to right.

✔ The Window➪Tile Top-Bottom command arranges all the windows top to bottom.

✔ The Window➪Cascade command arranges all the windows in a tidy stack in such a way that you can see their title bars (see Figure 8-3).

If you have so many windows open that you have trouble locating the one you want, choose the Window menu item and select the window you want from the list that appears.

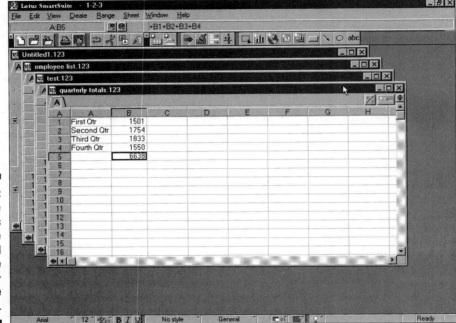

Figure 8-3:
These
windows
were
arranged
with the
Window⇨
Cascade
command.

The 1-2-3 File Menu: The Important Stuff

When you're working in 1-2-3, just about everything you do with your files is controlled through the File menu item (somewhat intuitive, eh?). As with all menu items, when you choose File from the menu (by clicking File or pressing Alt+F), 1-2-3 drops down a list that shows more commands, as shown in Figure 8-4. All these options can be somewhat intimidating at first, but they're all rather straightforward after you get used to them.

Using the File menu commands

Okay, here comes the meaty stuff — a summary of the important File menu commands and their functions.

Note: The File menu also offers several other commands that really don't have anything to do with files on your disk. These other commands are the ones that you use to print or view your worksheet, share work with other users, or work with add-ins. Because these commands are irrelevant to the current topic, I don't discuss them here.

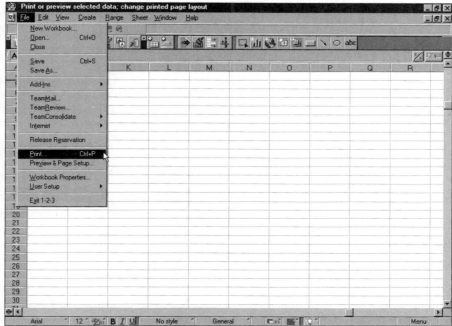

Figure 8-4:
The File
menu
commands
become
very
familiar to
you as you
gain more
experience
with 1-2-3.

File➪New Workbook

If you need to start another new project, choose File➪New Workbook. This
command brings up a dialog box, such as the one shown in Figure 8-5. You
can select a blank workbook or create a workbook by using a SmartMaster
template. (See the sidebar, "Don't reinvent the wheel," later in this chapter.)

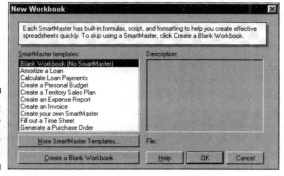

Figure 8-5:
The New
Workbook
dialog box.

The new workbook appears on your screen, but 1-2-3 doesn't save the workbook to disk. If you're already working on a workbook, this command starts a new one (called Untitled) but doesn't close the other one. A new workbook doesn't have a name until you save it.

When you start a new project and create a new workbook, saving it immediately (even though it's empty) is a very good idea. Saving it forces you to give it a name — I hope more meaningful than Untitled. Do this step with the File⇨Save command. (See the section entitled "File⇨Save".)

File⇨Open

Choose File⇨Open when you want to open a workbook that already exists on your hard disk so that you can work on it some more. If you already have one or more workbooks open, this command brings yet another one on-screen (and doesn't close any of the others). Figure 8-6 shows the Open dialog box.

Figure 8-6:
Choosing
File⇨Open
calls up this
dialog box,
where you
specify
which
workbook
file you
want.

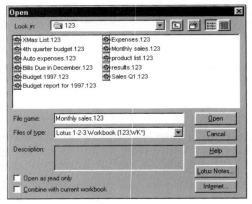

Just scroll through the list until you find the file you want. Sometimes, you may have to select a different directory or drive. When you change the drive or directory, you see a new list of files. When you find your file, double-click it or highlight it with the arrow keys and press Enter.

Here are some cool file-opening tricks:

- ✔ 1-2-3 remembers the names of the files you worked on recently and displays the filenames at the bottom of the File menu. To open one of these recent files, just click the filename once. This method is usually faster than trying to locate the file in the Open dialog box.

- ✔ You can open more than one file at a time by using the Open dialog box. The trick is to press Ctrl while you click on the filename. After you select all the files that you want to open, click the Open button. 1-2-3 opens all the files you selected.

Don't reinvent the wheel

1-2-3 includes a set of workbook templates called SmartMasters. What's a template? Well, a template is a workbook that's already set up to perform a common task. Say you're house hunting and you want to see what you can expect in the way of mortgage payments.

You can spend several hours trying to put together a loan amortization workbook in 1-2-3 — or you can use the loan amortization SmartMaster that's already on your hard drive. The accompanying figure shows how this SmartMaster looks.

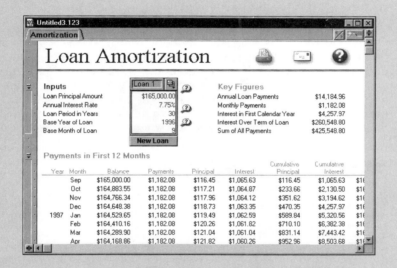

1-2-3 includes SmartMasters for the following tasks:

✔ Loan amortizations

✔ Loan payment calculations

✔ Personal budgeting

✔ Expense reports

✔ Time sheets

✔ Purchase orders

✔ Invoices

✔ Sales plans

If you're about to embark on a new spreadsheet project, seeing if a SmartMaster is available won't hurt. A SmartMaster can save you a great deal of time — or at least give you some ideas as to how to proceed with your own workbook.

✔ If you want to save a few milliseconds of time, you can bypass the File⇨Open command and press Ctrl+O — or you can simply click the SmartIcon named Open an existing file.

File⇨Save

The File⇨Save command saves your workbook to a file on-disk. If you've saved the file before, 1-2-3 uses the same name. If the file is a new worksheet without a name, 1-2-3 asks you for a name to use for the file. Just type a valid filename; the program supplies the .123 extension that identifies it as a 1-2-3 worksheet file. If you want to rename an existing file with a different name, choose File⇨Save As. (See the following section.)

The SmartIcon labeled `Save the current file` accomplishes the same thing as the File⇨Save command — but with a single mouse click. Also, you can press Ctrl+S to save the current file.

File⇨Save As

Choose File⇨Save As when you want to save the current workbook with a different name, or save it to a different directory or disk. In addition, you use this command when you want to save a 1-2-3 workbook in a different file format so that other programs can read the data. See the sidebar, "Foreign files," for more information about saving files in different file formats. Figure 8-7 shows the dialog box that appears when you choose File⇨Save As.

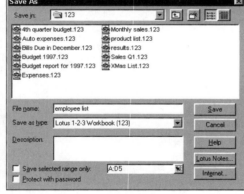

Figure 8-7: Choosing the File⇨ Save As command calls up the Save As dialog box.

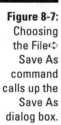

When you save a file for the first time by choosing the File⇨Save command, 1-2-3 is smart enough to know that you really meant to choose the File⇨Save As command. Consequently, you receive the dialog box you normally get when you choose the File⇨Save As command.

The latest version of 1-2-3 can open Excel files, up to and including Excel 97. This is good to know, because Excel is the most popular spreadsheet, and you're likely to run across such files. Be aware, however, that 1-2-3 can't translate advanced stuff, such as Excel macros.

File⇨Close

The File⇨Close command removes the current workbook from memory. If you haven't saved the workbook you're trying to close since you made any changes, 1-2-3 asks you whether you want to save it by displaying a dialog box similar to the one in Figure 8-8. To save the workbook before closing it, click Yes. To abandon your changes and close the workbook anyway, click No. Click Cancel if you get cold feet and decide not to close the file after all.

Figure 8-8:
If you try to close a file that includes unsaved information, 1-2-3 warns you with this message.

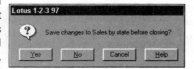

Foreign files

If you have a VHS videocassette player, you probably know that you can't play old Beta videocassettes in your machine. Besides being different physical sizes, the tapes are different formats. Even if you take the tape out of a Beta cartridge and spool it onto a VHS cartridge, your VHS machine can't understand it. Similarly, if you save a file from 1-2-3, you normally can't use that file in your word processor, because the two programs use different file formats. For example, if you try to load a 1-2-3 worksheet file into Word Pro, the word processor complains because it can't recognize the information — again, different file formats.

Actually, ways exist to save 1-2-3 files so that you can use the information in most other software programs. The trick is to save the file in a foreign file format — one that the other program can understand. You do so by choosing File⇨Save As. In the Save As dialog box, select the desired file format from the Save as type drop-down list.

1-2-3 can read worksheets produced by earlier versions of 1-2-3 and files produced by some other programs. After you choose File⇨Open, click the File of type drop-down list in the dialog box and select the file type that you want. This action displays only those types of files in the file list.

File⇨Exit 1-2-3

Choose File⇨Exit 1-2-3 after you're finished using 1-2-3 and are ready to call it quits. If you have any unsaved work, 1-2-3 lets you know about it and gives you the opportunity to save it to disk before quitting.

Alt+F4 is the standard Windows shortcut for File⇨Exit, and it works with 1-2-3.

A File Is Born

When you start 1-2-3, a copy of the program is loaded from your hard disk into your computer's memory. Actually, the complete program isn't loaded into memory — only the most important parts are. 1-2-3 leaves enough memory available so that you have room to work on your worksheets. As you use 1-2-3, your computer may need other parts of the program. The computer loads these parts from the hard disk in the background; you don't even notice what's going on unless you keep an eye on your hard disk access light.

When you start working on a new worksheet, you're storing information in your computer's memory. Therefore, if you turn off your PC, your work is gone to the big PC in the sky. To keep your work from being just an unpleasant memory, you need to save the worksheet that's in memory to a file on your hard disk.

Naming your workbooks

The first time you attempt to save a workbook to disk, you have to tell 1-2-3 what filename to use. After that, the program uses that same filename every time you save the file again, unless you specify a new and different filename (by choosing File⇨Save As). Every time you save the file, 1-2-3 replaces the file on disk with the updated information from memory. Saving your work at least every fifteen minutes or so is a good idea. Otherwise, an unexpected power outage or an ungainly coworker who kicks the plug out of the wall can destroy everything you've accomplished since the last time you saved your work.

The name you select for a 1-2-3 workbook must be a valid Windows filename. You must observe a few simple rules when naming your files, though. First, filenames must start with either a letter or a number. Second, you can't use the following characters in a filename:

- ✔ Backslash (\)
- ✔ Brackets ([ ])
- ✔ Colon (:)

- Comma (,)
- Equal sign (=)
- Period (.)
- Quotation marks (" ")
- Slash (/)
- Semicolon (;)
- Vertical bar (|)

All filenames include an extension, which is used to identify the type of file. Depending on how your computer is set up, you may or may not be able to see the file extensions. (They're hidden on some systems.) The file extension for the latest version of 1-2-3 is 123. When you save a file, this extension is added automatically.

Protecting your precious files

Use these two guidelines to avoid data loss when using 1-2-3 (or any computer program, for that matter):

- **Save your work to a disk frequently.** I've seen far too many people spend the whole day working on a workbook without saving it until they're finished. Most of the time, this practice doesn't get you into any trouble. But computers do crash occasionally, and power failures also have been known to occur. Both of these events cause you to lose everything that you haven't saved, and you have to restart your system.

  Saving a file takes a few seconds, but re-creating eight hours of lost work takes about eight hours. So to avoid headache, panic, confusion, fatigue, and general hysteria, save your work often!

- **Make a backup copy of all your important files.** Most people who back up their work religiously do so because they've been burned in the past (and you can count me among these folks). Hard disks aren't perfect — one bad byte, if that byte is critical, can make the entire disk unreadable. If a file has any value to you at all, make a copy of it on a backup disk and keep the disk in a safe place. And don't leave the backup disk next to your computer — if the building burns down during the night, a melted backup disk doesn't do you much good.

If You Mess Up Big-Time

At some point, you may realize that you made a major mistake. Maybe you accidentally deleted a critical range of numbers, and you discovered your error too late to choose the Edit➪Undo command. When you realize that you've made such an error, don't panic. Rather, take a deep breath and consider your options. You can

- ✔ Open the most recently saved version of the workbook. If it's a new workbook that you haven't saved yet, this action isn't an option.
- ✔ Do whatever is necessary to correct your mistake using the current version of the workbook.

Your choice ultimately depends on how much work you've done since you last saved the file. If you decide to scrap what you're doing and revert to the most recently saved copy, follow these steps:

1. **Choose File➪Save As and save the current (messed up) version of the workbook using a new name.**

   Type a name, such as **Messed up file**. Whatever you do, *don't save the file using the same name.* You don't want to overwrite the good copy that's on disk.

2. **Choose File➪Open to retrieve the last saved copy of your workbook.**

3. **Decide which of the two workbooks (the last saved version or the messed up version) is easier to fix up.**

4. **Do whatever is necessary to recover from your faux pas.**

   You may be able to save some work by copying information from one workbook to the other.

Backing Up Is Easy

One thing that almost all beginning computer users have trouble with is managing files on their hard disk and floppy disks.

Although this book isn't really the place for you to explore the ins and outs of managing your files, I do want to tell you how to make a backup copy of a file. That way, if you ever lose an important file, you can't blame me!

Making a backup of a file means placing a copy of the file in another location — usually a floppy disk. Some people make their backups to another hard drive on their system, to a network file server, or to magnetic tape. To keep things simple, I'm going to tell you just two ways to get a 1-2-3 worksheet file on a floppy disk:

Disk or memory: What's the diff?

One thing I've noticed over the years is that new computer users often get confused about memory and disks. This confusion isn't surprising, because both of these objects are places where you can store data. Here's the difference:

✔ **Memory:** A part of your computer that stores things you're currently working on. It also goes by the name of *RAM* (for random-access memory). Computer memory is very fleeting — a flick of the power switch and it's wiped out immediately.

✔ **Disks:** A disk stores information more or less permanently. Information stored on a disk is in files. If you turn off the power to your PC, the files that you've stored on-disk remain there. Disks come in a variety of sizes, which correspond to how much information they can hold. Your computer has a built-in hard disk (which holds a great deal) and can also use removable floppy disks (which hold less, and which

may or may not actually be floppy). You may also be connected to a network and have access to the disks on other systems.

✔ **CD-ROM:** Your computer is probably equipped with a CD-ROM drive. A *CD-ROM* is a removable storage device which can hold up to 640 megabytes of information. But unlike disks, a CD-ROM is read-only, meaning that you can read from it, but you can't write to it. Therefore, you can't use a CD-ROM to store your files or backups.

If you have several programs and data files stored on your hard disk, you may, at some time, get a `disk full` message. This message means that your disk is so full, it can't hold any more information (and this message has nothing to do with the amount of memory in your computer). You must erase unneeded files from your disk to free up some space. You can do so directly from 1-2-3, or you can use the standard Windows methods.

> ✔ Use the Save As dialog box.
> ✔ Use the Open dialog box.

You (or the office computer guru) may already have some procedures in place to make a complete backup copy of all the files on your hard disk. For example, you may own software that's designed specifically to back up all the files on your hard disk to a tape storage unit. I encourage you to make such backups regularly. But realize that you still need to make separate backups of important files that you work on. (What if someone's Ben & Jerry's melts all over the storage unit?) The procedures in this section tell you how to save your own files.

Backing up by using the Save As dialog box

You can search the 1-2-3 menus all day and never find the File⇨Backup command (because no such animal exists). However, you can still save your workbook to a floppy disk (if you haven't fallen asleep yet, you probably already have a pretty good idea of where this section is heading). The key is to use the File⇨Save As command and then specify drive A as the disk where you want to save your file.

Suppose you're ready to head for home after a long afternoon of working on your department's budget. You're tired and don't feel like thinking any more, but you're not too tired to remember that a hard disk mishap can easily destroy your day's work. Here's the easy way to save a copy of your file to a floppy disk:

1. **Save your worksheet to your hard disk as you normally do.**

2. **Insert a formatted floppy disk into drive A.**

3. **Choose File⇨Save As.**

4. **In the Save As dialog box, click the arrow in the box labeled Save in.**

5. **Select a: from the Save in list.**

   The drive may be labeled 3-$\frac{1}{2}$ Floppy (A:).

6. **Click Save.**

   1-2-3 saves your current workbook to the floppy disk in drive A.

7. **You can now choose File⇨Exit 1-2-3 to get out of 1-2-3.**

   You should be rejoicing because you have two exact copies of your file: the one on your hard disk and the one you just saved to the floppy disk.

8. **For good measure, stick that disk in your shirt pocket and take it home with you.**

   But watch out, someone may mistake you for a computer guru and ask you questions about TCP/IP protocols.

When you come back to work the next day, choose File⇨Open to open the file on your hard drive (don't use the backup disk). If you make any changes to the file, repeat the disk backup procedure after saving the file to your hard disk. Because the file already exists on your backup disk, 1-2-3 makes you verify the fact that you want to overwrite this file with your newer version.

Never work with a file that was opened from a floppy disk. Besides taking much longer to open and save the file, doing so can cause many problems if you remove the disk while you're still working on the file. If you *do* open a file from a floppy disk, make sure that you save it immediately to your hard disk.

Backing up by using the Open dialog box

Here's another way to make a copy of a 1-2-3 file:

1. Save your worksheet as usual by using the File⇨Save command.

If you haven't named the document yet, 1-2-3 asks for a name.

2. Insert a formatted floppy disk into drive A.

3. Choose File⇨Open.

You're not going to open a file — you're just going to take advantage of the list of files.

4. In the list of filenames, locate the file that you want to back up.

5. Right-click the filename.

1-2-3 displays a shortcut menu like the one shown in Figure 8-9.

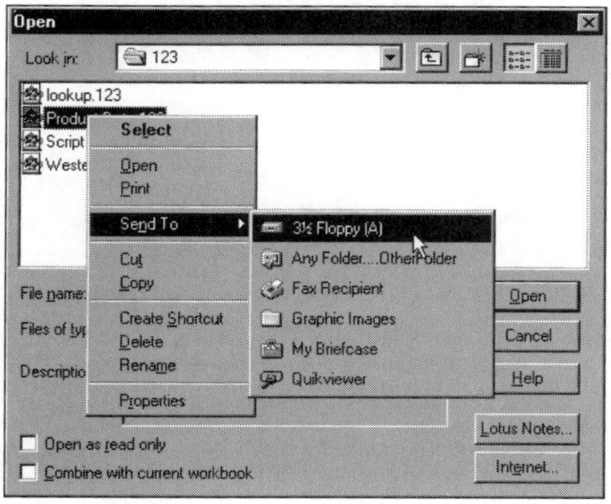

Figure 8-9:
Right-clicking a filename gives you a shortcut menu like this one.

6. In the shortcut menu, choose Send to and then select 3-¹/₂ inch Floppy from the list of send to locations.

Other ways to back up your work

Your computer may have other file-management programs on it. These programs can copy, organize, move, and rename files very easily. Consult the documentation that came with these programs (or buy a *...For Dummies* book!) to find out how to use them.

This chapter spends many pages telling you stuff that you won't fully appreciate until that fateful day comes when you realize that your only copy of an important file has bitten the dust. Take some precautions and practice safe spreadsheeting.

Chapter 9

Taking the Pain out of Printing

- -

- -

Many times, just looking at your spreadsheet efforts on-screen isn't enough — you want a hard copy. You basically have two choices: Use an instant camera to photograph your computer monitor, or send the worksheet to your printer. Most people choose the latter option, because snapshots are too small, and they're difficult to staple together in reports.

Both beginning and advanced users agree that dealing with printers can be one of the most frustrating parts of working with computers. But the effort pays off when you finally have something you can hold in your hand to show for the long hours you spent sweating over your keyboard.

Here are few observations about printers (maybe you recognize some of them):

- ✔ Your printer is never good enough for what you want it to do. And the day after you buy a new printer, the manufacturer comes out with a better model that's several hundred dollars cheaper than what you just plunked down.

- ✔ The paper jams or the toner cartridge dries up at the most inopportune times.

- ✔ Never start printing a 30-page job and then go to lunch. Printers know when you leave the office and purposely pick that time to jam.

- ✔ Printers have minds of their own. You may want to print in Arial typeface, but the document sometimes comes out in Courier for no apparent reason. (I think the explanation has something to do with the phase of the moon.)

✔ The ribbon dries up, the ink cartridge clogs up, or the toner cartridge bites the dust just as your boss yells, "I need that report NOW!"

✔ Nobody really knows what all those little buttons and lights are for. And the 700-page printer manual is printed in Japanese.

That instant camera is looking better and better, isn't it?

Simple Printing

To print a document in a perfect world, you simply issue your software's Print command, and everything instantly appears on paper just as you expect it to. Although the world is far from perfect, printing from 1-2-3 comes fairly close to perfection (except for the "instantly" part).

For basic printing (using the current settings), you can

✔ Choose File⇨Print.

✔ Press Ctrl+P.

✔ Click the Print SmartIcon.

Each of these commands displays the Print dialog box, shown in Figure 9-1. Click the Print button, and your print job is sent down the wire.

In the vast majority of cases, the current print settings work just fine. But using computers can't be that simple, right? As you may expect, *tons* of options (no exaggeration) are available so that you can change the way your work gets printed and do *tons* of other nifty things. That's why the rest of this chapter exists.

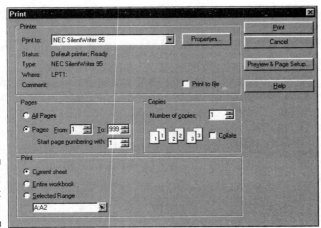

Figure 9-1:
The Print
dialog box.

Nothing's coming out!

Hundreds of printer models exist, and a book of this scope can't possibly provide detailed help for your particular printer. If you find that you can't print anything — or your printed output looks nothing like what's displayed in the print preview window (which I explain later in this chapter) — the problem has three likely causes:

✔ You have a connection problem. The printer isn't hooked up properly. If this is the case, you won't be able to print from any other Windows program either.

✔ Windows is using the wrong printer driver.

✔ Your printer is not configured correctly.

Try shutting down your system, turning off the power, and restarting the computer. This approach mysteriously fixes the problem sometimes. If that fails, your best bet is to bribe your favorite computer guru for help or make the dreaded call to the technical support department for your printer.

Slightly Less Simple Printing

Printing the current worksheet by using the default print settings is a no-brainer. At times, however, you need to make some changes in how 1-2-3 prints your worksheets. The following list contains examples of the printing adjustments you can make in the wonderful world of 1-2-3:

✔ The worksheet range to be printed (when you don't want to print everything)

✔ Print orientation — portrait (tall) or landscape (wide)

✔ Paper size — normal ($8^1/_2 \times 11$) and legal ($8^1/_2 \times 14$) are the most popular options

✔ The margins on the paper

✔ Headers or footers that appear on every printed page

✔ Page numbers

✔ The date or time printed

✔ The cell grid lines (printed or not)

✔ The row and column borders (printed or not)

✔ Certain worksheet rows or columns that print on each page

✔ Compressed print, so that everything fits on a single sheet of paper

✔ The number of copies to print

Generally, you perform the following steps when you're ready to print your work:

1. **Make sure that everything is ready for prime time — the formulas produce the correct results, the charts look good, the text is all spelled correctly, and so on.**

2. **Do a print preview of your output (see the next section in this chapter).**

   This step is optional but highly recommended.

3. **Specify any special print settings by using the Preview & Page Setup InfoBox.**

   This step is also optional. If you changed any settings previously for the sheet you are printing, you don't have to change them again.

4. **Click the Print SmartIcon to send your job off to the printer.**

1-2-3 saves your print settings along with the workbook. So the next time you load the workbook, all your settings come along for the ride. Clicking the Print SmartIcon prints the worksheet with these settings.

Psst . . . Wanna Sneak Preview?

One of the slickest features in 1-2-3 is its Preview & Page Setup window. This window does just what the name implies: It gives you a preview (in the privacy of your own screen) of what will be printed — and the InfoBox makes changing any print option you can think of very easy.

The advantages of previewing your print job before you send it off to the printer are obvious: You save time and paper. Before the days of print preview, the following scenario was not uncommon: You printed your work and discovered that the type didn't look very good — the column headings needed to be wider. So you went back to the worksheet and made some adjustments. You printed it again, and you discovered that one column gets printed on a page all by itself. And so on and so on. Thanks to print preview, you know what the output will look like before the printer spits it out.

Working with the preview window

To display the preview window, choose File⇨Preview & Page Setup (or just click the Print Preview SmartIcon). 1-2-3 responds by splitting the screen in half, showing your worksheet on the left and the preview window on the right. And, for your convenience, the program also displays the Preview & Page Setup InfoBox. Figure 9-2 shows an example of how your screen looks in print preview mode.

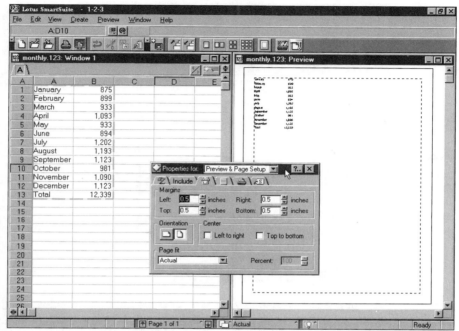

Figure 9-2:
Worksheet
on left,
preview
window on
right.

You can treat the preview window just like any other window. For example, you can resize it, move it, or even maximize it so that it fills 1-2-3's entire workspace.

When the preview window is active, 1-2-3 displays a new menu (the Preview menu) and also shows a new set of SmartIcons. You can also right-click anywhere in the preview window to get a shortcut menu of commands that are useful for previewing.

Viewing multiple pages

The preview window normally displays a single page of printed output. However, you can make the window show more pages at once — either two, four, or even nine pages. To do so, click the appropriate SmartIcon (or right-click and use the shortcut menu). Figure 9-3 shows the preview window displaying four pages at once.

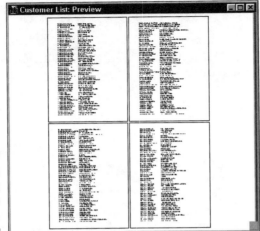

Figure 9-3:
Previewing
four pages
at once.

Blowing up your image

Depending on the size of your type and the number of pages being displayed, the previewed output may be illegible. Fortunately, magnifying the image is easy: Just click the preview window to enlarge the type (the area that you click appears in the center of the screen). Click again to enlarge it even more. Click a third time to return to normal. Figure 9-4 shows a preview window magnified.

Figure 9-4:
Zooming in
on a portion
of the
preview
window.

State	Projected	Actual
California	1,200	982
Oregon	500	432
Washington	600	733
Missouri	250	344
Illinois	500	542
Kansas	300	239
New York	1,000	872
New Jersey	600	744

Sales by state: Preview

Chekking your speling

If you use a word processor, you are probably on friendly terms with its built-in spelling checker. 1-2-3 isn't a word processor, but it does have a spelling checker, which can save you a great deal of embarrassment (but good spelers lyke me don't nede sutch thingz).

You access this feature by choosing Edit➪Check Spelling (or press Ctrl+F2). 1-2-3 then displays its Check Spelling dialog box. Click the Start button to begin. This dialog box

works pretty much as you would expect. If 1-2-3 finds a word it doesn't recognize, it displays a list of possible spellings for you to choose from.

The spelling checker isn't a substitute for a careful review of your worksheet. The checker can't identify words that are spelled correctly but used incorrectly in a sentence — butt of coarse, ewe already no that.

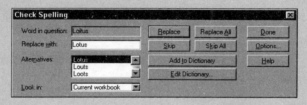

Switching among pages

If your printed output consists of more than one page, you probably want to take a peek at subsequent pages. Use the SmartIcons to go forward and backward among the previewed pages. Or right-click and use the shortcut menu, which includes commands to go to the previous or next page.

Printing Options

In this section, I describe some of the most common changes you need to make before printing. Although you can change some of these settings from the Print dialog box, using the Preview & Page Setup InfoBox offers a much easier method for setting all your printing options. Well, almost all. A few things still require the Print dialog box.

The Preview & Page Setup InfoBox appears automatically when you are previewing your work. If you dismiss the InfoBox and want to get it back, choose Preview➪Preview & Page Setup Properties.

Specifying what to print

When you're ready to memorialize your efforts on paper, you can print

- ✔ The current worksheet
- ✔ All sheets in the current workbook
- ✔ A selected range of cells

You select the setting you want to use in the Include tab of the Preview & Page Setup InfoBox, shown in Figure 9-5. If you want to print just a range of cells rather than the entire worksheet, select the range that you want to print. Then click the Print Preview SmartIcon. Click the Include tab of the Preview & Page Setup InfoBox and make sure that the Range option is selected.

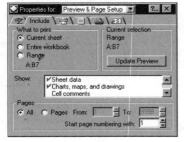

Figure 9-5: The Include tab of the Preview & Page Setup InfoBox.

You can also specify certain pages to be printed and the page number to start printing. For example, suppose you just printed a 40-page report and then discovered that you made a mistake on page 16. After you correct the mistake, you don't need to print the entire report again. Specify the page number to print (in this case, from 16 to 16) and tell 1-2-3 to start page numbering with 16. Then print the page and replace the bad one with the good one.

The Include tab also lets you specify what types of things you want to print. You can select as many of these options as you like (although usually the default settings are just right).

Your choices are

- ✔ **Sheet data:** This choice refers to the information that's in the cells. You almost always want to print this data.

- ✔ **Charts, maps, and drawings:** Sometimes you may want to omit these items.

✔ **Cell comments:** If you've inserted any cell comments, you may or may not want to print them. Refer to Chapter 5 for information on cell comments.

✔ **Formulas, cell contents:** Select this option if you want a printout of all your formulas. Looking at your formulas printed on paper can sometimes help you spot errors.

✔ **Buttons:** I don't know why anyone would want to print buttons that are inserted on a worksheet. But if you do, you can.

✔ **Sheet grid lines:** Some people like to see these lines in their printouts.

✔ **Sheet row and column headers:** Printing these makes determining the address of particular cells easy.

✔ **Outline frame:** If your worksheet includes an outline, you may want to print the outline frame. If you don't know what a worksheet outline is, check out Chapter 19.

Dealing with headers and footers

If you want information to appear at the top or bottom of every page you print, you need to know about headers and footers. *Headers* appear at the top of the page, and *footers* appear at the bottom.

Why use headers or footers? Well, some people like to identify what the printout is about. For example, your third-quarter report about tardiness can have a header that reads *Third Quarter Tardiness Report.* And if you need to number the pages of your output, the page numbers go in either the header or the footer.

Headers and footers each have three parts (all of which are optional):

✔ Information printed flush left

✔ Information centered

✔ Information printed flush right

When you check out the Headers and footers tab of the Preview & Page Setup InfoBox (see Figure 9-6), you see a drop-down box that lets you select the header or footer item of interest. Then you can type whatever you want into the boxes.

Figure 9-6:
The Headers
and footers
tab of the
Preview &
Page Setup
InfoBox.

The latest version of 1-2-3 supports multiline headers and footers. In previous versions, you were limited to a single line. You can also set the height of the header and footer. Do this by using the InfoBox, or by dragging the dotted line in the preview window.

Don't overlook the six icons directly below the text box. Clicking one of these icons puts special codes into the header or footer. These codes print specific information. Here's a list of the codes that are inserted when you click these icons:

- ✔ @ (current system date)
- ✔ + (current system time)
- ✔ # (page number)
- ✔ % (total number of pages to be printed)
- ✔ ^ (filename)
- ✔ / (contents of a particular cell)

If you want the contents of a particular cell to appear in a header or footer, click the Contents icon. 1-2-3 inserts a slash and the address of the active cell. You can edit the cell address if necessary.

After you make any changes to the headers or footers, press Enter, and the changes instantly appear in the preview window. If you want to change the font or text attributes of your headers or footers, use the Font, attribute, and color tab of the Preview & Page Setup InfoBox.

Printing title rows or columns on every page

Many worksheets are set up with titles in the first row and descriptive names in the first column. If such a worksheet requires more than one page to print, the first page looks fine. However, you may find reading subsequent pages difficult because the identifying text in the first row and first column isn't printed. 1-2-3 offers a simple solution: the capability to specify rows and columns that print on every page.

Printing row and column titles is similar in concept to freezing rows and columns for scrolling through your worksheet (by choosing the View⇨Titles command). However, these two operations are entirely different. Freezing the row or column titles on your worksheet does *not* cause the titles to be printed on each page. Chapter 11 discusses freezing rows and columns for scrolling purposes.

To specify the rows or columns to print on each page, access the Preview & Page Setup InfoBox and click the Headers and footers tab. In the section labeled Print as titles on each page, specify the rows and/or columns that you want to print on each page. To do so, click the arrow icon (which hides the InfoBox) and select rows or columns in the worksheet. You can select as many rows or columns as you like.

Don't confuse print titles with headers; the two concepts are different. Headers appear at the top of each page and contain information, such as the worksheet name, date, or page number. Print titles describe the data being printed, such as field names in a database table or list.

Adding page numbers

For lengthy reports, adding page numbers to the header or footer of your printout is a good idea. Then if someone opens the door on a windy day and the report blows all over the office, you won't have as much trouble putting the report back together.

To add page numbers, activate the Preview & Page Setup InfoBox and click the Headers and footers tab. Determine where you want the page number to appear and then click the corresponding text box. Then click the Page number icon. 1-2-3 inserts a pound sign (#), which is the code for page number.

You can combine any text with the codes produced by the icons. And you can enter the codes manually if you know them. For example, if you want your page number to appear in a format such as "Page 3 of 12," enter the following text into a header or footer box:

```
Page # of %
```

For a list of all these header and footer codes, refer to a previous section, "Dealing with headers and footers."

Printing multiple copies

Sometimes you may need to print more than one copy of your work. Rather than sending your job to the printer multiple times, you can tell 1-2-3 how many copies to print. You specify the number of copies in the Print dialog box right before you click the big button that sends your work to the printer. (This setting is one of those that doesn't appear in the Preview & Page Setup InfoBox.)

To specify the number of copies, enter a value in the Number of copies box. You can enter a number up to 9,999 (gee whiz, only 9,999!). Actually, if you need more than a dozen or so copies, you may want to check out the wonderful world of photocopiers.

When printing multiple copies of jobs that have more than one page, you may want to select the Collate option. Selecting this option causes 1-2-3 to automatically collate each copy printed. Then again, I've known some people who enjoy collating, so the choice is yours.

Changing the print orientation

You normally print a page in *portrait orientation,* where the printed page is taller than it is wide (like a typical portrait painting). Printing sideways on the page is called *landscape orientation* (like a typical landscape painting).

Your choice usually depends on how your data is arranged. You make your choice in — you guessed it — the Preview & Page Setup InfoBox. In this case, click the third tab (Margins, orientation, and placement), shown in Figure 9-7. Click the appropriate icon, and 1-2-3 redisplays the preview window to show you how your data looks in the selected orientation.

Figure 9-7:
The
Margins,
orientation,
and
placement
tab of the
Preview &
Page Setup
InfoBox.

Figure 9-7:
The
Margins,
orientation,
and
placement
tab of the
Preview &
Page Setup
InfoBox.

Adjusting margins

The margins on a page refer to the white space along the edges. As you may suspect, 1-2-3 lets you change the margins to whatever width you like. For example, if your company has a policy that all reports must have one-inch margins on all sides, you easily can set these particular margins. Or you may want to make the margins narrower so that everything fits on one page.

You adjust the margins in the Margins, orientation, and placement tab of the Preview & Page Setup InfoBox (refer to Figure 9-7). Click the arrows on the spinners to make your changes; 1-2-3 updates the preview window before your very eyes.

You can also center your output, either vertically, horizontally, or both. You do so in the Margins, orientation, and placement tab of the Preview & Page Setup InfoBox. Just select the appropriate option in the Center section of the InfoBox.

Sizing your printout

1-2-3 has some pretty spiffy options that shrink printed output so that the type is smaller and more data fits on a printed page. Or you can have the program automatically magnify the output so that the text is larger and less data fits on a printed page.

You perform this magic in the Margins, orientation, and placement tab of the Preview & Page Setup InfoBox (refer to Figure 9-7). Select one of the options from the Page fit drop-down list (see Table 9-1).

Table 9-1	Page Fit Options
Page Fit Option	**What It Does**
Actual	No scaling
Fit all to page	Scales the output so that it fits on a single page
Fit rows to page	Scales the output so that the rows fit on one page (the columns may extend to additional pages)
Fit columns to page	Scales the output so that the columns fit on one page (the rows may extend to additional pages)
Custom	Lets you specify a custom scaling factor from 15 percent (tiny) to 1,000 percent (huge!)

1-2-3 doesn't guarantee that your output will be legible! In some cases, reducing the scale factor makes your output so small that you can't read it.

Specifying paper sizes

Most of the time, you'll probably use standard-size paper (known as *letter size*), which is 8 $1/2$ x 11 inches, for printing. However, if you need to print something that's very tall or wide, you may opt for *legal-size* paper (8$1/2$ x 14 inches). Or you may have some oddball-size paper that you want to use for one reason or another.

1-2-3 lets you specify different paper sizes, assuming that your printer is capable of handling these different sizes. To specify the paper size, use the fifth tab (Printer and paper size) of the Preview & Page Setup InfoBox (see Figure 9-8).

Figure 9-8:
The Printer
and paper
size tab of
the Preview
& Page
Setup
InfoBox.

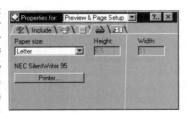

Selecting a printer

If you have access to more than one printer, you may need to select the correct printer before printing. You can do so in the Printer and paper size tab of the Preview & Page Setup InfoBox (refer to Figure 9-8). Click the Printer button, and you get another dialog box from which you can select the printer. Figure 9-9 shows an example of this dialog box.

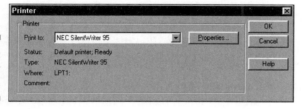

Figure 9-9:
The Printer
dialog box.

If you have a fax modem attached to your system, you can select the fax option from the list of printers. This option lets you send a fax directly from 1-2-3. The exact procedures vary with different brands of fax software, so that's about all I can say.

Creating and using print styles

You may have a workbook that you print in a number of different ways, depending on the circumstances. For example, sometimes you may want to print a summary range in portrait mode. But when you print the details, you may prefer landscape mode, scaled so everything fits on one page. Rather than change these settings every time you print, you can create print styles.

A *print style* is a just a named collection of print settings. You can recall all these settings simply by selecting a style before you print. Selecting a style not only saves time, but also makes your work more consistent (which is usually a good thing).

To create a named print style:

1. **Adjust the print settings to your liking by using the Preview & Page Setup InfoBox.**

2. **When you're satisfied with the print settings, click the Named style tab of the Preview & Page Setup InfoBox (see Figure 9-10).**

Figure 9-10
The Named
style tab of
the Preview
& Page Setup
InfoBox.

3. Click the Create Style button.

1-2-3 displays a dialog box asking you for a name for the style.

4. Enter a descriptive name and click OK.

Repeat these steps for each named print style that you want to create. After you create your print styles, you can recall all the settings by selecting a style name from the Named style tab in the Preview & Page Setup InfoBox.

Quick Reference for Printing

Unless you're a genius, you may be a bit overwhelmed by all these printing options. Wouldn't it be nice if someone put together a handy table of these options that told you exactly where to go to do what? Your prayers are answered in Table 9-2.

Table 9-2	Printing Options Quick Reference
Printing Option	*Where to Go**
Change paper size	InfoBox (Printer and paper size tab)
Change the margins	InfoBox (Margins, orientation, and placement tab)
Change the starting page number	InfoBox (Include tab)
Compress or expand the size	InfoBox (Margins, orientation, and placement tab)
Create or use a named print style	InfoBox (Named style tab)
Don't print graphs or drawn objects	InfoBox (Include tab)
Headers or footers	InfoBox (Headers and footers tab)
Insert page numbers	InfoBox (Headers and footers tab)

Printing Option	Where to Go*
Number of copies to print	Print dialog box
Paper orientation	InfoBox (Margins, orientation, and placement tab)
Print just part of your worksheet	InfoBox (Include tab)
Print just specific pages	InfoBox (Include tab)
Print rows/columns on every page	InfoBox (Headers and footers tab)
Print the date or time on each page	InfoBox (Headers and footers tab)
Print the filename on each page	InfoBox (Headers and footers tab)
Select a printer	InfoBox (Printer and paper size tab)

* InfoBox refers to the Preview & Page Setup InfoBox.

Printing Charts, Maps, and Drawings

Printing charts, maps, and other graphic objects is no big deal. If the objects are inserted on your worksheet, they are printed along with everything else on the worksheet. It's that simple.

If your charts don't print, access the Preview & Page Setup InfoBox and click the Include tab. In the box labeled Show, make sure that a check mark is next to the option labeled Charts, maps, and drawings.

Chapter 10
When One Sheet Just Isn't Enough

. . . .

In This Chapter

▶ Making the most of those 255 extra sheets

▶ Adding and removing sheets

▶ Moving and copying sheets

▶ Naming sheets

▶ Printing sheets

▶ Seeing more than one sheet at a time

▶ Navigating and selecting across multiple sheets

▶ Formatting a bunch of sheets at once using a sheet collection

. . . .

You may already know that 1-2-3, like all other Windows spreadsheets, lets you store more than one sheet in a single workbook file. In fact, you can have as many as 256 sheets in a single file. Each of these sheets has 65,536 rows and 256 columns.

Do your arithmetic (you can even use 1-2-3 for the calculation), and you discover that you have more than four billion cells at your disposal. This chapter explains how to use this powerful feature for fun and profit (well, at least for profit).

Why Use Multisheet Workbooks?

Jeepers, four billion cells! Don't get too excited, however, because you can never use all these cells. (Unless your system has a ton of memory, your computer system would slow to a crawl long before you even got close.) The benefit of using multiple sheets is *not* in the number of cells you can access. The benefit, rather, is in the great way you can organize your work and break it up into more manageable units.

TIP

You can break down many common spreadsheet projects into distinct chunks. For example, you may have a chunk that holds your assumptions, several different chunks that hold tables of values, a chunk to store data for graphs, and so on. Before the days of multisheet workbooks, one of the most difficult aspects of dealing with large spreadsheets was figuring out where to put all the various chunks. With 1-2-3, however, the task is simple: Put each chunk on a separate sheet.

Figure 10-1 shows an example of a workbook that contains six sheets. Notice that each sheet's tab is labeled with the name of a state; therefore, you can jump to the sales information for a state just by clicking the tab.

Figure 10-1:
This
workbook
stores sales
information
by state.
Each state's
data is in a
separate
sheet.

Monthly Sales by State						
California \ Oregon \ Washington \ Nevada \ Arizona \ Texas \						

	A	B	C	D	E	F	G
1		Projected	Actual	Difference			
2	January	15,000	16,211	1,211			
3	February	15,750	15,345	(405)			
4	March	16,538	17,822	1,285			
5	April	17,364	14,323	(3,041)			
6	May	18,233	18,722	489			
7	June	19,144	18,200	(944)			
8	July	20,101	24,873	4,772			
9	August	21,107					
10	September	22,162					
11	October	23,270					
12	November	24,433					
13	December	25,655					
14	Total	238,757	125,496	3,366			
15							
16							
17							

Clever Ideas for Using Multisheet Workbooks

Before you get into the meat of this multisheet stuff, let me whet your appetite with a few tasty ideas on how to put this concept to use. You may be able to use some of these ideas, or — better yet — maybe you can come up with some new ideas on your own. (If so, let me know. I'm always looking for good ideas that I can steal — er, borrow — for future books!)

✔ **Store results for different time periods.** If you use 1-2-3 to track information such as sales, orders, or new customers, you may want to organize your work by time periods. For example, you can have a separate sheet for each month or each quarter, enabling you to quickly locate what you want and still use formulas to get grand totals and summaries.

- **Put charts on separate sheets.** If your workbook file contains several charts, you can insert each chart onto a separate sheet and give each sheet a descriptive name. Then when your boss barges in and wants to see the production chart for July, you simply click the appropriate tab. The boss will think that you're very organized and give you a raise and a promotion.

- **Document your work.** If you're working on a fairly complex project, you may want to use a separate sheet to make notes to yourself to remind you of what you did, why you did it, and how you did it. And if you're really industrious, you even can keep a historical log that describes the changes you made to the worksheet over time. The person who takes over your job when you get promoted will appreciate your efforts.

- **Use a multisheet workbook in place of separate files.** If you're working on a project that uses five different single-sheet workbooks, for example, you may find it more practical to keep them all in one workbook file (each on a separate sheet). That way, when you're ready to work on the project, you load the one workbook file, and everything you need is handy.

- **Store different scenarios.** Many people use a spreadsheet to do "what-if" analysis, and multisheet workbooks can make this process easier. For example, you can copy an entire sheet to other sheets in the workbook. Then you just make some experimental changes in the assumptions for each copy and give the sheets names, such as *BestCase, WorstCase, LikelyCase, JoesScenario,* and so on.

If managing different scenarios is your bag, a better approach is to use the Version Manager feature in 1-2-3. Chapter 20 covers this 1-2-3 "what-if" feature.

Things You Should Know about Multisheet Workbooks

Keep the following concepts in mind when you work with more than one sheet in a 1-2-3 workbook file:

- The extra sheets in a workbook file don't appear automatically. Every file starts out with one lonely sheet, and if you want more sheets, you have to insert them yourself.

- ✔ The sheets are normally labeled with letters, starting with sheet A and continuing through sheet IV, which is the 256th sheet in a file. This labeling method is the same as the one used for columns. (Hey! Finally something is consistent!)

- ✔ Each tab displayed at the top of the screen represents a sheet. If you have lots of extra sheets with long names, you may not be able to see all the tabs at once, but you can scroll the tabs horizontally to get to the one you need.

- ✔ You can (and should) change the sheet letters to names that are more meaningful to you and that reflect the contents of the sheet.

- ✔ When you refer to cells or ranges on another sheet, you must precede the cell reference with the sheet letter (or sheet name, if it has one). For example, C:A1 refers to the upper-left cell on the third sheet (sheet C).

- ✔ Formulas that use range references can use ranges that cut across sheets. For example @SUM(A:A1..C:C3) adds up a $3 \times 3 \times 3$ cube of cells starting with the upper-left cell on the first sheet and extending through the cell in the third row and third column of the third sheet (27 cells in all).

- ✔ You can format all the sheets in one fell swoop with group mode — a real time-saver when you want all your sheets to look the same.

Fundamental Stuff

This section explains how to do some basic operations involving multisheet workbooks, including adding, removing, and naming sheets and other basic concepts.

Adding sheets

When you create a new workbook, it has only one sheet (sheet A). If you want to use additional sheets, you have to insert them yourself. Inserting additional sheets is actually pretty easy to do. Simply click the New Sheet button at the upper-right of the workbook window, as you can see in Figure 10-2. 1-2-3 inserts an empty sheet directly after the one you're currently working on and makes the new sheet the *active sheet*. (The active sheet is the one that you're working on and contains the cell pointer.)

For additional flexibility, choose Create➪Sheet. Doing so pops up the dialog box shown in Figure 10-3. You can specify how many sheets to add, and where to put them (before or after the current sheet).

Figure 10-2:
Clicking the
New Sheet
button adds
a new sheet
directly
after the
current
sheet.

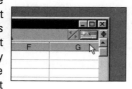

Figure 10-3:
The Create
Sheet
dialog box,
where you
tell 1-2-3 to
insert one
or more
new sheets.

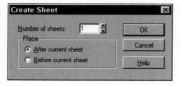

Removing sheets

If you want to get rid of an entire sheet (including everything that's on it, of course), activate the sheet that you want to zap and then choose Sheet⇨Delete. It'll be gone before you can say, "Hey, what happened to my data?"

Another way to delete the current sheet is to right-click the sheet's tab and choose Delete from the shortcut menu.

By the way, if you try to delete the only sheet in a workbook, 1-2-3 objects and displays a message telling you that you can't delete all sheets.

Deleting an entire sheet is a pretty drastic measure, because everything on the sheet is gone in an instant. If any of your formulas refer to cells on a deleted sheet, they'll return ERR (for *error*). So before you nuke a sheet, make sure that's what you really want to do. But if you do accidentally delete a sheet, don't forget about the 1-2-3 safety net: the Edit⇨Undo command.

Moving and copying sheets

Believe it or not, previous versions of 1-2-3 don't provide a way for you to move or copy a particular sheet. Fortunately, the designers at Lotus realized this omission and included this capability in 1-2-3 Millennium Edition. If your workbook contains multiple sheets, you may want to rearrange the sheets. Or, you may want to make an exact copy of one of your sheets. Both of these tasks are simple. Just choose the Sheet⇨Move or Copy Sheet command, and you see the dialog box shown in Figure 10-4.

Figure 10-4:
The Move or Copy Sheet dialog box lets you relocate a sheet, or make an exact duplicate of a sheet.

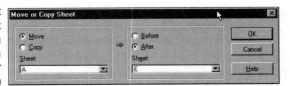

Just specify the operation (either Move or Copy), the sheet, and where to put it.

If you prefer, you can use handy drag-and-drop operations instead of the Move or Copy Sheet dialog box. To move a sheet, click its sheet tab. When the mouse pointer turns into a hand, drag the tab to its new location. To copy a sheet, press Ctrl while you drag the sheet tab.

Naming sheets

Giving a meaningful name to every sheet that you use is a good idea. Naming sheets makes identifying what's on each sheet easier for you (or anybody else who may inherit the file). After all, you'll have an easier time remembering that your boss's sales projections are on a sheet named *BOSS* than on a sheet named *R*. You can also use sheet names in formulas, which can make the formulas more understandable. Calculating a ratio with a formula such as +BOSS:A1/BOSS:A2 makes more sense than using +R:A1/R:A2, no?

To give a sheet a new name, just double-click the sheet's tab and then type a name. Sheet names can be up to 15 characters long (1-2-3 doesn't distinguish between upper- and lowercase letters in names). You can use spaces, but steer clear of commas, semicolons, periods, or any other nonletter or non-number characters. And finally, don't create sheet names that look like cell addresses (such as AB12); 1-2-3 may get confused — it's only human, you know.

You can continue to use the original sheet letter, even if you give the sheet a name. For example, if you name the first sheet *IntroScreen,* you can enter either of the following formulas:

```
@SUM(INTROSCREEN:A1..INTROSCREEN:A6)
@SUM(A:A1..A:A6)
```

1-2-3 recognizes both formulas as the same request for information, one using the sheet name and the other using the sheet letter. However, 1-2-3 always replaces a sheet letter reference that you enter with the sheet's name (if it has one).

Whenever you change a sheet name, 1-2-3 quickly checks all your formulas. If any of the formulas use the old sheet name, they are changed to the new sheet name automatically. Therefore, you can change the sheet names at any time and not have to worry about updating your formulas.

If you rename a sheet, 1-2-3 won't let you change the sheet name back to its original sheet letter. In fact, you can't rename a sheet using any single-letter names or two-letter names between AA and IV — these names are reserved.

Color-coding your sheet tabs

You don't need to settle for drab tabs. You can make your sheet tabs any color you like. Besides adding some pizzazz to your screen, using different colors for your sheet tabs makes it easier to identify various sheets.

Here's how to do it:

1. **Right-click the sheet tab and choose Sheet Properties from the shortcut menu.**

   This action displays the Sheet InfoBox.

2. **Click the Basics tab of the Sheet InfoBox and select a color from the Tab color list (see Figure 10-5).**

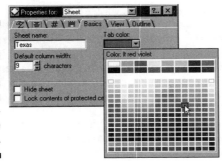

Figure 10-5: To make locating your sheets easier, you can color-code the sheet tabs.

Printing multiple sheets

Chapter 9 explains the nuts and bolts of printing a worksheet. But what about printing a workbook that has more than one sheet? Easy. Choose File⇨Print and then select the Entire workbook option in the Print dialog box. Each sheet begins printing on a new sheet of paper.

Navigating in the Third Dimension

You probably already know how to navigate through a single worksheet by using the arrow keys, mouse, scroll bars, and so on. Moving around in a multisheet workbook requires a bit more effort, however, because you have another dimension, so to speak, to be concerned about. In fact, thinking of a multisheet workbook as a 3-D workbook is often helpful.

Discovering how to move around a multisheet workbook is fairly logical after you get the hang of it. It's kind of like driving on the Los Angeles freeways, only infinitely safer (with much less gridlock and better air quality).

If you find that dealing with the third dimension is rather confusing, don't despair. The whole setup is very logical, and after you start playing around with multisheet workbooks, you're sure to get the hang of them. And when you do, you'll wonder how you ever got along without them. If you find yourself getting really frustrated, however, just stick with single-sheet workbooks. After all, some people have been using only one sheet for more than a decade — and they got along just fine.

Activating other sheets

Before you can scroll around on a sheet, you must activate it. The easiest way to activate a specific sheet in a workbook is to click the tab with your mouse. If you have many sheets or sheets with long names, the tab you want may not be visible. You can click the little arrows to the left of the New Sheet button, as shown in Figure 10-6, to scroll the tabs to the left or right until the one you want appears.

Figure 10-6:
Click to
scroll the
tab display
left or right.

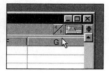

Sometimes, using the keyboard to activate a different sheet may be more efficient. Table 10-1 lists the keyboard combinations necessary to activate a sheet.

Table 10-1   Keyboard Combinations to Activate Sheets

Key Combination	*What It Does*
Ctrl+PgDn	Activates the preceding sheet, unless you're on the first sheet — in which case the key combination has no effect
Ctrl+PgUp	Activates the next sheet, unless you're on the last sheet — in which case the key combination has no effect
Ctrl+Home	Activates the first sheet and moves the cell pointer to the upper-left cell
End, Ctrl+Home	Moves to the last cell that contains data on the last sheet that contains data

A fast way to activate a far-off sheet is to press F5 — the Go To key. 1-2-3 asks you what address you want to go to. Enter a sheet letter followed by a colon and any cell address, and you're there in a jiffy. For example, if you want to activate sheet M, press F5, type **M:A1**, and then press Enter. If the sheet has a name, you can type the name instead of the sheet letter.

Selecting multisheet ranges

When you're building a formula that references information on more than one sheet, you can either enter the cell references manually, or you can use pointing techniques similar to those you use in a single sheet.

For example, assume that you're building a formula in cell A:A1 that adds up the figures in range B:A1 through F:A1, a common formula to consolidate the numbers in six sheets. You can, of course, type **@SUM(B:A1..F:A1)**. You may, however, prefer to point to the argument and let 1-2-3 create the range reference for you.

Do so by performing the following steps (if you're following along with the example, make sure that you start with a workbook that contains at least six sheets):

1. **Move to the cell that will contain the formula and type the formula to the point where the range reference is required.**

   If you're following the example, start in sheet A, activate cell A1, and type

   @SUM(

2. **Press Ctrl+PgUp or Ctrl+PgDn to move to the first sheet in the multisheet range and then select the cell reference.**

   If you're following the example, press Ctrl+PgUp to activate sheet B. Then move the cell pointer to cell B:A1, if it's not already there.

3. **Press the period to anchor the first cell in the selection.**

4. **Press Ctrl+PgUp or Ctrl+PgDn until you get to the last sheet in the multisheet range, and then select the last cell.**

   If you're following the example, press Ctrl+PgUp four more times until you get to sheet F. Then move the cell pointer to cell F:A1, if it's not already there.

5. **Type) to end the @function and then press Enter to finish the formula.**

   1-2-3 brings you back to the cell that holds the formula. In the example, the formula appears as @SUM(B:A1..F:A1).

Rather than press Ctrl+PgUp to activate other sheets while pointing, you can hold down the Shift key and click a sheet tab with your mouse.

Grouping Sheets

Before putting this chapter to bed, I want to discuss one more topic that's relevant and actually pretty useful at times when you need several sheets to look the same. 1-2-3 lets you create a sheet group that consists of two or more consecutive sheets. When you create a sheet group, you can specify one sheet as the master sheet. All the other sheets in the group then have the same formatting as the master sheet. Sound handy? It is.

For example, say you have a workbook with budget data for your company. Each sheet is set up the same way, and each sheet contains the budget information for a department. You decide that you want to change the formatting — use different fonts, sizes, colors, and number formats. One approach is to format each sheet separately, which would take quite a bit of time and would be subject to mistakes. A better solution is to format one of the sheets, create a sheet group, and apply the formatting to all the other sheets.

Creating a sheet group

To create a sheet group and copy the formatting from one sheet to all other sheets in the group, do the following:

1. **Make sure that all the sheets you want to group are set up identically.**

2. **Choose Sheet⇨Group Sheets.**

   1-2-3 displays the dialog box shown in Figure 10-7.

Figure 10-7:
Use the Group Sheets dialog box to copy formatting from one sheet to other sheets in a group.

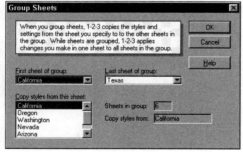

3. **Use the drop-down lists to select the first sheet in the group and the last sheet in the group.**

4. **Select the sheet from which you want to copy the formatting.**

5. **Click OK.**

Performing these steps copies the formatting from the sheet you specify in Step 4 to all the other sheets in the group.

When you close the Group Sheets dialog box, the sheet group remains in effect. (1-2-3 displays the word Grp in the status bar to remind you of this fact, and also displays the sheet tabs in italics.) Any formatting that you do while in group mode affects all the sheets in the group.

Working with sheet groups can be very handy, but it can also be a bit dangerous. For example, if you're working with a sheet group and you delete a column, the column is deleted from all sheets in the group.

Canceling a sheet group

To cancel a sheet group, choose Sheet⇨Clear Sheet Group. Everything returns back to normal.

Part IV
Making Yourself at Home

The 5th Wave   By Rich Tennant

"NO, THAT'S NOT A PIE CHART, IT'S JUST A CORN CHIP THAT GOT SCANNED INTO THE DOCUMENT."

In this part . . .

The five chapters in this part all deal with common spreadsheet tasks. In Chapter 11, find out how to customize 1-2-3 so that it looks and acts the way you want it to. Chapter 12 shows you how to format your sheets in a way that will impress your boss, your coworkers, and possibly even your cat. Chapters 13 and 14 deal with charts and maps. Finally, Chapter 15 explains how to get the most out of the time-saving SmartIcons and shortcut keys in 1-2-3.

Chapter 11

Making 1-2-3 Look and Act the Way You Want It To

. . . .

In This Chapter

▶ Adjusting how the screen looks by removing things you don't want to see

▶ Using the zoom feature to your advantage

▶ Splitting a worksheet window into panes

▶ Freezing rows or columns so that they always appear

. . . .

*I*f you're reading this book in a sequential fashion, you already have a great deal of nitty-gritty 1-2-3 knowledge — more than enough to do some meaningful work. This chapter is like the proverbial icing on the cake: You don't really have to know how to do the tasks I explain here, but they can make your life easier — and they're sort of fun, too. Several of these topics show you how to make 1-2-3 work or look differently than it normally does.

You may not be interested in everything I discuss in this chapter, but at the very least, I suggest that you glance through the pictures to see whether anything here strikes your fancy.

I don't go into a great deal of detail in this chapter, because this stuff is all fairly straightforward. If you're interested in more information, play around with the software or read the online help.

To View or Not to View

As you may know, 1-2-3 offers tons of options that affect what you see and how it looks. At times, you may want to change the way 1-2-3 looks. For example, when you want to see as much information on-screen as possible, you may want to remove the status bar and edit line, or hide the SmartIcons.

Fortunately, you have a great deal of freedom to put exactly what you want on-screen at any particular time, and you can drastically change the way your 1-2-3 screen looks. Unfortunately, the commands to view and hide items are scattered in several places. Table 11-1 tells you where to go when you want to hide or display certain items.

Table 11-1   Commands for Changing the Way Your Screen Looks

Item	How to Change It
Edit line	View⇨Hide (or Show) Edit Line
Outline frame	Sheet InfoBox (Outline tab)
Page break lines	View⇨Set View Preferences (View tab)
Row and column borders	Sheet InfoBox (View tab)
Scroll bars	View⇨Set View Preferences (View tab)
Sheet tabs	View⇨Set View Preferences (View tab)
SmartIcons	View⇨Hide (or Show) SmartIcons
Status bar	View⇨Hide (or Show) Status Bar
Worksheet gridlines	Sheet InfoBox (View tab)

Zooming Windows

If you have a video camera, it probably has a zoom lens, which lets you zoom in on your subject for a closer look (handy at your local nude beach) or zoom out to record the big picture (to fit all those "large" relatives in the scene). 1-2-3 isn't a video camera, but it does have a zooming feature. The View⇨Zoom to command leads to another menu with five zoom levels (25 percent, 50 percent, 75 percent, 100 percent, and 200 percent). These commands enable you to change the amount of magnification of the on-screen display.

The worksheet zoom level has nothing to do with printing. In other words, if you zoom in on your worksheet to make the text larger, the sheet doesn't print larger.

Figure 11-1 shows two worksheet windows. The one on the left is zoomed in to show close detail, and the other is zoomed out to give a bird's-eye view.

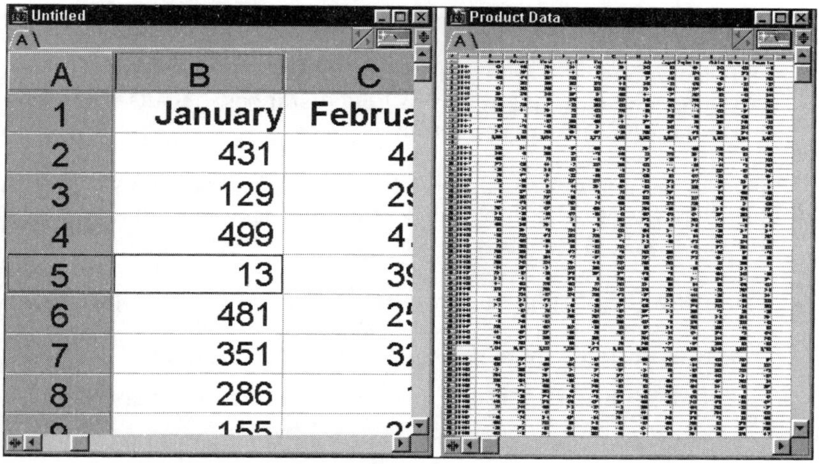

Figure 11-1:
Zooming
can show
the details
up close or
give you the
big picture.

Why would you want to zoom in or out? I can think of several reasons. If you're working on a chart (see Chapter 13) or using some of the drawing tools (see Chapter 16), zooming in gives you more control over the details. And if you have a large worksheet, you can zoom out to get a better idea of how the worksheet is laid out. Zooming out also makes selecting large ranges with a mouse easier, because you can reduce the amount of scrolling while you select cells.

You may have noticed another command on the View menu: Zoom to Custom Level. You can use this command to quickly zoom to a level that doesn't appear on the View➪Zoom to menu. Normally, the custom zoom factor is 87 percent (which is the 1-2-3 default zoom factor), but you can change it to whatever you want by choosing View➪Set View Preferences, which displays the Workbook Properties dialog box. Click the View tab and specify a custom zoom percent.

Splitting Windows — What a Pane!

If you have many rows and columns of information in a worksheet, scrolling through the sheet to examine all the cells can get tedious. The split windows option can help you out, however.

As you know, every worksheet is displayed in its own window. You can split this window into two panes or four panes so that you can see different parts of a worksheet at the same time. If you have a very large worksheet, this option can be handy because it lets you refer to one part while you work on another part that may be far away. If you like, you can even display a different sheet in each pane. The split windows option is also useful for copying cells and ranges across long distances, because you can quickly jump back and forth between the panes.

Figure 11-2 shows an example of a "paneful" worksheet window that has been split vertically into two panes. The left pane displays sheet A, and the right pane displays sheet C.

Choosing View⇨Split displays a dialog box with three options:

- ✔ **Top-Bottom:** Splits the screen into two stacked panes
- ✔ **Left-Right:** Splits the screen into two side-by-side panes
- ✔ **Four-way:** Splits the screen into four panes (two on top, two on bottom)

In all cases, the split occurs at the location of the cell pointer, so make sure that you move the cell pointer to the proper location before you choose View⇨Split.

To remove the split panes and return things to normal, choose View⇨ Clear Split.

A faster way to split and unsplit panes is to drag either the vertical or horizontal split bar. Just click the split bar and drag it to where you want the split to occur. To remove split panes by using the mouse, drag the pane separator all the way to the edge of the window. You can also change the location of the split by dragging the split bar. Figure 11-3 shows the location of the split bars.

Figure 11-2: This window has been split into two independently scrolling panes.

	A	B	C		C	G	H	I	J
1		January	February		30	229	348	432	
2	XB4-1	431	445		31	185	371	122	
3	XB4-2	129	297		32	262	0	391	
4	XB4-3	499	474		33	428	193	22	
5	XB4-4	13	398		34	42	154	292	
6	XB4-5	481	258		35	90	417	43	
7	XB4-6	351	326		36	126	320	341	
8	XB4-7	286	15		37	467	324	234	
9	XB4-8	155	235		38	173	155	229	
10	XB4-9	380	411		39	96	473	151	
11	XB4-10	58	3		40	417	292	347	
12	XB4-11	77	24		41	427	21	91	
13	XB4-12	192	176		42	289	145	444	
14	XB4-13	214	38		43	441	372	109	
15		3,266	3,100		44	362	316	97	
16					45	330	197	476	
17	XB4-14	339	341		46	11,003	10,712	10,018	12
18	XB4-15	346	40		47				
19	XB4-16	405	11		48				
20	XB4-17	272	480		49				

Horizontal split bar

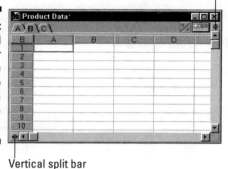

Figure 11-3:
Click and
drag either
of these
split bars to
split the
window into
two panes.

Vertical split bar

Normally, when you use split panes, scrolling isn't synchronized. In other words, the panes scroll independently of each other. If you want to synchronize the scrolling that occurs in split panes, select the Synchronize scrolling check box in the Split dialog box. Or you can choose View⇨Synchronize Split.

Press F6 to jump quickly between the panes in a split window.

If you don't like the idea of having your window split into pieces, you can always create a new window for the workbook by choosing Window⇨New Window. The new window is simply another view into your workbook. You can use it to view a different part of the worksheet or an entirely different sheet.

Freezing Rows and Columns (Brrrr!)

Many worksheets have row and column labels that describe the cells. A standard budget is a good example. Typically, the top row has month names and the left column has budget categories. However, after you start scrolling around through the worksheet, the first row and first column often are no longer visible, so you can easily lose track of what column and row a particular cell is in. If you have difficulty finding your bearings when the row and column labels scroll out of view, grab your winter coat and read on.

You can freeze rows and columns so that they remain visible as you scroll throughout the worksheet. Just another one of the magical tricks of 1-2-3. To freeze a row, a column, or both, follow these steps:

1. **Move the cell pointer to the cell below the row that you want to freeze and to the right of the column that you want to freeze.**

2. **Choose View⇨Titles.**

   1-2-3 displays the Titles dialog box, shown in Figure 11-4.

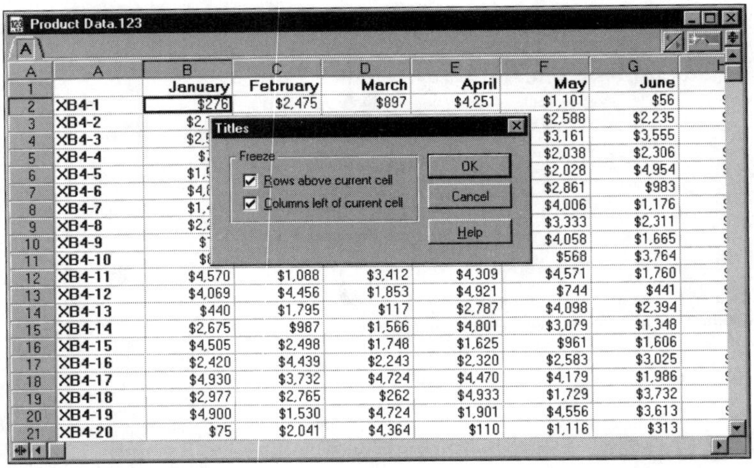

Figure 11-4:
The Titles
dialog box
lets you tell
1-2-3 what
to freeze.

3. Choose rows, columns, or both; then click OK.

1-2-3 freezes the row or column (or both) at the cell pointer position. Cells
that appear in the frozen rows or columns do not show gridlines.

Figure 11-5 shows a worksheet with the first row and first column frozen.
Notice that row 1 and column A are displayed, even though the cell pointer
is far away from the upper-left corner.

To thaw out the frozen rows or columns, choose View⇨Titles and remove
the check marks from the options in the Titles dialog box.

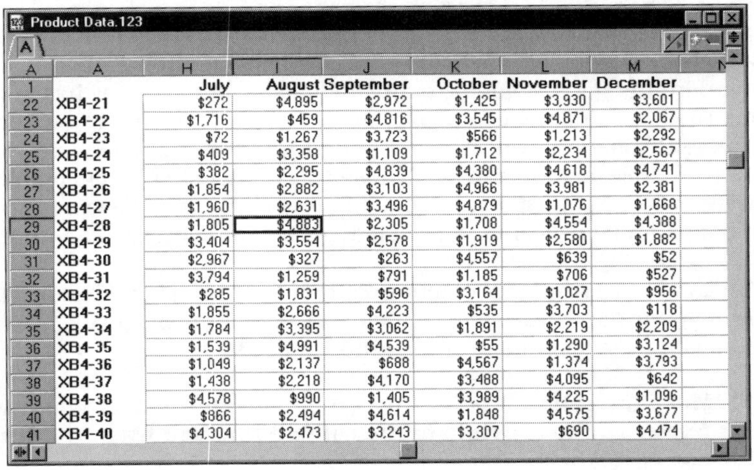

Figure 11-5:
An example
of a frozen
row and
column.

Chapter 12
Dressing Up Your Work

- -

In This Chapter
▶ Making your worksheets look great
▶ Knowing the ins and outs of dealing with fonts (making sure that WYS is really WYG)
▶ Drawing borders
▶ Changing cell colors
▶ Messing with cell alignment
▶ Saving time by using the style gallery and named styles
▶ Gathering some suggestions to keep you from going hog wild

- -

As they say in Hollywood, looks are everything. That philosophy may not be exactly true when it comes to spreadsheets, but a nicely formatted worksheet usually makes a much better impression. This chapter is about *formatting* — something that you do to improve the looks of your worksheet. When it comes to type fonts, sizes, colors, and fancy borders, many people are quite content to accept all the 1-2-3 default settings. Using these defaults produces a perfectly acceptable — but rather boring — worksheet.

If you want to add some pizzazz to your work (and give your creative juices a chance to flow — or trickle) this chapter tells you all about the stylistic formatting options at your disposal.

What Is Stylistic Formatting?

This chapter is mainly about aesthetics. In other words, I show you how to use the formatting commands that make your work look good and stand out in a crowd. By formatting, I'm not talking about the *numeric* formatting that you apply to numbers. Instead, I'm talking about the following types of formatting (sometimes referred to as *stylistic formatting*):

✔ Changing the type font

✔ Changing the size of the type

✔ Changing the type attributes (bold, italic, underlined)

✔ Adding borders, lines, and frames

✔ Changing the colors (or shading) of the text and the background

✔ Adjusting the alignment of cell contents

To Format or Not to Format?

The manner in which something is presented can often have a major influence on how it's accepted. Consider this scenario: Both you and your counterpart at a competing company submit a proposal to a potential client. One proposal uses plain old Courier type (like a typewriter), and the other is nicely formatted with different type sizes, attractive borders, and even some shading. Which one do you think the potential client will read first?

An attractive presentation commands more attention, is easier to read, and makes readers think that you really care about your work (little do *they* know, right?). Figure 12-1 shows an example of an unformatted report. Figure 12-2 shows that same report after applying some formatting. Which one do *you* prefer?

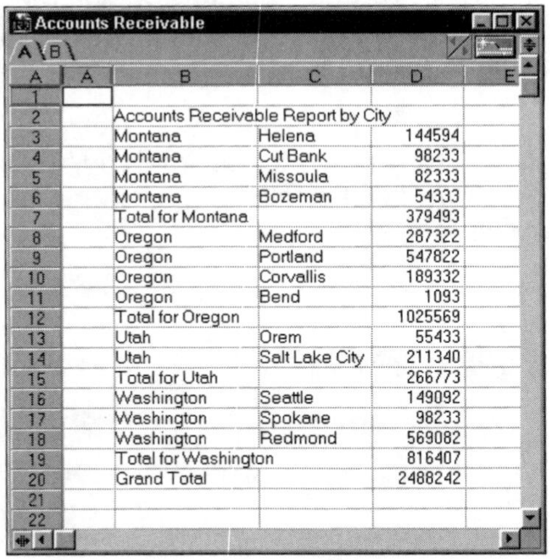

Figure 12-1:
An unfor-
matted
report.

	A	B	C	D	E
1					
2		Accounts Receivable Report by City			
3		Montana	Helena	144594	
4		Montana	Cut Bank	98233	
5		Montana	Missoula	82333	
6		Montana	Bozeman	54333	
7		Total for Montana		379493	
8		Oregon	Medford	287322	
9		Oregon	Portland	547822	
10		Oregon	Corvallis	189332	
11		Oregon	Bend	1093	
12		Total for Oregon		1025569	
13		Utah	Orem	55433	
14		Utah	Salt Lake City	211340	
15		Total for Utah		266773	
16		Washington	Seattle	149092	
17		Washington	Spokane	98233	
18		Washington	Redmond	569082	
19		Total for Washington		816407	
20		Grand Total		2488242	
21					
22					

Accounts Receivable

Accounts Receivable			
Accounts Receivable Report by City			
Montana	Helena	$144,594	
Montana	Cut Bank	$98,233	
Montana	Missoula	$82,333	
Montana	Bozeman	$54,333	
Total for Montana		**$379,493**	
Oregon	Medford	$287,322	
Oregon	Portland	$547,822	
Oregon	Corvallis	$189,332	
Oregon	Bend	$1,093	
Total for Oregon		**$1,025,569**	
Utah	Orem	$55,433	
Utah	Salt Lake City	$211,340	
Total for Utah		**$266,773**	
Washington	Seattle	$149,092	
Washington	Spokane	$98,233	
Washington	Redmond	$569,082	
Total for Washington		**$816,407**	
Grand Total		**$2,488,242**	

Figure 12-2:
A report, after applying some simple formatting.

I don't mean to imply that a nicely formatted report can compensate for a lousy analysis. In most cases, you must have the content before you add the flair. But if you take the time to do some stylistic formatting, at least you won't have a lousy analysis *and* a lousy-looking report.

One more reason to take the time to format your work nicely is that formatting can be fun. In fact, you'll probably find that formatting your work is a great deal more interesting than building formulas and copying ranges (at least *I* do).

General Principles of Formatting

Some people like to format their worksheets as they develop them. Others prefer to save the formatting for the final step — after they're sure that everything works the way it should. Neither of these approaches is better than the other. It's just a matter of individual preference. Like everything else you do in 1-2-3, nothing is carved in stone. You can change your formatting any time you want.

Screen versus printer

When it comes to formatting, the key word is WYSIWYG — *what you see is what you get.* The image that gets printed looks very much like the image you see on-screen. Change the font on the screen, and the worksheet prints with that new font. Add a border around a table of numbers, and the border appears in the printout. And so on and so on.

An important difference in printed versus on-screen appearance is color. If you don't have a color printer, your on-screen colors get translated into shades of gray when you print your work. This difference is important to keep in mind because some color combinations look great on the screen but look terrible — or are illegible — when you print them. If you need to have something that looks good on paper *and* looks good on-screen, the best approach is to experiment with various colors, printing out samples as you go.

General formatting how-to

The InfoBox makes your formatting as easy as possible. In general, you select the range of cells that you want to format and then use the appropriate tab of the Range InfoBox. Make your changes in the InfoBox and the results show up on-screen. If the change doesn't look like what you expected, go back and try it again. The InfoBox remains displayed, so you can easily experiment with various looks.

Besides the InfoBox, 1-2-3 gives you a few extra options for your formatting convenience:

- ✔ Use shortcut keys for some formatting operations.
- ✔ Use the SmartIcons for some formatting operations.
- ✔ Use the status bar at the bottom of the screen for some formatting operations.
- ✔ Use named styles (see "For Formatting Fanatics: Named Styles," later in this chapter).
- ✔ Copy existing formats to other cells.

Dealing with Fonts

One thing that can drastically change the look of your work is the font (or fonts) you use. *Font* refers to the typeface that's used for text and numbers. The actual fonts that you can use depend on which fonts you have installed on your computer system. The installed fonts appear automatically in the font lists that 1-2-3 displays in various dialog boxes.

Many different fonts are available from a variety of sources. Some are designed for ordinary work, and others can best be described as decorative.

Where did you get that font?

You may have seen a colleague's printed output that used some great-looking fonts. Chances are, this person acquired some new fonts from one of many sources.

The accompanying figure shows a sampling of some fonts that I have installed. As you can see, a good variety exists, although not all of them are appropriate for a board report.

So where do you get these new fonts? Sometimes, when you install a new software program, the program adds some new fonts. You can also buy separate font collections and install them in Windows. These collections often come on CD-ROMs and include hundreds of different fonts. Another excellent source for fonts is the Internet. Fire up your browser, jump to your favorite search site, and search for "Windows Fonts." You'll find hundreds of Web sites that provide free or inexpensive fonts that you can download.

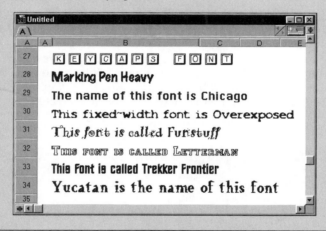

Two categories of fonts

Besides looking different, fonts differ in another characteristic — their horizontal spacing. With some fonts, every character takes up the same amount of horizontal space. These fonts are known as *monospaced* or *fixed-width* fonts. A common example of a monospaced font is Courier New. Other fonts use different amounts of horizontal space for each character. For example, the letter *i* doesn't take up as much horizontal space as the letter *W*. Figure 12-3 shows the same text in both Courier New (a monospaced font) and Times New Roman (a *variable-spaced* font).

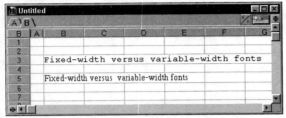

Figure 12-3:
Fonts vary
in the
amount of
horizontal
space
they use.

But the good news is that most fonts always use the same amount of horizontal space for *number* characters. Therefore, the numbers you put in a column of cells line up nicely regardless of which font you select.

Using the InfoBox to change fonts

The first step to formatting 1-2-3 cells is to select the cell or range that is to get the new font. Then access the Range InfoBox and click the Font, attribute, and color tab. If the Range InfoBox isn't displayed, press Alt+Enter to bring it up. Figure 12-4 shows what this box looks like.

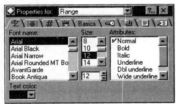

Figure 12-4:
The Font,
attribute,
and color
tab of the
Range
InfoBox.

This InfoBox lets you quickly adjust the following settings:

- ✔ The font used for the text
- ✔ The size of the text
- ✔ Text attributes (bold, italic, and so on)
- ✔ The color of the text

Your fault, my fault, or default?

In computer lingo, the term *default* is used to describe things that occur normally. When you enter data into a cell, 1-2-3 uses its default settings to display the information. For example, your information is entered in a default font with a default numeric format in default background color, and so on. If you don't like these default settings, you can easily change them for an entire worksheet. You may, for example, prefer that all cells in the sheet display in 14-point boldface type. If you set this formatting as the default, you don't have to format individual cells.

The secret to changing worksheet defaults is the Sheet InfoBox. To display this InfoBox, choose Sheet⇨Sheet Properties.

Like all InfoBoxes, the Sheet InfoBox offers a number of tabs. The following tabs all contain settings that let you change worksheet defaults:

✔ Font, attribute, and color (first tab)

✔ Alignment (second tab)

✔ Number format (third tab)

✔ Color, pattern, and line style (fourth tab)

Changing any of the default settings in the Sheet InfoBox affects only the current worksheet. Also, if you've already made any modifications to individual cells or ranges, these modifications are not affected by the changes in the default settings. For example, if you have selected a different font for a particular range, changing the default font doesn't affect that range.

Quick font changes via the status bar

Another way to change the font of your selected cells is to use the status bar. The status bar shows the font name for the cell or range you have selected. Simply click this font name to display a list of available fonts and then select a new one.

Directly to the right of the font name button in the status bar is the font size button. Clicking this button is a quick way to change the size of the font in your selection.

If your worksheet text is hard to read on-screen, you don't necessarily have to use a larger font to make it readable. You can always change the zoom factor to enlarge the screen image. Choose View⇨Zoom to adjust the zoom factor. Zooming has no effect on the printed output.

Lines and Borders and Frames (Oh My!)

The grid lines that normally appear on your screen help you see where the cells are. Normally, you don't print the grid lines (although you can, if you want). But 1-2-3 lets you add all sorts of additional lines to your worksheet, and you have plenty of control over how they look.

Adding lines or borders can greatly enhance your worksheet, as you can see in Figure 12-5. This figure shows an example of a range before and after adding some lines and borders.

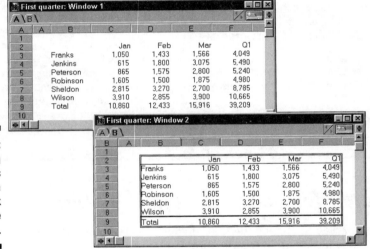

Figure 12-5: Adding borders can make a table look much more organized.

If you add lines and borders to your worksheet, you may want to turn off the cell grid display. Turning off the display makes the added lines easier to see. To get rid of the cell grid display, use the Sheet InfoBox (choose Sheet⇨ Sheet Properties). Click the View tab and remove the check mark from the Grid lines check box.

Bordering on beautiful

The Range InfoBox (what else?) is the place to go when you need to add some lines or borders. More specifically, you use the Color, pattern, and line style tab — which is shown in Figure 12-6. When working with lines and borders, you can ignore the top half of this InfoBox (the part labeled "Interior"), which deals with what's inside the cell, not what's around it.

Figure 12-6:
The Color, pattern, and line style tab of the Range InfoBox.

When you work with the Range InfoBox, remember that the borders you specify apply to the entire range selected. Applying a border consists of the following steps:

1. **Select the cell or range around which you want to draw a border.**

2. **Make sure that the Range InfoBox is displayed. If it isn't, choose Range⇨Range Properties.**

3. **Click the fourth tab (Color, pattern, and line style).**

4. **Select a border style by clicking one of the icons in the Border section.**

5. **Select a line style (you won't see the border if the Line style box is set to none).**

6. **Select a line color (optional).**

As always, the selected cells take on these new formats as soon as you make your choices in the InfoBox.

You can add borders to as many parts of the selection as you like, and each line part can be a different line style. In other words, you can go crazy with line drawing options.

To remove all lines from a selection, click the first border icon and select none from the list of line styles.

Adding designer frames

The Color, pattern, and line style tab of the Range InfoBox has another part at the bottom. Click the Designer frame check box, and the InfoBox displays two additional controls: Frame style and Frame color.

These options let you put one of 16 designer frames around your selection. Figure 12-7 shows a workbook that uses a designer frame.

Figure 12-7:
For special
effects,
select one
of the 16
designer
frames. This
worksheet
shows
a few
examples.

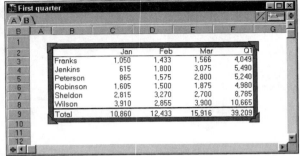

Color My World

When I first started out in computing (shortly after dinosaurs became extinct), a color monitor was considered a luxury item, and the color monitors that were available were pretty wimpy by today's standards. Nowadays, practically every system is equipped with a decent-quality color monitor.

Color has some great benefits:

🖝 You can use color to make certain text stand out from the crowd.

🖝 Coloring the background of a range helps you remember that those cells belong together.

🖝 Color is easier on the eyes than solid black and white.

1-2-3 lets you change the color of the text in the cells, as well as the background color and pattern of the cells. I can't really demonstrate this effect in a black-and-white book, but suffice it to say that you can get some nice-looking worksheets — as well as some very gaudy worksheets — by changing the color of the text and background.

You change colors by using the Color, pattern, and line style tab of the Range InfoBox. A picture of this tab of the InfoBox appears in the previous section, so you may want to turn back to refresh your memory (refer to Figure 12-6).

Start by selecting the cell or range you want to color. In the selected range, you can make the following changes:

✔ **Pattern:** Here's where you select the pattern for the background. You have 64 choices (the first three choices don't actually display the selected pattern). The choices show up using the background color and pattern color that are currently selected. Be careful; most of these patterns make your text illegible, so patterns are most useful for empty cells.

✔ **Background color:** The background of cells can use two colors, combined in a pattern. Use this option to select the background color (if desired). You can select from 255 glorious colors.

✔ **Pattern color:** This option is for the second background color. You can choose from the same 255 glorious colors.

✔ **Text color:** This option lets you change the color of the text — again, you have 255 (mostly glorious) color choices.

When you print your worksheet on a black-and-white printer, different colors appear as shades of gray. Some combinations of text colors and background colors that look great on the screen look terrible when you print them. And to make things even more unpredictable, the results you get depend on the printer you're using. All I can say here is to experiment and see what you get.

Alignment and Misalignment

Chapter 4 describes the most common ways of aligning information in cells: flush-left, flush-right, or centered. The status bar pop-up menu makes these types of formatting a breeze. But you may find some other alignment options interesting in your stylistic pursuits. Additional choices appear in the Alignment tab of the Range InfoBox, which is shown in Figure 12-8.

Figure 12-8:
The Alignment tab of the Range InfoBox lets you drastically change the way cells appear.

Word wrap

One of my favorite features in 1-2-3 is its wrap-text option. Each cell formatted with this option works like a tiny word processor. In other words, when you type a long label into the cell, the words wrap around and the row height increases to accommodate the extra lines. Figure 12-9 shows an example of this option. As you can see, it's great for the headings in tables.

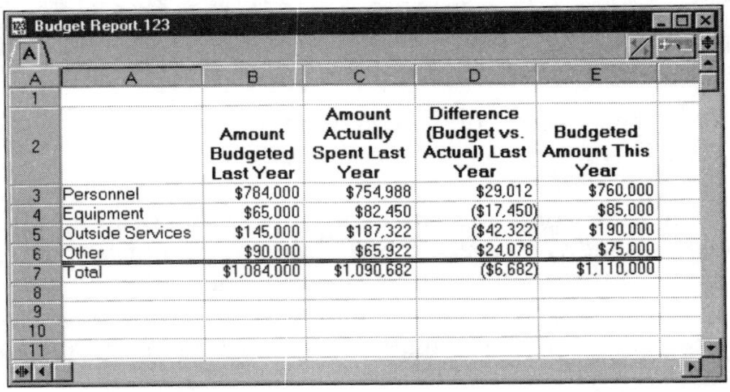

Figure 12-9: Using the wrap-text alignment option makes long labels wrap around within a cell.

	A	B	C	D	E
1					
2		Amount Budgeted Last Year	Amount Actually Spent Last Year	Difference (Budget vs. Actual) Last Year	Budgeted Amount This Year
3	Personnel	$784,000	$754,988	$29,012	$760,000
4	Equipment	$65,000	$82,450	($17,450)	$85,000
5	Outside Services	$145,000	$187,322	($42,322)	$190,000
6	Other	$90,000	$65,922	$24,078	$75,000
7	Total	$1,084,000	$1,090,682	($6,682)	$1,110,000

Centering across cells

Another handy feature lets you center a label across a horizontal range of cells. Figure 12-10 shows a label that's actually in cell A1 but is centered across the range A1:E1. Using this feature is a good way to put titles across a multicolumn table of numbers. Back in the dark ages (circa 1989), people used to add spaces to their labels (by trial and error) to get this effect. Now it's automatic.

To center a label across a group of columns, first enter the label in the left-most cell of the range in which you want the label. Then select that cell and

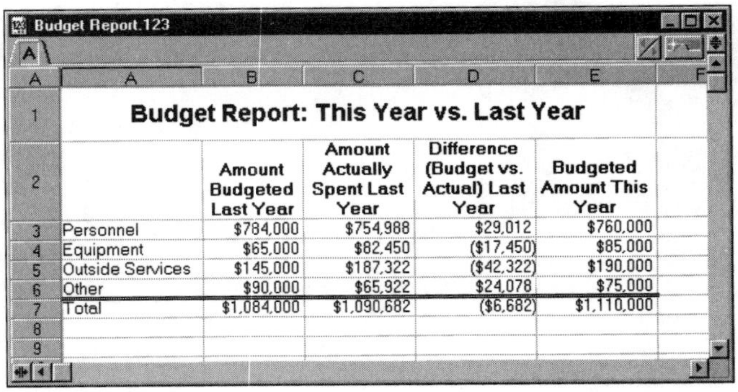

Figure 12-10: The label is actually in cell A1, but it's centered across a bunch of columns.

	A	B	C	D	E	F
1		Budget Report: This Year vs. Last Year				
2		Amount Budgeted Last Year	Amount Actually Spent Last Year	Difference (Budget vs. Actual) Last Year	Budgeted Amount This Year	
3	Personnel	$784,000	$754,988	$29,012	$760,000	
4	Equipment	$65,000	$82,450	($17,450)	$85,000	
5	Outside Services	$145,000	$187,322	($42,322)	$190,000	
6	Other	$90,000	$65,922	$24,078	$75,000	
7	Total	$1,084,000	$1,090,682	($6,682)	$1,110,000	

the cells to the right — enough to cover the entire area that you're centering across. In the Alignment tab of the Range InfoBox, select the Align across columns option and then click the center horizontal alignment icon (the third icon).

Even spacing

Yet another option lets you space the letters in a label to fill an entire cell or an entire horizontal range. Figure 12-11 shows a few examples of this feature. To space out the label, select the last icon in the Horizontal alignment section. If you want to space a label out across a bunch of cells, also check the Align across columns check box. Text formatted using even spacing almost always looks terrible, and I've never seen anybody actually use this option.

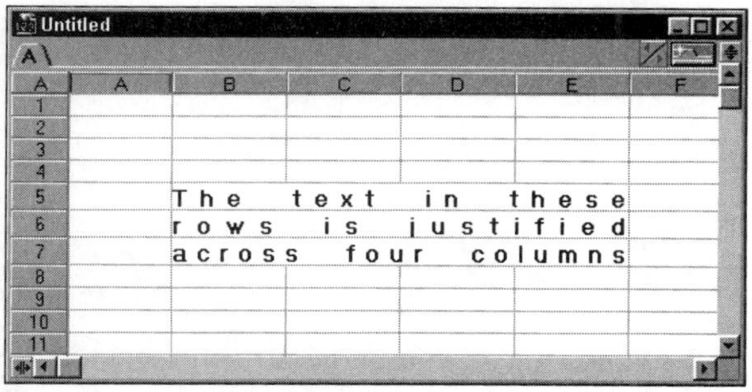

Figure 12-11:
Another alignment option lets you space the letters in a label to fill a cell or a range.

Vertical spacing

Normally, information you enter in a cell sits at the bottom of the cell. Even if you make the row height very high, the cell contents still remain at the bottom of the cell. You can change the status quo by using the vertical alignment options in the Alignment tab of the Range InfoBox. Figure 12-12 shows some examples.

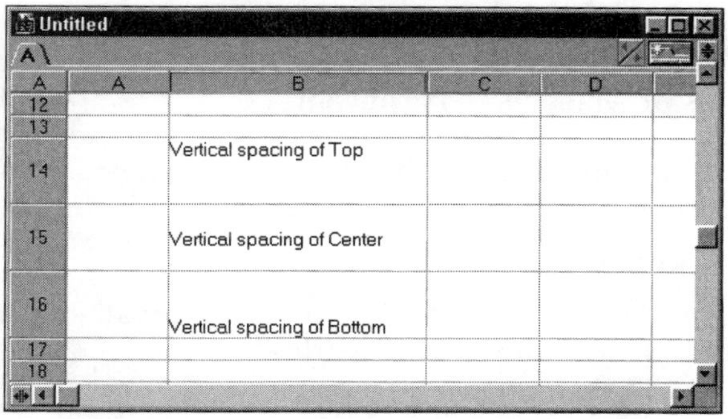

Figure 12-12:
1-2-3 also lets you adjust the vertical alignment of cell contents.

Changing orientation

Another interesting feature lets you change how the text is oriented in a cell. You have five choices, which you can make by choosing the Orientation pull-down menu in the Alignment tab of the Range InfoBox. If you select the diagonal option, you can even adjust the angle. Figure 12-13 shows several examples of text with various orientations.

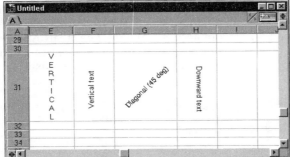

Figure 12-13:
You have lots of choices as to the orientation of the text in your cells.

For Formatting Fanatics: Named Styles

If you work with 1-2-3 long enough, you find yourself doing the same sorts of formatting over and over. For example, you may like to make your column headings 14-point, bold, italic, with a light yellow background color. Applying these formats isn't difficult, just tedious. Wouldn't it be nice if you could just click a button to apply all those formats in one fell swoop?

Your prayers are answered. 1-2-3 offers a nifty feature known as *named styles*. You create a named style that consists of format settings for several different attributes. Then you can apply that named style quickly and consistently to a cell or range.

Advantages of using named styles

Using named styles provides three big advantages:

- ✔ You save time because using a named style is much faster than applying a bunch of different formatting commands.
- ✔ Your work looks more consistent.
- ✔ If you modify a named style, 1-2-3 automatically updates all the cells that use that style with the new formatting.

Creating a named style

The easiest way to create a named style is *by example.* Format a cell to have the style characteristics that you want and then let 1-2-3 create the style from that cell. To create a style by example, follow these steps:

1. **Select a cell and apply the formatting to make up the style.**

2. **Bring up the Range InfoBox and click the last tab (Named style).**

3. **Click the Create Style button.**

   1-2-3 displays a dialog box asking you for a name for the new style (see Figure 12-14).

Figure 12-14:
The Create
Style dialog
box lets you
give a
name to a
collection
of formats
that you
create.

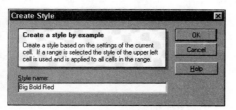

4. **Enter a name for the style (come up with something descriptive) and click OK to create the new style.**

   The new style is available, and you can apply it to other cells or ranges.

Modifying a named style

If you change your mind about a style — for example, if you want the style to include the italic attribute — no problem. Use the same steps I outline in the preceding section but, in Step 3, click the Redefine Style button (instead of the Create Style button). 1-2-3 displays a list of named styles. Choose the style that you're redefining, and click OK. All the cells with that style automatically change to the new style formats.

Applying a named style

After you create a named style, applying the style to a cell or range is easy. Just select the cell or range that you want to format and then click the style name in the Named style tab of the Range InfoBox.

One-Click Table Formatting

Suppose your worksheet contains a table of numbers. You could use any or all of the techniques I discuss in the previous sections to turn your table into a pretty spiffy-looking masterpiece. Of course, you may spend a good 15 minutes or more. Or you can take the express route and have 1-2-3 do the work for you — in about 4.2 seconds (or faster, when you get some practice under your belt).

To format a table automatically, follow these steps:

1. **Select the entire range that holds the table.**

2. **Make sure that the Range InfoBox is displayed. If it isn't, choose Range⇨Range Properties.**

3. **Click the Named Style tab (the last one on the right) of the Range InfoBox.**

4. **Click the Style Gallery button.**

   1-2-3 displays the Style Gallery dialog box shown in Figure 12-15.

Figure 12-15:
You can select one of 14 canned styling templates.

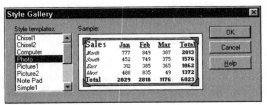

5. **Select one of the 14 style templates from the list.**

6. **When you find one you like, click OK.**

Remember: The sample that you see in the Style Gallery dialog box doesn't correspond to your actual data. It's just a sample to give you a rough idea of what you can expect.

Figure 12-16 shows an example of how data appears before and after using the style gallery.

Budget Report.123: Window 1

	Budget	Actual	Difference	New Budget
Personnel	784000	754988	29012	760000
Equipment	65000	82450	-17450	85000
Outside Services	145000	187322	-42322	190000
Other	90000	65922	24078	75000
Total	1084000	1090682	-6682	1110000

Budget Report.123: Window 2

	Budget	Actual	Difference	New Budget
Personnel	784000	754988	29012	760000
Equipment	65000	82450	-17450	85000
Outside Services	145000	187322	-42322	190000
Other	90000	65922	24078	75000
Total	$1,084,000	$1,090,682	($6,682)	$1,110,000

Figure 12-16:
A range of data before and after using the style gallery to apply formatting.

Applying one of these style gallery templates to a selected range can cause some drastic changes in the look of your worksheet. For example, the column widths may change, the fonts and attributes may change, and you may get many new colors. If you don't like the look of things after you close the dialog box, choose Edit⇨Undo immediately to reverse the effects. As an alternative to scrapping the whole formatting job, you can simply reformat the part of the table that you don't like.

Be Careful Out There

I find that getting carried away with formatting is all too easy. After you discover what you can do (and you can do a great deal), wasting too much time trying to get everything just perfect is tempting. You need to weigh the value of what you're doing against the value of your time. In other words, don't spend three hours formatting a report that took you 15 minutes to develop — especially if no one will ever read it anyway. Also, bad formatting is worse than no formatting. So don't go overboard with colors and lines.

If your system has dozens of fonts installed, go easy on them. Just because you have 96 fonts available doesn't mean that you need to use them all in a single worksheet. As a general rule, you shouldn't use more than two different fonts in a document. If you want variety, changing the size of some of the text or using italics or bold is often better.

Finally, remember that substance is what really counts. Spending your time making sure that your analysis is correct is better than making your report look good. 'Nuff said.

Chapter 13

Presto Change-o: Turning Numbers into Charts

In This Chapter

▶ Turning a range of common, everyday numbers into an attention-grabbing chart
▶ Customizing a chart by changing some of the chart parts
▶ Exploring some of the more interesting chart types you can create in 1-2-3

*P*eople tend to be visual by nature. Because of this fact, we often grasp a concept better if it's in the form of a picture or a diagram. Take a look at Figure 13-1, which shows a range of numbers on the left, and the same numbers expressed as a chart on the right. Which presentation tells the story better?

1-2-3 offers some great charting capabilities, and with them you can create some awesome-looking charts. Making simple charts is easy, and if you spend some time playing around, you'll soon discover how to tweak them a bit and make your charts even better.

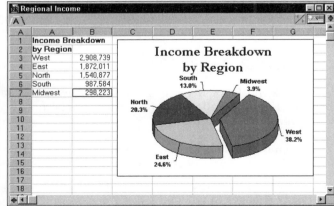

Figure 13-1:
Boring old numbers or a titillating chart? You decide.

What Makes Up a Chart?

Figure 13-2 shows a simple chart that I created in 1-2-3, with all the major parts labeled. Many of these parts are optional, and you can get rid of them if you don't want to see them. For example, if you're plotting only a single series of data, you probably don't want a legend. I refer to various parts of a chart throughout this chapter, so you may want to familiarize yourself with these terms.

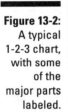

Figure 13-2:
A typical
1-2-3 chart,
with some
of the
major parts
labeled.

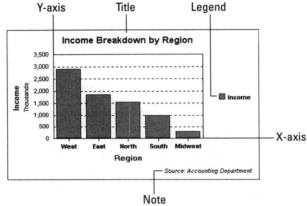

Chart parts

A chart displays one or more series of numbers graphically. A series of numbers is stored as a range in your worksheet. You can display the series as lines, bars (or columns), pie slices, and several other options. The example shown displays a company's income in each region, depicted as bars, but many other types of charts are possible.

Chart-making essentials

Before you create a chart, you need to understand a few things about how 1-2-3 deals with charts. The following list includes points that every chart-maker should know:

- ✔ To create a chart, 1-2-3 needs to use numbers that are stored in a worksheet. The numbers can be values or the results of formulas.

- ✔ When you change any of the numbers used by a chart, the chart automatically changes to reflect the new numbers.

✔ A 1-2-3 chart can show as many as 23 different series of numbers in a single chart — but don't go overboard.

✔ You can select from a long list of chart types: bar charts, line charts, pie charts, doughnut charts (yes, that's right), and more. And a single chart can be a *mixed* type — containing both lines and bars, for example. You can easily change the chart to a new type.

✔ You don't have to include a legend if you don't want one. A *legend* (like on a map — not the King Arthur type) explains what each color or line represents.

✔ You have almost complete control over the colors used, hatch patterns, line widths, line markers, fonts used for titles and labels, and so on.

✔ Charts live right on your worksheet, enabling you to print a chart along with the data it uses. You can also move a chart and change its size.

✔ You can store any number of charts in a single worksheet.

Making Your First Chart

The good news is that creating a chart using 1-2-3 is easy. Very easy. Figure 13-3 shows a range of data that's practically begging to be turned into a chart.

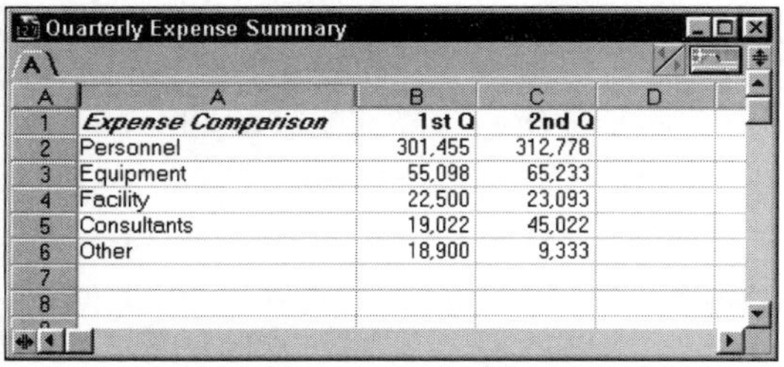

Figure 13-3:
This
information
would make
a very
nice chart.

	A	B	C	D
1	*Expense Comparison*	**1st Q**	**2nd Q**	
2	Personnel	301,455	312,778	
3	Equipment	55,098	65,233	
4	Facility	22,500	23,093	
5	Consultants	19,022	45,022	
6	Other	18,900	9,333	
7				
8				

Quarterly Expense Summary

Easy as 1-2-3

Here's how to turn numbers like those in Figure 13-3 into a chart.

1. Select the data that you want to make up your chart.

Include in your selection all cells that hold labels and legends. In Figure 13-3, you select A1..C6.

2. Click the Create a Chart SmartIcon (it has a picture of a chart on it).

The following message appears in the title bar: `Click where you want to display the chart`. Also, the mouse pointer turns into a small cross.

3. Click anywhere in your worksheet.

The location isn't important — you can always move or resize the chart later. 1-2-3 displays the chart in the area you outlined (see Figure 13-4).

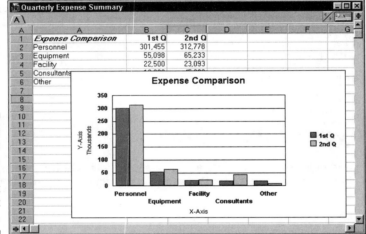

Figure 13-4: 1-2-3 creates the chart using its default chart format.

That's all it takes. After selecting the data, all you need is a click of a SmartIcon and another click in your worksheet — and you've got yourself a chart.

The chart that 1-2-3 creates may not be exactly what you had in mind. But fear not, you can very easily transform a chart into another chart type.

A look at the chart

If you look at the chart in Figure 13-4 and the data that 1-2-3 uses to create the chart, you notice the following things about the chart:

- 1-2-3 gets the chart's title from the upper-left cell in the range.
- Because the first column has labels, these labels end up as the x-axis labels.
- The text for the legend comes from the first row of the selected range.
- 1-2-3 creates a column chart — which is its default chart type.

✔ 1-2-3 examines the values in the range and decides how large to make the y-axis values. (The program also "scales" the y-axis values and inserts a label that tells you that these values are in thousands.)

✔ Just in case you decide to label the x-axis and y-axis, 1-2-3 inserts dummy labels for you.

If you want to find out how to change some of these things, don't stop now. Keep reading. The fun is just beginning.

Taking Control of Your Charts

After 1-2-3 draws a chart on your worksheet, *you* have control over it. You can change its chart type, modify the colors, move the chart around, change its size, print it, and even wipe it off the face of the planet if you don't like it.

Before you can make any of these wonderful changes to a chart, you must select the chart by clicking its border. When you select a chart, 1-2-3 does the following:

✔ Displays eight small *handles* on the chart's borders — little square draggable boxes

✔ Displays the chart's name in the edit line

✔ Displays a set of SmartIcons that are appropriate to charts

✔ Adds a new menu: Chart

✔ Changes the buttons in the status bar to chart-oriented buttons

If you click on a chart in a place other than its border, you may select a particular part of the chart rather than the entire chart. The edit line tells you the name of the part you selected or displays Chart x if you select the entire chart. To select the entire chart only, click the border.

Moving and resizing charts

To move a chart, select it and drag it to its new location; the mouse pointer turns into a hand when you can drag it. You can also use the Windows Clipboard to move charts to places where you can't drag them. For example, if you want to move a chart from one sheet to another, you can choose Edit⇨Cut to cut it and then Edit⇨Paste to paste the chart into another sheet.

To resize a chart, first select it and then grab any of the eight handles and drag it. You can make a chart as large or as small as you choose.

Annihilating charts

To remove a chart from your worksheet, select the chart and press Del. If you instantly regret nuking your chart, choose Edit⇨Undo to get it back.

Printing charts

You don't have to do anything special to print a chart; it works just like printing a worksheet. As long as you include the chart in the range to be printed, the chart prints out the way it appears on-screen.

If your chart doesn't print, choose File⇨Preview & Page Setup. In the Preview & Page Setup InfoBox, click the Include tab. Examine the Show list and make sure that the option labeled Charts, maps, and drawings is selected.

If you don't want a particular embedded chart to appear on your printout, hide it before printing. Select the chart and then choose Chart⇨Chart Properties to display the Chart InfoBox. Click the Basics tab and then place a check mark next to the Hidden check box.

Introducing the Chart InfoBox

It probably comes as no surprise to you that 1-2-3 includes a beast called the Chart InfoBox. After all, just about everything else in 1-2-3 includes an InfoBox, so why not charts?

If you do any amount of chart formatting, the Chart InfoBox is sure to become your friend. In the subsequent sections, I cover basic chart editing and formatting — and I refer to the Chart InfoBox many times.

To display the Chart InfoBox, select the chart and choose Chart⇨Chart Properties.

The Chart InfoBox is very handy because it also enables you to select a particular chart part to work with. See the drop-down list in the Chart InfoBox title bar? You can select any part of the chart from this list (see Figure 13-5). For example, if you want to work with the chart's title, select Title from the drop-down list. Two things happen:

- ✔ The InfoBox transforms itself to show options appropriate for working with the chart title.
- ✔ The chart's title is selected for you (automatically).

Figure 13-5:
The Chart
InfoBox
makes it
easy to
select a
part of
a chart.

You can also select a particular part of a chart by clicking it, which also transforms the Chart InfoBox to display commands relevant to the selected chart element.

Changing the Chart Type

1-2-3 offers 12 chart types for your viewing pleasure, and each of these chart types includes several variations *(subtypes)*. Because you can customize each of these chart types in a nearly infinite number of ways, you really have more flexibility than you are ever likely to need.

A quick overview of chart types

Table 13-1 lists all the 1-2-3 chart types, with a few comments about each one. These chart types all have subtypes.

Table 13-1	1-2-3 Chart Choices
Chart Type	*Description*
Bar	A very common chart type that shows each data point as a vertical bar (or a horizontal bar, depending on the subtype you choose).
Stacked Bar	Like a bar chart, but the data series are stacked on top of one another. This type also has horizontal subtypes.
100 percent Stacked Bar	Like a stacked bar chart, but the corresponding points for each data series are shown as percentages. This chart type has a horizontal subtype.
Line	A very common chart type that shows each data point as a marker, and the markers are connected by lines.

(continued)

Table 13-1 *(continued)*

Chart Type	Description
Area	Like a line chart, but the area below the line is colored in.
Pie	A very common chart type, with each data point corresponding to a slice of pie. If you plot more than one data series, 1-2-3 draws a separate pie for each series (up to a maximum of four pies).
Hi/Low/Close/Open	A chart type you use for displaying stock market data. You can display as many as four series, with the series corresponding to the stock's high, low, closing, and opening price.
XY (Scatter)	This chart displays data as dots. Each dot corresponds to an x-value (in the first data series) and a y-value (in the second data series).
Radar	A weird-looking chart that hardly anyone ever uses.
Mixed	A chart that uses both bars and lines.
Number Grid	This choice isn't really a chart. It's just a grid of numbers.
Doughnut	The low-calorie version of a pie chart. It has a hole in the middle.

Ways to make your chart look different

How do you know which type of chart to create? Sorry, I can't tell you the answer to this one. No hard and fast rules exist for choosing chart types, but I do have some general advice: Use the chart type that gets your message across in the simplest way possible. To display quantities over time, a line, bar, or area chart is a good choice. To show percents of a total, use a pie chart.

To change the chart type, follow these steps:

1. **Select the chart.**

2. **Choose Chart⇨Chart Type.**

   This action displays the Chart InfoBox (if it isn't already standing at attention) and also selects the Type tab. See Figure 13-6.

Figure 13-6: The Type tab of the Chart InfoBox.

3. **Select a chart type from the list and a subtype from the icons displayed on the right.**

   The subtype icons change for each chart type. Even more exciting: As you make your selection, the chart changes before your very eyes. Try a few different types and see what happens. When you find a chart type that looks good, you can stop.

Several SmartIcons enable you to quickly change to a particular chart type. However, for maximum flexibility, use the InfoBox to change chart types.

Rearranging Your Chart's Furniture

Like practically everything else you do in 1-2-3, you can change things in the charts you generate. You can change a chart by using the InfoBox. In this section, I discuss some of the more common chart changes you can make.

To make any changes to a chart, the InfoBox must be displayed. To bring the InfoBox to life, select the chart and choose Chart⇨Chart Properties.

Changing chart titles and labels

Charts can have a great deal of text in them: Three lines for the title, two lines for notes, and axis labels. To change any of the chart's text, just click the text. The InfoBox changes to show options appropriate to what you clicked.

Figure 13-7 shows the Options tab of the InfoBox for the chart's title. Generally, the title for the chart comes from a cell (the check box is checked). If you want to override this title, remove the check mark from the Cell check box and then type whatever text you want for the title. You can use as many as three lines of text for the title.

You can use other tabs in the InfoBox to adjust colors and font characteristics. These options all work just as you would expect (having a consistent user interface has its advantages).

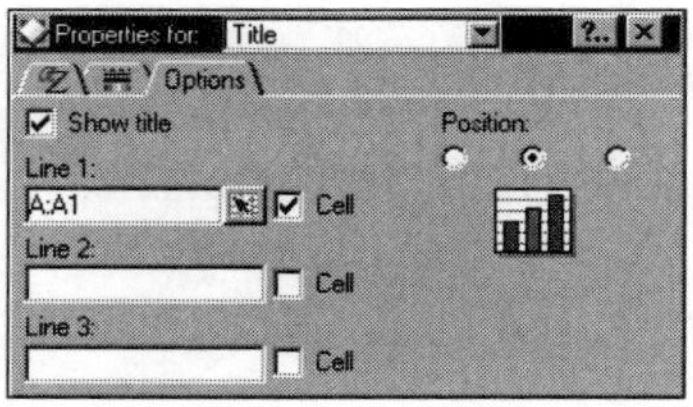

Figure 13-7:
The Title
InfoBox.

Moving a chart element

You can move a few of the chart parts around: Title, Legend, Plot Area, and Note. Moving one of these parts is a snap:

1. **Select the chart.**

2. **Click and drag the chart element to the desired location in the chart.**

If you don't feel like dragging, you can also use the InfoBox to position any of these chart items. Select the chart element and then click the Options tab in the InfoBox. Then select the position and 1-2-3 does the moving for you.

Adding a new data series to a chart

After you create a chart, you may discover that you need to add another data series to it. Rather than re-create the chart, you can use this procedure:

1. **Select the chart and choose Chart⇨Chart Properties to display the Chart InfoBox.**

2. **Select any series in the chart.**

   Doing so transforms the InfoBox into a Series InfoBox.

3. **Click the Options tab of the Series InfoBox.**

4. **In the drop-down list (which isn't labeled), select the first empty series.**

   You can recognize an empty series because it's labeled something like

   ```
   [Series 2]- Empty
   ```

5. **Click the range select button next to the Range box.**

   1-2-3 displays its Range Selector dialog box, which asks you to select a range for the new series.

6. **Select the range in the worksheet.**

Voilà! The range that you selected appears in the chart as a new data series.

Changing a chart's data series

You may need to change a chart's data series for two reasons:

✔ You add new data to the worksheet and want these new values to appear in the chart.

✔ You delete some data from the worksheet, and you don't want the empty cells to appear in the chart.

For example, you may have a chart that shows monthly sales. After the new sales figures arrive, you need to update the chart to display the new month's data. But after you enter the new number into your worksheet, you discover that 1-2-3 isn't as smart as you would like. It ignores your new value, and the chart doesn't get updated.

Or you may delete some of the data points in a range that is plotted. You find that the chart displays the deleted data as zero values — even if you delete the values from the beginning or end of the data range.

In either of the preceding scenarios, you need to change the chart's data series.

You *can* re-create the chart. But if you added a great deal of formatting to the chart, you probably want to modify the chart series to correspond to the new data range. Here's how to do it:

1. **Select the chart and choose Chart⇨Chart Properties to display the Chart InfoBox.**

2. **Select the series that you want to modify.**

3. **Click the Options tab of the Series InfoBox.**

   Figure 13-8 shows what this tab looks like.

4. **In the Range box, edit the range reference to refer to the new data series.**

   Or click the range select button next to the Range box and select the range by pointing.

The chart's data series is based on the range that you specify. If you need to change the ranges for additional series in the chart, repeat Steps 2 through 4 for each series.

Figure 13-8: The Options tab of the Series InfoBox.

Changing a chart's scale

A chart's scale refers to the beginning and ending numbers on its y-axis. Adjusting the scale of a y-axis can dramatically affect the appearance of a chart. If you don't believe me, take a look at Figure 13-9. These two charts both use the same data series — but they use different y-axis scales.

Figure 13-9: The same data, plotted using different y-axis scales.

1-2-3 always determines the scale for your charts automatically. You can, however, override the choice that 1-2-3 makes. Here's how:

1. **Select the chart and choose Chart⇨Chart Properties to display the Chart InfoBox.**

2. **Click the axis that you want to modify.**

   Usually, you want to modify the y-axis scale, but you can also change the x-axis scale of an XY *(scatter)* chart. The InfoBox changes to display options for the axis that you select.

3. **Click the Scale tab in the InfoBox (see Figure 13-10).**

4. **Adjust the Minimum and/or Maximum values for the scale.**

   The chart's axis changes according to your modifications.

If you don't put a check mark next to Maximum or Minimum, 1-2-3 performs the scaling automatically.

Figure 13-10: The Scale tab of the Y-axis InfoBox.

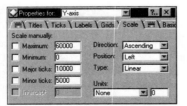

You can adjust the x-axis scale only if the chart is an XY (scatter) chart.

The Scale tab provides the following additional options:

- ✔ **Major Ticks:** You can enter the number of units between major tick marks. If the check box is not checked, 1-2-3 determines this value automatically.

- ✔ **Minor Ticks:** You can enter the number of units between minor tick marks. If the check box is not checked, 1-2-3 determines this value automatically.

- ✔ **Direction:** Select Ascending (the default option) to make the scale go from bottom to top; select Descending to make the scale go from top to bottom.

- ✔ **Position:** You can choose to display the axis on the left side of the chart (the default option), on the right side of the chart, or on both sides of the chart.

- ✔ **Type:** You can make the scale linear (the default option), logarithmic, or 100 percent. A logarithmic scale is primarily useful for scientific applications in which the values to be plotted have an extremely large range.

- ✔ **Units:** You select how the values on the axis are scaled, choosing from a variety of settings. This setting is most useful if you have large values and you don't want them to take up so much space on the axis.

Displaying series labels in a chart

Sometimes, you want your chart to display the actual data values for each point on the chart. Or you may want to display the category label for each data point. Figure 13-11 shows a chart with series labels displayed.

Figure 13-11: This chart uses series labels to identify each data point.

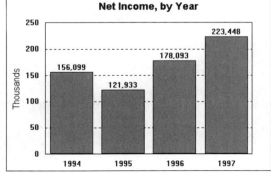

To add series labels to a chart series, follow these steps:

1. **Select the chart and choose Chart⇨Chart Properties to display the Chart InfoBox.**

2. **Select Series Labels from the drop-down list in the title bar of the InfoBox.**

   If Series Labels doesn't appear in the list, the chart type can't display series labels. If you really want series labels, select another chart type.

3. **Click the Options tab (see Figure 13-12).**

Figure 13-12:
Use the
Options tab
of the Series
labels
dialog box
to add data
labels to
a chart.

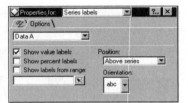

4. **Select the data series from the drop-down list.**

5. **Place a check mark next to one or more of the check boxes to indicate the type of labels that you want.**

   If you select the option labeled Show labels from range, you need to select a worksheet range with labels that correspond to the data points.

6. **Optionally, you can change the label placement, orientation, or both.**

Hungry for More Chart Power?

You can do a whole lot more with charts than I have room to cover in this book. I just barely scratch the surface when it comes to customizing charts.

If you want to expand your chart-making powers, try digging in and playing around with the various options yourself. Not to put myself out of business as a computer-book writer, but you may progress faster by doing than by reading — at least, after you read this chapter for the basic tools you need. You'll find that the process is quite logical.

If you want to change something in a chart, just follow these four steps:

1. **Select the chart and make sure that the InfoBox is displayed.**
2. **Click the part on the chart that you want to modify.**
3. **Check out the tabs in the InfoBox until you find one that looks appropriate.**
4. **Adjust the settings until things look right.**

Ninety-nine percent of the time, you are able to do what you want to do by following these steps.

Table 13-2 lists all the various elements of a chart (not all these parts appear in every chart). These elements are selectable (using either the direct-click method or by selecting the element from the drop-down list in the InfoBox title bar).

Table 13-2	Chart Parts
Part	*Description*
Doughnut Labels	Labels that describe each slice of a doughnut
Doughnut Titles	Subtitles (multiple doughnuts only)
Doughnut	A doughnut chart (a single chart can have multiple doughnuts)
Legend	The chart's legend
Note	The chart's note
Pie Labels	Labels that describe each pie slice
Pie Slice	A slice of a pie
Pie Titles	Subtitles (multiple pies only)
Pie	A pie chart (a single chart can have multiple pies)
Plot	The plot area of the chart
Series	A data series in the chart
Slices	Corresponding slices (multiple pies or doughnuts only)
Table	A table of data values
Title	The chart's title
X-Axis	The horizontal axis (or, the vertical axis if the chart is oriented horizontally)
Y-Axis	The vertical axis (or, the horizontal axis if the chart is oriented horizontally)
Z-Axis	The depth axis (3-D charts only)

Charming Chart Choices

I close this chapter by filling the pages chock-full of choice charts that you can check out and choose from (cheap). These examples demonstrate some of the things you can do with charts and may give you some ideas that you can adapt to your own situation.

A 3-D bar chart

The chart in Figure 13-13 shows a different slant on bar charts. This chart consists of two series of data. This three-dimensional, bar chart subtype is useful if you want to add some extra visual appeal to a normal bar chart.

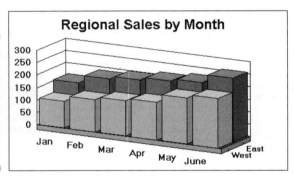

A horizontal bar chart

Bar charts don't always have to start from the ground and work their way up. The chart in Figure 13-14 shows a bar chart — but with the Horizontal orientation option selected. This chart type is particularly useful if the x-axis labels are long.

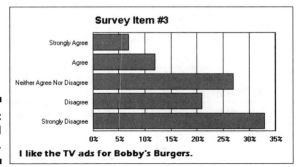

A chart that knows how to accessorize

Figure 13-15 shows a chart that has some stuff added to it. Chapter 16 shows you how to add great accessories like these using the drawing tools. I used two text boxes and two arrows to annotate this chart. Using the drawing tools is a good way to make a chart say more than mere numbers can.

Figure 13-15:
Adding comments to a chart using drawing tools is often useful.

A mixed chart

When is a bar chart not a bar chart? When it also includes lines. The chart in Figure 13-16 is usually called a mixed chart. Notice that this chart has two different scales. The bars belong with the left y-axis and show the monthly sales. The line goes with the right y-axis and shows the percent of sales goal reached. If I used the left scale for both series, the line would not have even showed up, because all the values are less than 1.2 (120 percent).

Figure 13-16:
This mixed chart contains bars and a line (hence the name).

This chart began life as an ordinary bar chart. Then I changed the second series to be shown as a line. To do so, select the series and click the Options tab of the Series InfoBox. Then select Line from the Mixed type drop-down list. To use the second y-axis for a series, check the box labeled Plot against 2nd Y-axis.

I also moved the legend inside of the plot area so that it doesn't take up much extra space. This adjustment makes the chart more compact.

Multiple doughnuts (mmm-mmm good)

The chart in Figure 13-17 is actually two charts in one. Each data series is shown as its own doughnut. For the readers who don't know their way around the kitchen, a doughnut chart is basically a pie chart with a hole in the middle. In this case, each doughnut has one slice *exploded* for emphasis. Exploding a slice is as simple as clicking it and dragging it.

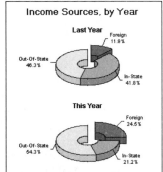

Figure 13-17:
Two
doughnut
charts.

An XY chart

The chart in Figure 13-18 is an XY (scatter) chart. Each dot represents one person and shows his or her height and weight. You can see the upwards linear trend: Taller people generally weigh more than shorter folks. I also used the drawing tools (a text box and an arrow) to make a tasteless comment about the person who belongs to one of the dots.

A stock market chart

The chart in Figure 13-19 shows stock performance over a period of time. (Stock market analysts love this sort of thing.) For each day, the chart shows the daily high, the daily low, and the closing price. Another option (not shown in the example) plots the daily opening price.

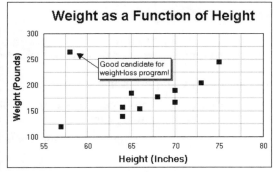

Figure 13-18:
An XY chart
can show
whether
your data
has any
discernible
trend.

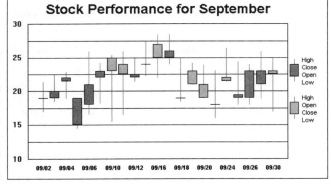

Figure 13-19:
This chart
shows the
month's
performance
of this stock
at a glance.

A 3-D line chart

Figure 13-20 shows another twist on 3-D charts — this one's called 3-D Line
(although *ribbon chart* may be a more appropriate name).

Figure 13-20:
A 3-D line
chart is
another 3-D
variation
offered by
1-2-3. (This
chart
shows that
Jill seems
to crush
Bob fairly
regularly.)

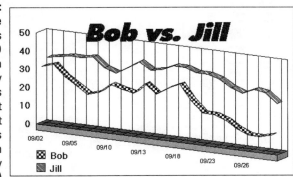

A picture chart

Figure 13-21 shows a common bar chart that was enhanced with a picture. Here are the steps you take to create such a chart of your very own:

1. **Create a standard bar chart using the normal methods.**

2. **Enter a left parenthesis character into a cell (any empty cell will do) and format the cell using the Wingdings font.**

   That particular character happens to look like a telephone in the Wingdings font.

3. **Copy the cell to the Clipboard by choosing Edit⇨Paste.**

4. **Select the data series in the chart.**

5. **Click the Pictures tab on the Series InfoBox and then click the Paste Picture button.**

6. **In the Pictures tab, specify the number of units for one picture.**

   In the case of Figure 13-21, the number of units is 100.

7. **If you want, you can create a legend manually.**

   In Figure 13-21, the legend consists of two objects: a pasted picture of the telephone, plus a text box.

You can paste any picture using this method, but you'll find quite a few interesting images hiding right there in the Wingdings font.

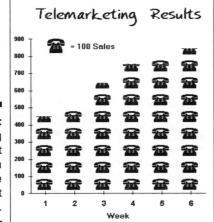

Figure 13-21:
Converting
a bar chart
into a
picture
chart
is easy.

Chapter 14

Presto Change-o II: Turning Numbers into Maps

. . . .

In This Chapter

▶ Finding out about the slick mapping feature in 1-2-3

▶ Creating a map with only a few mouse clicks

▶ Using techniques to help make your map look the way you want it to

. . . .

Charts are great, but sometimes you need a map to really tell your story. Although the maps generated by 1-2-3 won't cause the folks at Rand McNally to lose much sleep at night, you'll find that these maps can really make your data tell a story. And the best part is that you don't have to fiddle with messy marking pens that always seem to run out of ink at the wrong time.

To Map or Not to Map?

As I discuss in Chapter 13, 1-2-3 can create a bewildering variety of charts to help you display your data graphically. But not all data benefits from a chart. Take a look at the chart in Figure 14-1, which shows the median household income for each state in the United States. This result was the best I could do to show this data in a chart. Doesn't really tell you much, eh?

1-2-3 gives you a better option: maps. A map is another method to present your data graphically. People use maps for many purposes. Maps are suitable for data with a basis in geography. If you classify something by state, province, or country, chances are you can make a map out of the data. A common example is to display sales figures on a map. If your company sells its products all over the United States, showing the annual sales by state may be useful.

Figure 14-2 shows the same data as Figure 14-1, but the information is presented in a map. You probably agree that the map is much easier on the eye.

Figure 14-1:
This chart
shows
median
income for
each state
and is
almost
more
confusing
than looking
at a huge
table of
numbers.

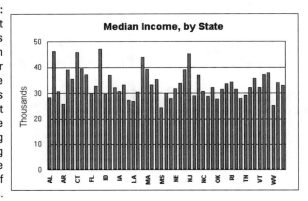

Figure 14-1:
This chart
shows
median
income for
each state
and is
almost
more
confusing
than looking
at a huge
table of
numbers.

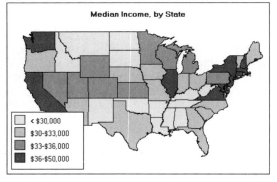

Figure 14-2:
This map
shows
median
income for
each state,
color
coded.

The map view of the data conveys quite a lot of information. For example, (with the exception of Illinois) the higher income states tend to be in the Northeast and the West. If you looked at the data in a standard chart, noticing any geographic trends would be impossible.

Types of Maps Available

The U.S. map (by state) is just one of many maps built into 1-2-3. The maps you can use include the following types:

- ✔ Alaska
- ✔ Canada
- ✔ Europe

> ✔ Hawaii
>
> ✔ United States (excluding Alaska and Hawaii)
>
> ✔ World countries

Don't ask me why Alaska and Hawaii aren't included in the U.S. map by state. Last time I checked, they were still part of the United States.

Depending on how 1-2-3 was installed on your machine, you may have some additional maps available. The following geographical regions are installed as an option: Japan, Mexico, Southern Africa, Central and Northeast Asia, Australia and New Zealand, Eastern Europe, and Scandinavia. If you need one of these maps and it's not available, rerun the 1-2-3 (or SmartSuite) Setup program and select the Custom installation option.

If this map selection isn't good enough for you, you can purchase more from Strategic Mapping, Inc. For example, you may want a map for your state, divided by zip code. Such a map is available. Contact Strategic Mapping for details about ordering (contact information is provided in the 1-2-3 documentation).

Map-Making Overview

Making a map is easy — just as easy as making a chart. You start out with your data, identified by map *region*. If you're creating a map of the United States, your regions are states. If you're making a map of Canada, your regions are provinces. If you're making a map of the world, your regions are countries — and so on.

Creating a map is similar to creating a chart. However, you must make sure that you set up your data properly. Map making in 1-2-3 is a four-step process (the fourth step is optional):

1. **Enter your region names in a column.**

2. **Enter the data for each region in the column directly to the right of the region names.**

3. **Choose Create⇨Map (or click the Create a Map SmartIcon) and click the location in the worksheet where you want the map to go.**

   1-2-3 creates the map before your very eyes.

4. **Customize the map in any number of ways.**

Ready, Set . . . Create That Map

In this section, I show you how to prepare your data for mapping and how to create a map.

Ladies and gentlemen, prepare your data

When entering data into 1-2-3 that you want to turn into a map, the important rule to remember is to identify the regions for the map using words that 1-2-3 can interpret. 1-2-3 is pretty flexible here; you can use either the official region name or an abbreviated map code.

For example, the official region name for the state where I live is *California,* and the abbreviated map code is *CA* (U.S. state map codes just happen to correspond to the official post office abbreviations). If I try to use an unrecognized region name or map code (such as *Calif* or *Cal*), 1-2-3 complains.

Before generating the map, 1-2-3 scans each region name and pops up a dialog box if it doesn't recognize the name. You have an opportunity to select from a list of all regions for the particular map.

Each map consists of regions, and the regions are different for each map. When you're preparing your data, you don't need to include data for every region on the map. For example, if you're creating a map of sales by state, you can omit the states in which you don't do business. Omitted regions are considered to have a value of 0.

To find out the region names that 1-2-3 can deal with, use the online help system. You may not need to resort to this step for states in the United States, but for unfamiliar regions you'll want to consult the online help system. For example, off the top of your head, can you name the map code for Azerbaijan? Time's up. It's AZ. Note that a particular map code has a different meaning depending on which map you're using. (For a U.S. map, AZ is the map code for Arizona.)

For the eternally curious, Figure 14-3 pinpoints the exact location of Azerbaijan. With 1-2-3 on your computer, you have a new tool to help you prepare for your next appearance on *Jeopardy!*

Besides a column of region names, you need to supply one or two columns of data. Figure 14-4 shows a small set of data for U.S. states, plus the resulting map. Notice that sales (the first column of data) is plotted as colors, and region (the second column of data) is plotted as different patterns.

Figure 14-3:
Yes,
Virginia,
there really
is an
Azerbaijan.

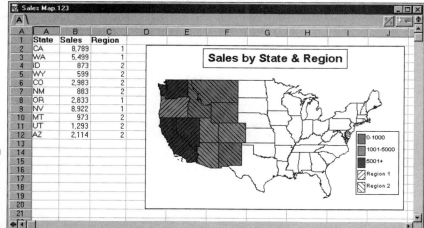

Figure 14-4:
Data and its
resulting
map.

The second column of data is optional. Most maps you make are likely to have only a single column of data.

Creating your mapsterpiece

After you have your regions and data set up in your worksheet, you're ready to create the map:

1. **Select the worksheet range that contains your data. If the data has column headings, *do not* select the headings (1-2-3 isn't smart enough to recognize them as headings).**

2. **Choose Create⇨Map (or click the Create a Map SmartIcon).**

   If 1-2-3 doesn't recognize one or more of your region names, or if any ambiguity exists, you are prompted to supply more information. Otherwise, the mouse pointer changes to a small cross.

3. **Click the area of the worksheet where you want the map to be.**

   A single click does the trick. Or you can drag to define the size of the map.

1-2-3 quickly analyzes the region names and map codes and chooses the appropriate map. In a few moments, you have a map suitable for framing. Mapping is as easy as that.

In some cases, the default map that 1-2-3 spits out will be just fine as is. More often, however, you need to do some tweaking to make the map look better. Later in this chapter, in the section "Modifying a Map," I describe the types of map modifications you can make.

Getting your bearings

Notice that 1-2-3 doesn't display any region names within a map, making it easy to get lost. Fortunately, a way exists to find out the name of a particular map region — as well as some other information about the region.

Right-click a region, and you get 1-2-3's shortcut menu. However, this shortcut menu is a bit different because it displays some useful information in addition to menu commands.

Figure 14-5 shows an example of the shortcut menu that appears when you click on the state of Montana. The menu displays the region name, its map code, and even its latitude and longitude. Choosing any of these commands copies the information to the Clipboard.

Modifying a Map

The following list offers a quick overview of the types of changes you can make to a map:

✔ You can change the size and location of the map after the fact.

✔ If you have data for more than six regions, 1-2-3 creates six categories (which are called *bins*) and color-codes the regions. You can adjust these categories or the colors used.

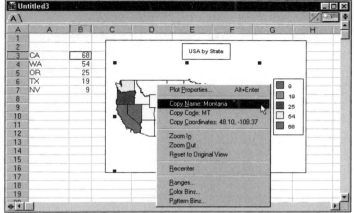

Figure 14-5:
Right-click
a region to
find out the
region's
name.

✔ You can change the map's title and adjust the font of the title and legend.

✔ You can zoom a map to show more detail and change the map's center position — perfect if you don't have data for all map regions (you may have data for only the western United States, for example).

✔ You can use patterns in your map to further identify characteristics of a region. For example, you can identify sales territories by different patterns.

✔ You can add *pin characters* to a map. These characters look like push pins you insert on a wall map to mark locations.

Selecting a map

Before you can do anything to a map, you must select it. You do so by clicking the map's border. When you select a map, 1-2-3 does the following (see Figure 14-6):

✔ Displays eight small handles on the map's borders

✔ Displays the map's name in the edit line

✔ Displays a set of SmartIcons that are appropriate to maps

✔ Adds a new menu: Map

✔ Changes the buttons in the status bar to map-oriented buttons

Map's name   Map menu   Map SmartIcons   Handles

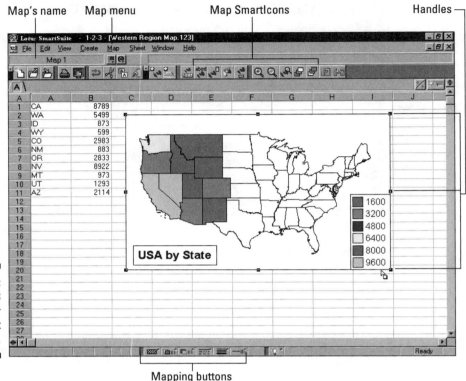

Figure 14-6:
Your 1-2-3
screen after
you select
a map.

Mapping buttons

If you click a map in a place other than its border, you may select a particular part of the map rather than the entire map. The edit line tells you the name of the part you selected or displays Map x if you've selected the entire map. To select the entire map only, click the border.

The Map InfoBox

When you make changes to a map, you usually use the Map InfoBox. Like all InfoBoxes, this one has a series of tabs that let you perform various tasks with the map. If the Map InfoBox isn't displayed, select the map and choose Map⇨Map Properties.

Moving and resizing a map

Maps, like charts, aren't fixed in size or position. You can move a map anywhere you want by clicking and dragging it. However, make sure that you select the map itself — not the plot area within the map (see the next section).

And, as you may expect, you can also change a map's size. Just click the map's border once to select it; then drag any of its eight handles to make the map the size you want. If you want to keep the same proportions, press Shift while you drag any of the four corner handles.

Adjusting the plot area

A map, like a chart, has a plot area. The *plot area* of a map is the main area that contains the map (the title and legend are outside the plot area). You can change the size or location of the plot area within a map. To do so:

1. **Select the map.**

2. **Select the plot area of the map by clicking the map image itself (not the surrounding area).**

3. **Click and drag any of the plot area handles to change the size of the plot area, or drag any of the borders to change the position of the plot area.**

If you make the plot area smaller, the map image itself shrinks. On the other hand, making the plot area larger makes the map image larger. Although the size of the map image changes, this adjustment is not the same as zooming the map — which I describe in the next section.

To restore the plot area to its default size and position, choose Map⇨Plot Properties to display the Plot InfoBox (if it isn't already on-screen) and click the Basics tab (see Figure 14-7). Then select the Default settings option.

Figure 14-7:
The Basics tab of the Plot InfoBox.

Zooming and recentering

You can zoom a map to make it larger or smaller. Zooming doesn't change the size of the plot area — only the size of the image inside the plot area.

To zoom your map, select the map's plot area. Then use any of the following techniques:

✔ Access the Plot InfoBox and click the Basics tab. Change the value in the Zoom % box. Values less than 100 make the map smaller; values greater than 100 make the map larger (and you see less of it). You can zoom a map down to 1 percent (minuscule) or up to 10,000 percent (humongous).

✔ Click either of the two zoom SmartIcons to change the zoom factor by 10 percent.

✔ Right-click and choose Zoom In or Zoom Out from the shortcut menu. Each of these commands changes the zoom factor by 10 percent.

When you zoom in on a map, you may find that the main area of interest zooms right out of the picture. If that happens, you need to zoom back out and specify a new center point for the map. The easiest way to recenter a map is

1. Right-click the map point that you want to be in the center.

2. From the shortcut menu, choose Recenter.

1-2-3 redraws the map, centered over the region that you right-clicked.

You can also recenter the map using the Basics tab of the Plot InfoBox. But to recenter using this tab, you need to specify the latitude and longitude of the area to be centered (information that most people don't have at their fingertips). Using the right-click technique I describe in the preceding steps is *much* easier.

After you recenter your map, you can zoom the map and your region remains centered. Figure 14-8 shows a U.S. map zoomed in on Kentucky. Before zooming, I recentered the map on Kentucky.

Figure 14-8:
Zooming in on the Bluegrass State.

Changing the title

Changing the title is one of the most frequent changes made to a map. 1-2-3 sticks in a title that merely describes the map — for example, "USA by State." You probably want to change the title to describe the data that you're mapping. For example, "Number of Nasty Letters Received by State."

To change the title of a map:

1. **Select the map and, if necessary, choose Map⮞Map Properties to display the Map InfoBox.**

2. **Click the map's title.**

   The Map InfoBox magically changes into a Title InfoBox.

3. **Under the Basics tab of the Title InfoBox, change the text for the title.**

   Your title can use up to three lines of text. Figure 14-9 shows the Basics tab of the Title InfoBox.

To change the font or color of the map title, use the other tabs in the Title InfoBox.

Figure 14-9:
The Basics
tab of the
Title
InfoBox.

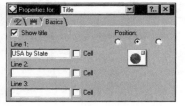

Modifying the map bins: values and colors

If your map has data for six or fewer regions, each region's exact value appears in the map legend. But a map's legend is limited to only six items, so if you have more than six regions with data, 1-2-3 automatically creates *bins* for the data values. 1-2-3 then creates a legend using these bins. A bin represents a *range* of data values rather than a single data value. If the data for a region falls within the range for a particular bin, the data is mapped with that bin's color.

Figure 14-10 shows an example of a map that shows sales data for eleven regions (states). Because the map has more than six regions, 1-2-3 creates six equal-sized bins, each of which represents a range of sales values. The number shown in the legend is the *upper* value for the bin. In this case, the bins are set up as follows:

0–108,000

108,001–216,000

216,001–324,000

324,001–432,000

432,001–540,000

540,001–648,000

Figure 14-10:
This map's
legend
shows the
six bins
created
by 1-2-3.

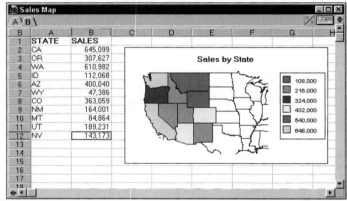

Because Montana and Wyoming both show sales figures between 0 and 108,000, these states fall into the first bin and are colored accordingly. Four states show sales between 108,001 and 216,000, so they fall into the second bin.

In many cases, the automatically created bins are just fine, but you may want to make some adjustments. In fact, you can adjust any or all of the following settings:

- ✔ The number of bins used in the map (fewer than six, if you like)
- ✔ The upper limit for each bin (You can enter these limits manually, or point to a worksheet range that holds these values.)
- ✔ The color used for each bin
- ✔ The legend label for each bin (You can enter these labels manually or point to a worksheet range that holds the labels.)

Changing the bin values

To change the values for the bins used in your map:

1. **Select the map and choose Map⇨Map Properties to display the Map InfoBox.**

2. **Click the Colors tab in the Map InfoBox (see Figure 14-11).**

Figure 14-11:
The Colors
tab of the
Map
InfoBox.

3. **In the center of the dialog box, make sure that the Values drop-down box is set for Manual.**

   This setting allows you to change the bin values manually.

4. **In the drop-down box labeled** `Put in bins by`**, select Upper limit (to create bins that include a range of values) or Exact match (to create bins that consist of single values).**

5. **Modify the numbers in the center column of the InfoBox. Each number that you enter represents the upper value for the bin.**

   If you want fewer than six bins, leave some of the value fields empty.

You can also get the bin values from a worksheet range. To do so, select From range in the drop-down box labeled Values. Then use the Values range box to select the worksheet range that contains the upper values for the bins.

Changing the bin colors

If you don't like the colors used in your map, change them by using the following procedure.

1. **Select the map and make sure that the Map InfoBox is displayed (choose Map⇨Map Properties).**

2. **Click the Colors tab in the Map InfoBox.**

3. **In the left side of the dialog box, make sure that the Colors drop-down box is set for Manual.**

   This setting allows you to change the colors manually.

4. **In the left column of the InfoBox, change the color used for any of the bins.**

   Modify the color for any of the bins by selecting from the drop-down list of colors.

You can also get the colors from a worksheet range. To do so, select From range in the drop-down box labeled Colors. Then use the Colors range box to select the worksheet range that contains the color codes. You need to experiment to determine which color codes to use.

If your map uses two sets of data, the second set is represented as patterns rather than colors. You can adjust the patterns using the same procedures — just use the Patterns tab instead of the Colors tab.

Changing the legend labels

You may want to change the legend labels to make them more descriptive. Here's how to do it:

1. **Select the map and choose Map⇨Map Properties to display the Map InfoBox.**

2. **Click the Colors tab in the Map InfoBox.**

3. **In the right side of the dialog box, make sure that the Legend labels drop-down box is set for Manual.**

   This setting allows you to change the legend text manually.

4. **In the right column of the Map InfoBox, enter the legend text for each bin.**

You can also get the legend text from a worksheet range. To do so, select From range in the drop-down box labeled Legend labels. Then use the Legends range box to select the worksheet range that contains the text for the legend.

Figure 14-12 shows the sales map after I made the following adjustments:

- ✔ I reduced the number of bins from six to three.
- ✔ I changed the upper limit for each of the bins.
- ✔ I changed the colors used.
- ✔ I changed the legend text.

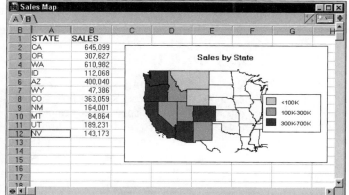

Figure 14-12:
This map
has had
its bins
adjusted.

Modifying a map legend

By default, each map that you create displays a legend that describes the colors and patterns used in that map. To make changes to the map legend:

1. **Select the map and choose Map⇨Map Properties to display the Map InfoBox.**

2. **Select the legend.**

   Make sure that you select the entire legend — not just one item in the legend. You may want to select Legend from the drop-down list in the Map InfoBox.

3. **To determine what to display in the legend and where to display the legend, click the Basics tab (see Figure 14-13).**

4. **To change the font size, click the first tab (Font, attribute, and color).**

Figure 14-13:
The Basics
tab of the
Legend
InfoBox.

Got map-making fever?

As with most things in 1-2-3, creating maps gets easier with practice. But to practice making maps, you need some data, right? You may not realize it, but you already have a great deal of map-worthy data on your hard disk.

When you install 1-2-3, the Setup program places some sample files on your hard disk. You can open some sample mapping workbooks stored in your SAMPLES\MAPS directory. This directory contains several worksheet files with tons of useful data. Check it out!

Chapter 15
SmartIcons and Shortcuts: Saving Precious Minutes Each Day

In This Chapter

▶ Making the most of those weird little pictures at the top of your screen

▶ Finding out what a SmartIcon does

▶ Putting SmartIcons somewhere else (or making them disappear temporarily)

▶ Creating your very own SmartIcon bar

▶ Discovering other keyboard shortcuts

*N*ew 1-2-3 users are usually curious about those cryptic little pictures at the top of their screens. What do the pictures mean? Are they some form of computer hieroglyphics or secret messages from aliens? As you've probably figured out by now, those pictures are called *SmartIcons*. SmartIcons can save you a great deal of time and trouble if you know what they're all about and how to take advantage of them for all they're worth.

In addition to SmartIcons, many other time-saving tricks are hiding up the ample sleeves of 1-2-3. The following pages give you enough shortcuts to more than make up for the time you spend reading this chapter.

Why SmartIcons?

Somewhere along the line, someone figured out that software users tend to use some commands more often than others. Because clicking an icon (that is, a small picture) is usually faster than accessing the menu and dealing with a dialog box, software companies put together collections of icons to serve as shortcuts for the more commonly used commands.

They're everywhere

Today, most Windows programs include a collection of such icons. If your software is not made by Lotus, these collections are usually referred to as toolbars. But Lotus designers have a thing about the word *smart*, so they call them SmartIcons — and a collection of SmartIcons is known as a *SmartIcon bar.*

Belly up to the SmartIcon bar

Before getting down to the details, take a minute to digest the following appetizers:

- ✔ The only way to access a SmartIcon is with your mouse.

- ✔ Normally, the SmartIcon bars appear directly below the edit line, but you can move them to the left, right, or bottom of your screen. Or you can have bars floating around so that you can move them wherever you like. You can even hide them altogether if you want.

- ✔ 1-2-3 is smart enough to know what you're working on and displays the appropriate SmartIcon bar automatically.

- ✔ Many additional SmartIcons that don't appear in the predefined SmartIcon bars are available.

- ✔ You can create custom SmartIcon bars by using the extra SmartIcons or SmartIcons that appear on other bars.

- ✔ If you're really industrious (or just want to have some fun), you can even edit the little pictures with the icon editor built into the program.

So Many SmartIcons, So Little Time

One of the SmartIcon bars is called *Universal.* This bar, which contains generally useful SmartIcons, is normally displayed at all times. Figure 15-1 shows this SmartIcon bar.

Including the Universal SmartIcon bar, 1-2-3 has a total of 24 predefined SmartIcon bars. The appropriate set of icons is displayed for you automatically, depending on which type of object is selected. You can display several other SmartIcon bars if you need them. Table 15-1 lists and describes all the SmartIcon bars.

Figure 15-1:
The
Universal
SmartIcon
bar.

Table 15-1	The 24 SmartIcon Bars and Their Uses
Bar	*Contents and Uses*
Active Document	Miscellaneous tools for working with worksheets
Chart*	Tools for working with charts (see Chapter 13)
Database	Tools for working with lists and databases (see Chapter 17)
Display	Tools that enable you to change various aspects of how 1-2-3 looks
Draw*	Tools for working with drawn objects (see Chapter 16)
Editing	Tools that are useful when editing cells
Formatting	Tools used for formatting cells
Internet Tools*	Tools for connecting to Internet Web sites (see Chapter 21)
Map*	Tools for working with maps (see Chapter 14)
Navigation	Tools for navigating through worksheets or workbooks
OLE Object*	Tools for working with embedded OLE objects
OLE Server	Tools for working with embedded OLE server objects
Outlining	Tools for working with outlines (see Chapter 19)
Print Preview*	Tools for working in the preview window (see Chapter 9)
Printing	Tools that change various printing options
Query Table*	Tools for working with database query tables (see Chapter 17)
Range*	Tools for working with cells and ranges
Record	Tools for recording your actions into scripts (see Chapter 18)
Scripting	More tools for working with scripts
Sheet*	Tools for working with a worksheet
Team	Tools useful when doing group projects
Universal*	General-purpose tools that are always useful
Versions	Tools for working with the Version Manager (see Chapter 20)
Web Table	Tools for working with Web tables (see Chapter 21)

* 1-2-3 automatically displays this SmartIcon bar when appropriate.

Moving and Hiding SmartIcon Bars

You can put the SmartIcon bars anywhere you like: along any of the edges of the screen, or just free-floating. Or, you can hide them altogether to maximize the amount of information you can see on-screen.

Moving SmartIcon bars

To change the location of the SmartIcon bar, first locate the bar's title bar. If the bar is oriented horizontally, the title bar is on the left. If the bar is oriented vertically, the title bar is on the top. Title bar is a misnomer, because no title exists, but you know what I mean.

When you locate the SmartIcon bar's title bar, click it and drag (the mouse pointer turns into a hand). You can drag the title bar

- ✔ To one edge of the screen (left, right, top, or bottom)
- ✔ To a location in the middle of the screen (make it a *floating* toolbar)

If you drag the toolbar to one edge, it changes its orientation and sticks there.

Figure 15-2 shows what the screen looks like after you drag the Universal SmartIcon bar to the left side of the screen and make the Range SmartIcon bar float freely in the middle of the screen.

Sometimes when you move a SmartIcon bar to a floating position, the bar isn't displayed in its full size. In other words, some of the SmartIcons may be hidden. You can change the size of a floating SmartIcon bar by dragging any of its borders.

Now you see it, now you don't

If you want to hide all the SmartIcons, choose View⇨Hide SmartIcons. Or you can right-click any SmartIcon and choose either Hide this bar of SmartIcons or Hide all SmartIcons.

To make your SmartIcons reappear, choose View⇨Show SmartIcons.

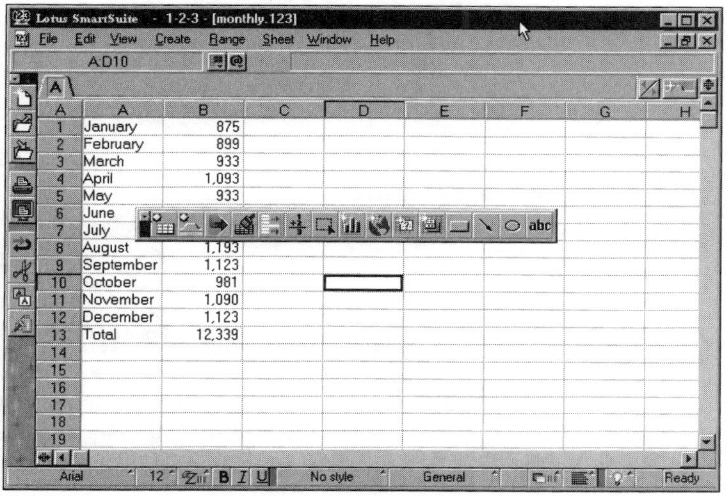

Figure 15-2:
1-2-3, after
moving
a few
SmartIcon
bars to new
locations.

Knowing Which SmartIcon Does What

After all the votes are tallied, 1-2-3 offers around 300 SmartIcons — some good, some bad, some ugly. Oddly enough, many of these SmartIcons are unemployed and don't appear on any of the 24 predefined SmartIcon bars.

I won't even try to describe all the SmartIcons that exist. If I did, the description would take up a few dozen pages — and nobody would read it anyway. Throughout the book, I do point out particularly useful SmartIcons.

When 1-2-3 displays a SmartIcon bar, you can discover what a particular icon in that bar does by moving the mouse pointer over the icon and pausing for about one second. A description of the SmartIcon appears in a cartoon-like bubble. Figure 15-3 shows one such description for a SmartIcon.

Whatever you do, don't be afraid to use SmartIcons. If you aren't sure whether a SmartIcon does the job you want done, read the description. If you're still not sure, but the SmartIcon seems appropriate, just go for it. If the SmartIcon does something unexpected, you can always rely on the Edit⇨Undo command (or press Ctrl+Z) to reverse the effects.

Figure 15-3:
Pausing the
mouse
pointer over
a SmartIcon
pops up a
description.

Copy a range's styles to
other ranges

Making Your Own SmartIcon Bar

The final topic in this SmartIcon discussion may not appeal to everyone, but those who like to tinker with things may find it pretty interesting. I'm talking about creating a custom SmartIcon bar that includes only the icons that you like and use most. If this SmartIcon bar were a compact disc, you would call it *SmartIcons' Greatest Hits*.

In this example, you create a SmartIcon bar with a bunch of drawing icons. Chapter 16 shows you how to make drawings on a worksheet using the Create⇨Drawing command. But that's not the only way to make drawings. 1-2-3 has hidden SmartIcons that make creating drawings easy and enable you to bypass the menu.

You can follow these instructions to create this bar or — if you're really bold and daring — read through this section to get an idea of how to make your own. Then do it.

1-2-3 doesn't have an easy way to create a new set of SmartIcons. Rather, you have to start with an existing set and save it using a new name. That task is what you do first:

1. **Choose File⇨User Setup⇨SmartIcon Setup.**

   1-2-3 displays the SmartIcons Setup dialog box shown in Figure 15-4. At this point, one set of SmartIcons is selected and appears at the top of the dialog box.

2. **Click Save Set.**

   1-2-3 displays another dialog box that asks whether you want to overwrite the existing SmartIcon bar.

3. **Reply to the dialog box by clicking the Save as New button.**

   You get yet another dialog box, shown in Figure 15-5, that asks for a name and a filename.

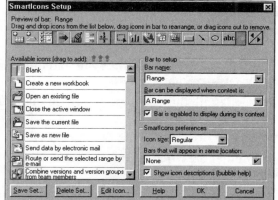

Figure 15-4:
The
SmartIcons
Setup
dialog box.

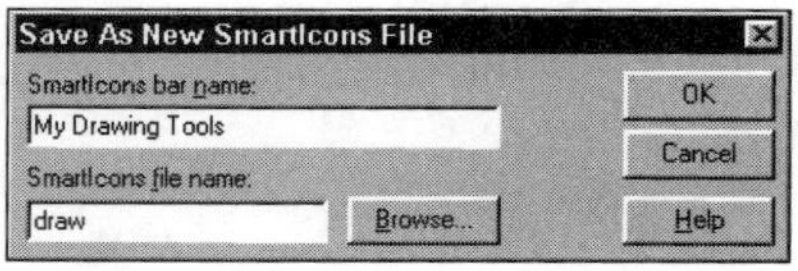

Figure 15-5:
Use this
dialog box
to save your
SmartIcon
bar to a file.

4. **Enter a name for your new SmartIcon bar and a filename for saving it; then click OK to save the file.**

   For the example, enter **My Drawing Tools** as the SmartIcon bar name and **DRAW** as the filename. You are returned to the SmartIcons Setup dialog box. Notice that the active SmartIcon bar is now called My Drawing Tools.

Removing SmartIcons

The next step is to remove all the SmartIcons from the bar, leaving it empty so that you can add your own SmartIcons.

1. **To remove a SmartIcon, click it and drag it away.**

   The SmartIcon disappears from the bar at the top of the SmartIcons Setup dialog box.

2. **Repeat this process for all the SmartIcons.**

   After you remove all the SmartIcons, the bar is empty.

Adding new SmartIcons

The next step is to add the new SmartIcons to the empty bar:

1. **Scroll down the list of available icons until you find one that you want to use in your custom SmartIcon bar.**

   If you're following along with the example I present in this chapter, look for the icon called Create a text block.

2. **Click the SmartIcon and drag it to the bar at the top of the dialog box.**

3. **Click and drag any other SmartIcons you want into the bar at the top of the dialog box.**

   For the example, add other SmartIcons until the bar looks something like Figure 15-6.

Figure 15-6:
This
SmartIcon
bar is
customized.

You can add a Blank SmartIcon (the first one in the list) to leave a gap between icons. Using spaces can help you organize the SmartIcons on a bar into logical groups.

Displaying the SmartIcon bar

The next step is to determine when you want your new SmartIcon bar to appear. Because my example creates a SmartIcon bar containing drawing tools that you can use in many different situations, the bar should be displayed all the time:

1. **Locate the drop-down list labeled** Bar can be displayed when context is, **and select Always from the list.**

2. **Make sure that a check mark appears in the check box labeled** Bar is enabled to display during its context.

Saving the SmartIcon bar

The final step is to save your custom SmartIcon bar again:

1. **Click the Save Set button to save your changes.**

   1-2-3 asks you if you want to overwrite the existing file. Answer in the affirmative.

2. **Click OK to close the SmartIcons Setup dialog box.**

   Your new SmartIcon bar is displayed and ready for action.

Trying out the new SmartIcon bar

After you close the SmartIcons Setup dialog box, the new SmartIcon bar appears. Drag the bar to a position you like and try it out (see Chapter 16 for details on creating drawings).

Mouseless Shortcuts

SmartIcons are great time-savers, but 1-2-3 gives you other easy ways to save time — and you don't even have to move your hand from the keyboard to grab your mouse.

Menu shortcuts

Many of the commands in the File and the Edit menus have shortcut keys assigned to them. When you choose one of these menus, the shortcut keys are displayed next to their commands. Figure 15-7 shows the Edit menu. Ten of these commands provide shortcuts; for example, Ctrl+X is the shortcut for the Edit⇨Cut command.

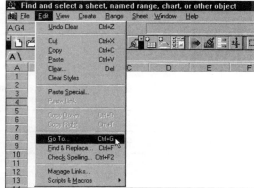

Figure 15-7:
The Edit
menu and
its shortcut
keys.

Table 15-2 lists all the shortcut keys that 1-2-3 recognizes.

Table 15-2	The Shortcut Keys
Key	*What It Does*
Ctrl+C	Copy the selection to the Clipboard
Ctrl+D	Copy down
Ctrl+F	Find and replace
Ctrl+G	Go to a cell or range
Ctrl+O	Open a file
Ctrl+P	Print
Ctrl+S	Save the current workbook
Ctrl+T	Copy to the right
Ctrl+X	Cut the selection to the Clipboard
Ctrl+Z	Undo

Stylistic shortcuts

Several shortcut keys exist for formatting your work stylistically (see Chapter 12). By getting into the habit of using these shortcuts, you can save yourself a great deal of time — and get home at a reasonable hour. Table 15-3 lists these shortcuts.

Table 15-3	Stylistic Shortcuts with the Control Key
Key Combination	*What It Does*
Ctrl+B	Adds or removes boldface
Ctrl+E	Centers cell contents
Ctrl+I	Adds or removes italics
Ctrl+L	Left-aligns cell contents
Ctrl+N	Removes bold, italics, and underlining from the current selection
Ctrl+R	Right-aligns cell contents
Ctrl+U	Adds or removes underlining

Function keys

Many shortcuts don't have menu equivalents; instead, use the function keys on your keyboard. These keys are located along the top of your keyboard, on the left side, or in both locations. Table 15-4 lists these function keys and their uses.

Table 15-4	The Function Keys
Key	*What It Does*
F1 (HELP)	Displays online help that's usually relevant to what you're doing
F2 (EDIT)	Switches the program into Edit mode so that you can change the contents of the current cell
F3 (NAME)	Lists names of files, charts, ranges, collections, query tables, drawn objects, versions, and @functions
F4	In Edit, Point, or Value mode, cycles the cell references in formulas from absolute to mixed to relative; in Ready mode, anchors the cell pointer so that you can select a range of cells
F5 (GOTO)	Moves the cell pointer to a cell, named range, worksheet, chart, drawn object, query table, version, or active file (equivalent to Edit⇨Go To)
F6 (PANE)	Moves the cell pointer between panes in split windows
F7 (QUERY)	Performs a query on the selected query table (equivalent to Query Table⇨Refresh)
F8 (TABLE)	Repeats the last Range⇨Analyze⇨What-if Table command
F9 (CALC)	In Ready mode, recalculates all formulas; in Edit mode, converts a formula to its current value
F10 (MENU)	Activates the menu bar so that you can use the keyboard

Some of the function keys do different things when you use the Alt key with them. Table 15-5 contains a list of the Alt+function key shortcuts.

Table 15-5	Ctrl+ and Alt+Function Key Shortcuts
Key Combination	*What It Does*
Alt+F1 (COMPOSE)	Creates characters that you cannot enter directly from your keyboard. For example, Alt+F1 followed by the letters c and o generate a copyright symbol
Alt+F3 (RUN)	Displays the Run Scripts and Macros dialog box (equivalent to Edit⇨Scripts & Macros⇨Run)
Alt+F4	Closes 1-2-3 (equivalent to File⇨Exit 1-2-3)
Ctrl+F2	Starts the spell checker
Ctrl+F4	Closes the active window
Ctrl+F6	Activates the next workbook window

Part V
Expanding Your Horizons

The 5th Wave By Rich Tennant

"I asked for software that would biodegrade after it was thrown out, not while it was running."

In this part . . .

The chapters in Part V address features that are sometimes considered advanced. You may never *need* to use these features, but they can make your life a little easier. In this part, you get the scoop on using drawing tools, creating databases, recording scripts, outlining worksheets, using the Version Manager, and even launching into the Internet right from 1-2-3.

Chapter 16

Using the Drawing Tools: Artistic Talent Not Required

. . . .

In This Chapter

▶ Adding lines, arrows, shapes, diagrams, and freehand drawings to your worksheet

▶ Pasting clip art into your worksheet

▶ Discovering serious uses for the drawing tools to justify the fun you have playing with them

. . . .

1-2-3 is known primarily as a spreadsheet. As the earlier chapters in this book attest, the cells are pretty handy for holding numbers and formulas. But did you know that you can use 1-2-3 to draw geometric shapes, too? In fact, you can add all sorts of art (lines, arrows, and other shapes) to spruce up any 1-2-3 spreadsheet.

You can do a variety of things with the 1-2-3 drawing tools — ranging from constructive and industrious (such as organizational charts) to whimsical and silly (such as doodles). In many cases, you may find that 1-2-3 includes all the drawing software you need — so you can save your company from spending big bucks on special drawing software.

Discovering the Secret Draw Layer

You can imagine that every worksheet contains an invisible *draw layer,* like a transparency on which you can add drawings and other items. If you've created a chart or a map in 1-2-3, then you've already used the draw layer. Charts and maps reside on the draw layer, and they can be moved around freely, independent of the cells in the worksheet.

In addition to charts and maps, you can add geometric shapes, boxes that hold text, and pictures from graphics files. You even can draw freehand, if you're so inclined. As with charts, you can move and resize all these objects as much as you want. You can also combine several elements into one. Figure 16-1 shows some examples of what you can do on the draw layer.

Figure 16-1: The draw layer enables you to add all sorts of "art" to your worksheet.

Introducing the Drawing Tools

To access the 1-2-3 drawing tools, choose Create➪Drawing. Doing so takes you to the cascading menu shown in Figure 16-2.

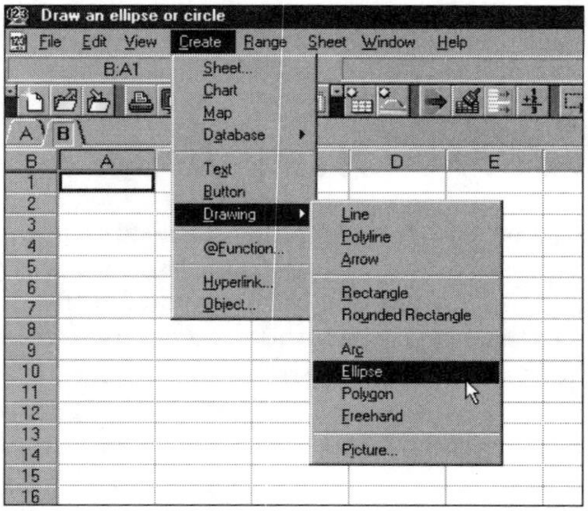

Figure 16-2: Accessing the drawing tools.

Note: 1-2-3 also provides a text tool, which you can access by choosing Create⭧Text.

In Chapter 15, I describe how to create a new SmartIcon bar that enables you to select any of the drawing tools by clicking a SmartIcon.

Table 16-1 describes the drawing tools.

Table 16-1	The 1-2-3 Drawing Tools
Drawing Tool	*What It Does*
Line	Draws a straight line
Polyline	Draws an object with multiple lines
Arrow	Draws a line with an arrowhead
Rectangle	Draws a rectangle (including a perfect square)
Rounded Rectangle	Draws a rectangle with rounded corners
Arc	Draws an arc
Ellipse	Draws an ellipse (including a perfect circle)
Polygon	Draws a *polygon* — an irregular-shaped closed object
Freehand	Enables you to draw freehand
Picture	Inserts a graphics file
Text	Inserts a free-floating text box

Drawing with the Drawing Tools

The drawing tools are easy to use, and they work pretty much as you may expect. To use the drawing tools, all you have to do is choose the appropriate command and then click and drag in the worksheet. I suggest that you jump right in and play around. I guarantee that you'll get the hang of using the drawing tools in no time flat.

Here's an example of how to draw a rectangle (the steps you follow to draw other shapes are pretty much the same as those for drawing a rectangle):

1. Choose Create⭧Drawing⭧Rectangle.

Notice that brief instructions appear in the title bar: Click and drag; for a square hold down SHIFT as you drag. Also, the mouse pointer changes shape to remind you that you're drawing an object.

2. **Click the place in the worksheet where you want the upper-left corner of the rectangle to appear and drag.**

    You see the rectangle growing as you drag.

3. **When the rectangle is the size you want, release the mouse button.**

    After you draw the object, it is selected (you can tell by the handles around it), and its name appears in the edit line.

When you're drawing an object, don't be too concerned about placing and sizing it exactly. You can always select an object and then change its size and position at any time.

When you draw an object using the Text tool (which you access by choosing Create➪Text), you can type text inside of the object. The Text tool is the only tool that can contain text.

Moving and copying objects

To move an object on the draw layer, click the object to select it and then drag it to its new position. Just make sure that you don't drag one of its handles (the tiny dark squares on the object).

If you want to make an exact copy of a drawn object, click the object to select it. Then press Ctrl and drag the object (you're dragging a copy of the object; the original stays put).

You can also use the Windows Clipboard to cut, copy, and paste objects on the 1-2-3 draw layer. Select the object you want to manipulate and then choose Edit➪Copy, Cut, or Paste.

You can also drag objects to a different workbook or to a different sheet in the same workbook. If you want to drag an object to another sheet in the same workbook, you must first open a new window for the workbook (by choosing Window➪New Window) and display the destination sheet in the new window.

Resizing drawings

To change the size of an object on the draw layer, click the object's border to select it and then drag one of its handles to change its size. You drag toward the center of the object to reduce its size and drag away from the object to increase the size. To maintain the same relative proportions, press Shift while you drag one of the corner handles.

Changing the look of your drawings

When you put an object on the draw layer, you have control over the object's color, line width, pattern, and so on. To change any of these attributes, use the options on the Color, pattern, and line style tab of the object's InfoBox. If the InfoBox isn't displayed, select the object and choose Drawing⇨Drawing Properties (or just double-click the object's border).

Figure 16-3 shows an example of the InfoBox for a rectangular object. Use the controls in the InfoBox to adjust how the drawing looks.

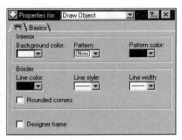

Figure 16-3:
The Color, pattern, and line style tab of the Draw Object InfoBox.

Besides changing the colors, patterns, and line styles, 1-2-3 enables you to make a few other changes to the look of a drawn object:

- ✔ **Rotate the object:** Use the Basics tab of the Draw Object InfoBox to specify an angle.
- ✔ **Flip the object horizontally:** Choose Drawing⇨Flip Top-Bottom.
- ✔ **Flip the object vertically:** Choose Drawing⇨Flip Left-Right.

Restacking objects

You can add any number of objects to the draw layer. The objects can overlap each other; in fact, the objects are stacked on top of each other. You can manipulate this stack of objects by selecting one of the objects and then sending it to the top or bottom of the stack.

To change an object's position in the stack of objects, first select the object and then do one of the following, depending on whether you want the object to be on top or underneath another object:

- ✔ Choose Drawing⇨Bring to Front to move the selected object to the top of the stack. You can also right-click and choose Bring to Front from the shortcut menu.

  ✔ Choose <u>D</u>rawing⇨<u>S</u>end to Back to move the selected object to the bottom of the stack. You can also right-click and choose Send to Back from the shortcut menu.

Figure 16-4 shows some objects stacked on top of each other.

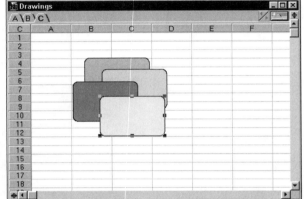

Figure 16-4:
These
objects are
stacked on
top of each
other.

Sometimes, an object may be completely obscured by another object that's stacked on top of it. In that case, you need to adjust the stack order of the objects to get to the object at the bottom. One way to adjust the stack order is to send the top-most object to the bottom of the stack.

Combining objects

If you create a diagram by using several different objects, you may find it advantageous to combine the objects into a single object so that you can manipulate the diagram (move it or resize it) as a single object. For example, if you create a simple flowchart that uses several rectangles and arrows, you can combine the elements into one object. To combine several objects into one object, follow these steps:

1. **Select all the objects that you want to combine.**

   Press Shift while you click each object that you want to add to the group.

2. **Choose <u>D</u>rawing⇨<u>G</u>roup to join the objects in holy matrimony.**

   Now this group of objects contains only one set of handles. You can move or resize the group just like any other single object.

   You can always divorce (ungroup) the objects by selecting the grouped object and choosing <u>D</u>rawing⇨<u>U</u>ngroup.

When you're working with drawn objects, the right mouse button is quite handy. After selecting one or more objects, right-click to display a shortcut menu. In most cases, this menu contains the command that you want to use.

Working with text boxes

A text box (unlike the other drawing objects) can contain text. Therefore, a text box has a few additional formatting options. The InfoBox for a text box has two additional tabs: the Alignment tab and the Font, attribute, and color tab. You can use these tabs to change how the text appears in the text box. Unlike other drawing objects, you can't rotate a text box. You can, however, rotate the text inside of a text box. Figure 16-5 shows a text box that has some formatting applied to it.

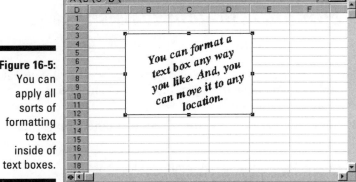

Figure 16-5: You can apply all sorts of formatting to text inside of text boxes.

Adding Graphic Files to a Worksheet

The drawing layer can also hold graphic images that are stored in files (sometimes known as *clip art*). Graphic files range from simple line drawings to detailed, photographic-quality color images.

You can easily import graphic files from a variety of sources. Your other software (especially graphics packages) may include some graphic files, and thousands of files are available from online services and on the Internet.

Understanding graphic file formats

Graphic files come in several different file formats; you can usually identify the file's format by its file extension. The most common clip-art file types are BMP, PCX, GIF, JPG, CGM, TIF, and WMF.

1-2-3 Millennium Edition can import GIF and JPG files. Previous versions of 1-2-3 don't support these popular graphic file formats.

Bitmapped graphics files, such as BMP, PCX, GIF, TIF, and JPG, are composed of individual dots. They usually look best at their original size, and if you make them larger or smaller, they sometimes look distorted. Picture graphics files, on the other hand, are composed of lines that are described mathematically. These types of files usually look very good even if you shrink or enlarge them. The most common picture file formats are CGM and WMF.

Inserting clip art into your worksheet

You can insert clip art into your worksheet in the following two ways:

✔ Open the file directly by choosing Create⇨Drawing⇨Picture. Just locate the file that you want and click the Open button. 1-2-3 inserts the graphic image on the worksheet's draw layer.

✔ Use the Windows Clipboard to copy the file from another application and then paste it into your worksheet.

Figure 16-6 shows a worksheet with an added BMP file.

Figure 16-6:
I chose
Create⇨
Drawing⇨
Picture to
insert this
BMP image
into the
worksheet.

Another use for drawing tools is to add pizzazz to your printed reports (and impress your boss at the same time). For example, you may want to add your company's logo to your reports. If you don't have an electronic version of your company's logo, most office or photocopy shops now have the capability to scan images and create graphic files from these images. After the image is stored in a graphic file, you can copy and paste it to your worksheet.

Getting Down to Business with the Drawing Tools

What good is all the information about the draw layer, the drawing tools, and graphic files that I discuss ad nauseam in this chapter? Well, besides being fun to play with (and great for doodling when you're on the phone), these tools can add some useful enhancements to your work.

Hey! Look at me!

If you want to draw attention to a particular cell or range (for example, when the information in it is particularly good or bad), you can change the font or attributes — make the information bold or italic — to make the range stand out from the others. But if you want to make the cell or range even more attention-grabbing, consider using the draw layer.

Figure 16-7 shows an example of how you can use the draw layer to emphasize values in three cells. In the figure, I drew an oval around a range and used a text box and arrow to make the range really stand out.

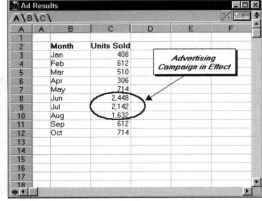

Figure 16-7:
Using the
draw layer
to draw
attention to
a particular
range.

Improving your charts

Any art work that you can add to your regular worksheets, you can add to charts as well. Because a chart also lives on the draw layer, you can stack other objects on top of it. This capability enables you to enhance a chart by adding all sorts of interesting objects and images to it. Figure 16-8 shows an example of a chart that has been beefed up with some annotations.

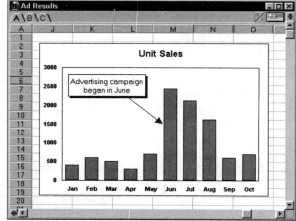

Figure 16-8: A chart after the addition of some artwork.

Creating diagrams

You can use the drawing tools to create flow diagrams, like the one in Figure 16-9. This diagram uses text boxes and arrows. I saved some time by creating one text box and formatting it the way I wanted it; then I made copies of the text box and changed the text. The result? A consistent-looking diagram with minimal formatting required.

Creating vertical labels

In Chapter 12, I discuss how to align text within cells. One of the alignment options enables you to display the text in a cell vertically. However, displaying text vertically has a serious side effect: You must increase the row height to accommodate the vertical text. More often than not, doing so messes up other information in your worksheet.

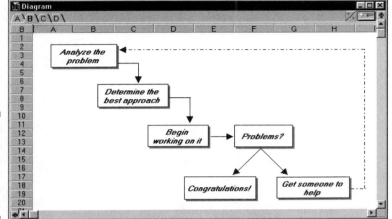

Figure 16-9:
Text boxes
and arrows
used to
create a
diagram.

Using a text box for vertical labels is a good alternative. Figure 16-10 shows an example of vertical text alignment in a cell (top) and another example that uses a text box to hold the vertical label (bottom). The top example looks terrible because the row height needs to be increased to handle the vertically aligned text in cell B5. In the bottom example, the Month label is actually a text box with no border and no background color. The bottom example looks much better, don't you think?

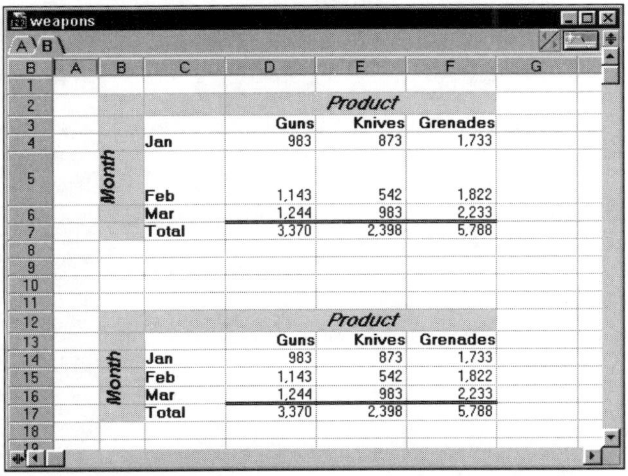

Figure 16-10:
Using a test
box to
display a
vertical label
(bottom
example) is a
good
alternative to
formatting a
cell with
vertical
alignment
(top
example).

Chapter 17

Dealing with Lists and Databases

. . . .

In This Chapter

▶ Noting why 1-2-3 is good for keeping track of things

▶ Explaining the difference between a simple list and a database

▶ Creating a query table and displaying database records that meet certain criteria

▶ Using 1-2-3 to work with data stored in an external database

. . . .

*I*f you're like most 1-2-3 users, you use a word-processing program on your computer. And you've probably used your word processor to store lists of things. Compared to spreadsheets, typical word-processing programs can best be classified as dumb. That is, most word processors don't let you use formulas to do calculations. In addition, these programs require you to know about tab settings and other boring topics when working with tables and multicolumn lists.

Spreadsheets — including 1-2-3 — are great for dealing with lists, as this chapter describes. In this chapter, I explain how to use 1-2-3 to create and manage these lists and keep track of the data in them.

Considering a List versus a Database: What's the Diff?

Before going any further, let me throw out two definitions:

▶ A *list* is a collection of items, each of which is stored in a separate row in a worksheet. Each item may consist of more than one part (that is, contain more than one column). The order of the items may or may not be important.

▶ A *database* is an organized collection of items. Each item is called a *record,* and each record consists of multiple parts called *fields.* Furthermore, each field has a designated *field name.*

Here's a list

Figure 17-1 shows a list that's stored in a 1-2-3 worksheet. This particular list contains 11 items. Each item occupies two columns (actually, two of the items use three columns), and a few blank rows are in the middle of the list. Notice that the numeric formatting isn't the same for all items. (The item in row 12 has no decimal places.) This list also happens to use a formula that calculates the total.

	A	B	C	D
1	Bills to pay this month			
2				
3				
4	Mortgage	1852.32		
5	Telephone	??	Bill hasn't come yet	
6				
7	Car Payment	289.32		
8	Cable TV	34.11		
9	Gas & Electric	89.45		
10				
11	Spreadsheets Today Mag Sub	24.95		
12	Visa Card	100		
13	Internet service	19.95		
14				
15	Health Insurance	198.22		
16	American Express	201.56		
17	Compuserve	9.95	←Need to cancel this	
18				
19	Total Damage:	2819.83		
20				

Figure 17-1: A simple list stored in 1-2-3.

Making a list in 1-2-3 is a snap. Just start entering numbers or text, change the column widths if necessary, insert new rows if you need them, and do anything else you can think of to make the list do what you want it to do. Feel free to move elements around; do whatever makes you happy. The only rule for this type of list is that there are no rules.

Because informal lists are pretty easy to handle (and don't involve any rules), allow me to drop this subject and move on to the next one: databases.

Here's a database

Figure 17-2 shows a database set up in a 1-2-3 worksheet. This particular database stores sales information for a company. The database tracks sales by month, region, product, quantity, and sales amount. This database consists of 16 records and 5 fields. Notice that the first row contains labels that list the field names; this row is not counted as a record.

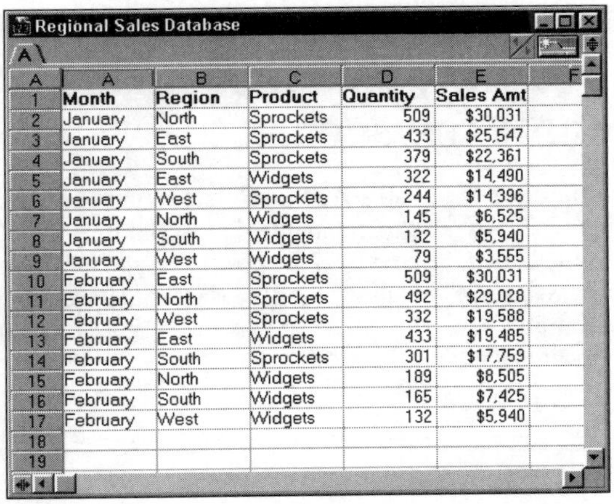

Regional Sales Database

	A	B	C	D	E
1	Month	Region	Product	Quantity	Sales Amt
2	January	North	Sprockets	509	$30,031
3	January	East	Sprockets	433	$25,547
4	January	South	Sprockets	379	$22,361
5	January	East	Widgets	322	$14,490
6	January	West	Sprockets	244	$14,396
7	January	North	Widgets	145	$6,525
8	January	South	Widgets	132	$5,940
9	January	West	Widgets	79	$3,555
10	February	East	Sprockets	509	$30,031
11	February	North	Sprockets	492	$29,028
12	February	West	Sprockets	332	$19,588
13	February	East	Widgets	433	$19,485
14	February	South	Sprockets	301	$17,759
15	February	North	Widgets	189	$8,505
16	February	South	Widgets	165	$7,425
17	February	West	Widgets	132	$5,940
18					
19					

Figure 17-2: A small database stored in 1-2-3.

At this point, the difference between a list and a database may be rather fuzzy to you. To make a long story short, a database is basically a more *organized* list. In the example shown, every record is laid out identically, with the same number of fields and the same numeric formats. Because of this added degree of organization, a database makes locating the exact information you want easier. The trade-off, however, is that setting up a database takes a bit more work up front, and the information that you put into the database must conform to the fields that you define.

Diving More Deeply into Databases

You can use a database to track and update customer information, account information, budget plans, inventory items, sales figures, and myriad other important (and unimportant) data.

Because a database is more organized than a list, a database enables you to do tasks that would be more difficult (or impossible) with a simple list. For example, with a database you can

- **Extract all records that meet certain criteria and put them in another place.** This procedure is known as *querying* a database. In a customer database, you can easily find all your customers who live in a certain state, those customers who have spent more than a specific amount of money with your company, those customers who haven't purchased anything in the past year, and so on (assuming, of course, that your database actually includes fields that store the information for which you're querying).

Lotus's approach to database deeds: Behind the scenes

1-2-3 calls on the powers of Lotus Approach to help out with its database activities. This process happens pretty much behind the scenes. In other words, you don't need to actually start up Approach; the operation is automatic. (A delay may result, however, while 1-2-3 does all of this behind-the-scenes work.)

Lotus Approach is one of the applications included in the Lotus SmartSuite. If you purchase 1-2-3 separately, you find that Approach comes along for the ride. (Gee, thanks, Lotus!)

Querying a database enables you to make a database subset that contains only the records of immediate interest. You may want to extract a bunch of records and use them in a mail-merge letter that you create in your word processor. When you extract data, you don't have to extract all the fields — just the fields that you need.

✔ **Create a summary report.** You can turn a huge database of information into a (usually) comprehensible summary table.

✔ **Enter or view data with a form.** For data entry chores, some people prefer to use a form rather than type data directly into the worksheet. If you're one of those people, 1-2-3 accommodates you. You can also use a form to browse your data, one record at a time.

✔ **Crosstabulate data.** You can create summary tables of your database. In a sales database, for example, you can create a crosstab table that shows the total amount of each product sold in each sales region. And you can crosstabulate data without building any formulas.

To name a database, select the entire database (including field names) and choose Range⇨Name. Type the name in the Name box and click OK. For more information about naming ranges, refer to Chapter 6.

Note: This chapter covers database queries. You can perform other database operations in the preceding list by using 1-2-3, but these procedures are beyond the scope of this book.

Creating a Worksheet Database

If you decide that you want to be able to do database tasks (such as extract specific data) and your data is structured enough to qualify as a database, you need to be aware of a few rules. Understanding the following rules pays off in the long run:

- Each field in the database must have a name, and no two names can be the same.

- Don't leave blank rows between the field names and the actual data.

- Don't leave blank rows in your database.

- Use the same type of data in each column. In other words, give some thought to what kind of data each field holds; generally, it's not a good idea to mix text and values in a single column.

- Give your database a name. To do so, choose Range⇨Name (include the field names in the named range). This step is optional, but specifying a name makes working with your database easier.

Entering data into a database doesn't require a special procedure; just type the information into the cells.

The size of a database stored in a worksheet is limited to the dimensions of the worksheet. Therefore, the database can have no more than 65,535 records (the top row is reserved for the field names). In addition, your database can't have more than 256 fields. If you need to work with more data than fits into a single worksheet, look to Lotus Approach. And, as you see later in this chapter (in the section "Working with External Database Files"), you can use 1-2-3 to extract data from an external database file and dump the data into a worksheet.

Querying a Worksheet Database

The examples in this section demonstrate the mechanics involved in performing common operations based on the used car inventory database shown in Figure 17-3. This particular database (named INVENTORY) consists of 24 records and 5 fields. For this example, assume that you're the owner of the used car lot (but don't let it go to your head!).

The INVENTORY database has the following fields:

- **Make:** The car's manufacturer

- **Model:** The model of the car

- **Year:** The year the car was manufactured

- **Acquired:** The date the car was acquired by the used car dealer

- **Price:** The listed selling price of the vehicle

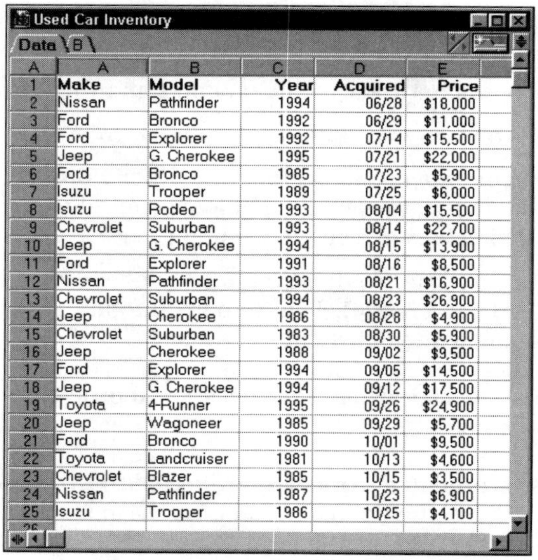

Used Car Inventory

	Make	Model	Year	Acquired	Price
2	Nissan	Pathfinder	1994	06/28	$18,000
3	Ford	Bronco	1992	06/29	$11,000
4	Ford	Explorer	1992	07/14	$15,500
5	Jeep	G. Cherokee	1995	07/21	$22,000
6	Ford	Bronco	1985	07/23	$5,900
7	Isuzu	Trooper	1989	07/25	$6,000
8	Isuzu	Rodeo	1993	08/04	$15,500
9	Chevrolet	Suburban	1993	08/14	$22,700
10	Jeep	G. Cherokee	1994	08/15	$13,900
11	Ford	Explorer	1991	08/16	$8,500
12	Nissan	Pathfinder	1993	08/21	$16,900
13	Chevrolet	Suburban	1994	08/23	$26,900
14	Jeep	Cherokee	1986	08/28	$4,900
15	Chevrolet	Suburban	1983	08/30	$5,900
16	Jeep	Cherokee	1988	09/02	$9,500
17	Ford	Explorer	1994	09/05	$14,500
18	Jeep	G. Cherokee	1994	09/12	$17,500
19	Toyota	4-Runner	1995	09/26	$24,900
20	Jeep	Wagoneer	1985	09/29	$5,700
21	Ford	Bronco	1990	10/01	$9,500
22	Toyota	Landcruiser	1981	10/13	$4,600
23	Chevrolet	Blazer	1985	10/15	$3,500
24	Nissan	Pathfinder	1987	10/23	$6,900
25	Isuzu	Trooper	1986	10/25	$4,100

Figure 17-3: The sample database.

Note: As databases go, this database is pretty skimpy. In real life, this type of database probably contains many more records and fields (for example, price paid for the auto, features, mileage, condition of the vehicle, and so on). However, the same techniques apply, regardless of the size of the database. Using this simple example helps you get the hang of things.

To perform a query, you must first create a query table. Then you use the query table to specify the query. A query table is a special object that you insert on a worksheet. This object communicates with Lotus Approach and does all the work required to perform a query.

Suppose that you (the owner of a used car lot) want to see a list of all vehicles manufactured in 1989 or earlier. You turn on your computer, fire up 1-2-3, and open the Used Car Inventory workbook. All the information is in the database; you just need to isolate all the older models. In other words, you need to query your database. This process requires two steps:

1. **You create a query table.**
2. **You tell 1-2-3 the types of records that you want to find.**

Note: If you've already created a query table, you don't need to create another one — which makes this task a one-step process. Can life get any simpler?

Creating a query table

Creating a query table is the first step in performing a query on a worksheet database. The following steps are required for creating a query table:

1. **Open or activate the worksheet that contains the database.**

2. **Choose Create➪Database➪Query Table.**

   1-2-3 displays the Query Table Assistant dialog box, shown in Figure 17-4.

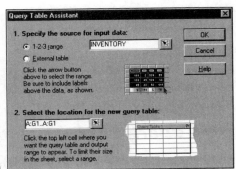

Figure 17-4:
The Query
Table
Assistant
dialog box.

3. **In the Query Table Assistant dialog box, select the option labeled 1-2-3 range.**

4. **Specify the worksheet range that contains the database.**

5. **Specify a location for the query table (a single cell is sufficient).**

   The location you choose can be on the same worksheet that contains the database or on a different worksheet.

6. **Click OK to close the Query Table Assistant dialog box.**

   You may note a short pause while Lotus Approach launches in the background. Eventually, you see the Worksheet Assistant dialog box, which displays a list of all the fields in your database.

7. **In the Worksheet Assistant dialog box, specify the database fields that you want displayed in the query table.**

   To add a field, select it and then click Add. Add as many fields as you like (usually, you want to add all the fields). Figure 17-5 shows how this dialog box looks after adding all the fields.

8. **After you add all the fields you want, click Done.**

   1-2-3 inserts a query table at the location you specified and displays a toolbar with several buttons.

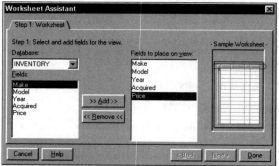

Figure 17-5:
The
Worksheet
Assistant
dialog box
lists all the
fields in
your
database.

9. Click anywhere in your worksheet.

Clicking outside the query table *deactivates* (or deselects) the table. Your worksheet returns to normal — except for the new query table.

Understanding the query table

A query table is a special kind of object that floats on your worksheet. You can think of a query table as a window into your database, and the window displays records that meet a certain criteria. When you first create a query table, the table displays all the records in the database.

Here's a list of things to keep in mind when working with a query table:

✔ When you create a query table, the query table is activated. Use the scroll bars in the query table to scroll through the records.

✔ When a query table is activated, menus that enable you to work with the query table replace the 1-2-3 menus. Also, a new bar of SmartIcons appears automatically (see Figure 17-6).

✔ To deactivate a query table, click in the worksheet. The 1-2-3 menus reappear.

✔ To reactivate a query table, double-click the gray title bar on the query table. (The title bar may be at the top or bottom of the query table.) You need to activate a query table before you can perform a query.

Creating a query by using a query table

After you create a query table for your database, you can use the query table to create a query.

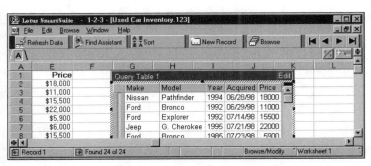

Figure 17-6:
New
SmartIcons
appear
below the
menu bar
when you
activate a
query table.

A *query* is essentially a request that asks 1-2-3 to show only the records that meet certain criteria. For example, the used car dealer may create a query that asks 1-2-3 to show all the Fords, or to show all the cars with a price greater than or equal to $15,000.

You use the following steps to create a query:

1. **Make sure that you've already created a query table for the database.**

   If you haven't, refer to the previous section, "Creating a query table."

2. **Double-click the title bar in the query table to activate it.**

3. **Choose Browse⇨Find⇨Find Assistant, or click the Find Assistant SmartIcon.**

   1-2-3 displays the Find/Sort Assistant dialog box, shown in Figure 17-7. This dialog box contains four tabs. The Find Type tab (which is the one you want) is always displayed when this dialog box appears.

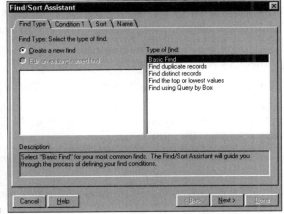

Figure 17-7:
The Find
Type tab of
the Find/
Sort
Assistant
dialog box.

4. In the Find Type tab of the Find/Sort Assistant, select Basic Find from the list labeled Type of find.

1-2-3 offers several types of finds. Usually, the Basic Find is just fine.

5. Click Next to move on to the next step.

1-2-3 displays the Condition 1 tab of the Find/Sort Assistant (see Figure 17-8). Now you tell 1-2-3 which records you want to retrieve.

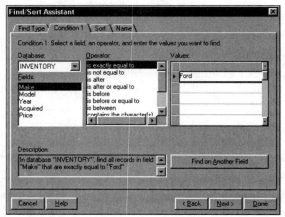

Figure 17-8:
The
Condition 1
tab of the
Find/Sort
Assistant
dialog box.

6. Select a field from the Fields list, select an operator from the Operator list, and then enter one or more values in the Values list.

Figure 17-8 shows an example of how to specify a query. The process is quite logical, and 1-2-3 displays an English language description of the query in the Description box.

7. If your query involves an AND operator, click the Find on Another Field button and repeat Step 6.

An example of such a query is, "Find all records in which the Make is Chevrolet AND the Year is greater than or equal to 1990."

8. After you specify the query, click Next to move on to the next step.

1-2-3 displays the Sort tab of the Find/Sort Assistant dialog box (see Figure 17-9). In the Sort tab, you can specify one or more fields on which to sort the results of the query.

9. Select a field and click Add to add the field to the list labeled Fields to sort on.

10. Change the sort order, if necessary (either Ascending or Descending).

11. Click Next to move on to the final step.

1-2-3 displays the Name tab of the Find/Sort Assistant dialog box (see Figure 17-10).

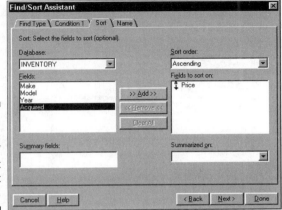

Figure 17-9:
The Sort tab
of the Find/
Sort
Assistant
dialog box.

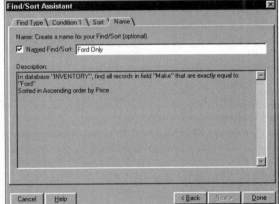

Figure 17-10:
The Name
tab of the
Find/Sort
Assistant
dialog box.

12. **In the Name tab, enter a name for the query (if desired) and click Done.**

    Naming your query (as shown in Figure 17-10) enables you to repeat the query at a later time without having to go through all the preceding steps.

    Note: The Name tab also displays your complete query in the Description box. If the query isn't what you had in mind, click the Back button to retrace your steps and make corrections as needed.

After the Find/Sort Assistant dialog box closes, the query table displays only those records that match the criteria you specified. Figure 17-11 shows an example of a query table that's displaying the results of a query.

	D	E	F	G	H	I	J	K	L
1	Acquired	Price							
2	06/28	$18,000		Query Table 1				Output	
3	06/29	$11,000		Make	Model	Year	Acquired	Price	
4	07/14	$15,500		Ford	Bronco	1985	07/23/98	5900	
5	07/21	$22,000		Ford	Explorer	1991	08/16/98	8500	
6	07/23	$5,900		Ford	Bronco	1990	10/01/98	9500	
7	07/25	$6,000		Ford	Bronco	1992	06/29/98	11000	
8	08/04	$15,500		Ford	Explorer	1994	09/05/98	14500	
9	08/14	$22,700		Ford	Explorer	1992	07/14/98	15500	
10	08/15	$13,900							
11	08/16	$8,500							
12	08/21	$16,900							
13	08/23	$26,900							
14	08/28	$4,900							
15	08/30	$5,900							
16	09/02	$9,500							

Figure 17-11:
The query
table shows
the results
of a query.

Reusing queries

You can use a single query table for any number of queries. If you provide
a name for a query (in the Name tab of the Find/Sort Assistant dialog box),
you can easily execute the query again.

To execute a named query:

1. **Double-click the query table to activate it.**

2. **Choose Browse⇨Named Find/Sort.**

   1-2-3 displays the dialog box shown in Figure 17-12.

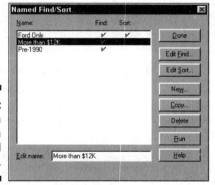

Figure 17-12:
Choosing a
query from a
list of named
queries.

3. **Select the query from the list.**

4. Click **R**un.

The query table is updated with the results of the query you selected.

Deleting certain records

Sometimes you want to clean up your database by deleting certain records that you no longer need. Here's how to perform a query to select unwanted records and then remove them from the database:

1. **Make sure that you've created a query table for the database. (See the section "Creating a query table," earlier in this chapter.)**

2. **Activate the query table (double-click its title bar) and choose Browse⇨Find⇨Find Assistant or click the Find Assistant SmartIcon.**

3. **Create a query that selects the records that you want to delete.**

    See the section "Creating a query by using a query table," earlier in this chapter.

4. **Activate the query table and make sure that it's displaying only the records that you no longer need.**

5. **Choose Browse⇨Delete Fo**u**nd Set.**

    1-2-3 asks you to verify your intentions and, if you stick to your guns, removes the records from your database.

Be careful when deleting records because you can't undo this operation. As a safeguard, you may want to save your workbook before deleting records from a database. Make sure that you have a backup copy just in case something goes wrong.

Working with External Database Files

In some cases, you may need to work with data that resides in a separate database file. Your company may have a centralized database that stores customer data. You can use 1-2-3 to perform a query on the database and bring in only the data that you need.

For example, you may want to analyze customers who live in a particular state. To perform this task, set up a query table, define your query, and execute your query. 1-2-3 goes out to the database, retrieves the records you need, and places the data into your worksheet. Then you can do what you want with the information.

Now for the good news: Performing a query on an external database works just like performing a query on a worksheet database.

Note: The following discussion assumes that you know how to perform a query on a worksheet database. I cover that information in the section "Querying a Worksheet Database," earlier in this chapter.

Creating a query table for an external database

Before you bring in data from an external database, you must create a query table on your worksheet. Here's how:

1. **Activate the worksheet that is to contain the query table.**

   This worksheet can be empty or contain data.

2. **Choose <u>C</u>reate⇨<u>D</u>atabase⇨Query <u>T</u>able.**

   1-2-3 displays the Query Table Assistant dialog box.

3. **In the Query Table Assistant dialog box, select the option labeled <u>E</u>xternal table.**

4. **Select a cell for the location of the query table.**

5. **Click OK to close the Query Table Assistant dialog box.**

   1-2-3 displays the Open dialog box (see Figure 17-13). This dialog box is where you select the database that you want to work with.

6. **In the box labeled Files of <u>t</u>ype, select the type of database file that you are using.**

   1-2-3 supports a wide variety of database file formats.

Figure 17-13:
Use the Open dialog box to specify the database file.

7. **In the box labeled Look <u>i</u>n, specify the location for the file.**

   This location can be a local drive or a network drive.

8. **Select the database file from the list and click <u>O</u>pen.**

   1-2-3 displays the Worksheet Assistant dialog box.

9. **In the Worksheet Assistant dialog box, specify the database fields that you want displayed in the query table.**

10. **After you add the fields that you want, click <u>D</u>one.**

    1-2-3 inserts a query table at the location you specified.

After you complete the preceding steps, your worksheet contains a query table that uses the database file you specified.

Creating an external query by using a query table

After you create a query table for your external database, you can use the query table to create a query. This process is *exactly* the same as that used for a worksheet database. Refer to the section "Creating a query by using a query table," earlier in this chapter, for details on creating a query.

Chapter 18

Recording and Running Scripts: What Every User Needs to Know

M any years ago, Kodak had a popular slogan: *You press the button; we do the rest.* That statement pretty much sums up the appeal of using scripts. A *script* is a great timesaving feature that enables you to perform many custom tasks with a single command.

Knowing about scripts is not essential to using 1-2-3; in fact, most spreadsheet users ignore this feature completely. But you owe it to yourself to at least find out what scripts can do, so that you know what you're missing.

Lotus introduced scripting in 1-2-3 97. If you develop a script, you can't use that script if you save the file in an older version of 1-2-3.

Scripting: It's Not Just for Playwrights Anymore!

A *script* is simply a list of instructions that tell 1-2-3 what to do. Scripts can be simple (like those I cover in this chapter) or extremely complex (like those I *don't* cover in this chapter).

Imagine that you have a worksheet set up and you need to enter the name of your company in several different places throughout the worksheet. You can type the company name each time you need it, or you can type the company name once and then use the normal copy-and-paste techniques to copy the name to the other locations. Another way to save time is to create a script that types the company name for you automatically upon command.

A script by any other name . . .

You may have heard the term *macro,* and you may be wondering how scripting relates to macros. Well, the two concepts are similar — but different. Previous versions of 1-2-3 used macros to automate some procedures. With 1-2-3 97, Lotus introduced a brand-new way of automating spreadsheet work. The new way uses LotusScript, which is essentially a programming language that works across all the applications in the Lotus SmartSuite.

1-2-3 can still execute macros that were developed in previous versions. So if someone gives you an older 1-2-3 file that uses macros, you're not out of luck.

If your company's name is Integrated Biotechnical Research Resources of New Zealand, you can develop a script that types these words for you automatically. You can then assign the script to a key combination, such as Ctrl+I. Then, whenever you press Ctrl+I, 1-2-3 locates the script and executes the instructions that the script contains. In this case, pressing Ctrl+I causes 1-2-3 to type the company name instantly (and correctly, assuming that you spelled the name correctly when you created the script).

And — believe it or not — using scripts gets even better. You also can create scripts that execute a series of commands for you in one fell swoop. For an example of this capability, refer to the section "Changing Your Point of View," later in this chapter.

Scripting Basics

If you're going to be working with 1-2-3 scripts, you need to know the following factoids:

- You can create a script by recording your actions or by entering the script manually. This chapter focuses exclusively on the recording method (the much easier method).

- After you create a script, you can assign it to a key combination (such as Ctrl+N), attach it to a menu item, or attach it to an object on your worksheet (such as a button) to execute the script.

✔ Playing back the script is called *running the script* or *executing the script*. To run the script, press the specific key combination that you assigned to the script, select the script from the menu, or click the object to which you attached the script.

✔ Scripts are stored in workbooks. You can view them and even edit them, if you know what you're doing.

✔ You can use a script as many times as you want; the script always does exactly the same thing. Better yet, scripts never complain of boredom or being overworked.

Giving Birth to Your First Script

Ready to create your first script? You may be pleasantly surprised at how easy this process is. Just follow the step-by-step directions in the next section to get the hang of script creation.

In the following sections, I explain the steps required for

✔ Recording a script

✔ Testing the script to see whether it works properly

✔ Assigning the script to a key combination

Recording a script

In this section, I detail the steps you take to record a script. To make these steps more meaningful, I describe how to record a script that types your name into a cell and then moves the cell pointer to the next row:

1. **Save your workbook, if you haven't already done so.**

2. **Move the cell pointer to an empty cell.**

3. **Choose Edit⇨Scripts & Macros⇨Record Script.**

   1-2-3 responds with the Record Script dialog box, shown in Figure 18-1.

4. **Type a name for your script in the box labeled Script name.**

   The name cannot use any spaces. For this example, type **EnterMyName** for the script name.

   For now, you want to record the script in the current workbook, which is already selected in the box labeled Record script into.

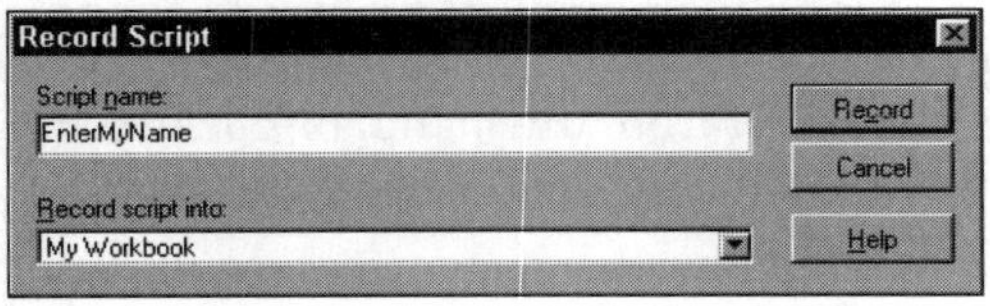

Figure 18-1:
The Record
Script
dialog box.

5. Click Record.

From this point on, all your actions are recorded. (Don't be nervous!)
Notice that 1-2-3 displays a floating SmartIcon bar with two SmartIcons
(one icon stops recording; the other pauses or restarts recording —
just like a tape recorder).

**6. Using your mouse or your keyboard, perform the actions that you
want to record.**

To create a script that types your name, for example, you simply type
your name in the active cell and press the down-arrow key to move to
the cell below.

7. Click the Stop Script Recording SmartIcon.

1-2-3 stops recording your actions, the SmartIcon bar disappears, and
the Scripts window appears on your screen (see Figure 18-2). Don't
worry about trying to understand the script. The script is just computer language stuff, and you don't really have to understand the script
in order to use it.

8. Close the Scripts window to get it out of the way.

Otherwise, the window stays on top, obscuring your view of the
workbook.

That's all there is to recording a script. You just recorded a simple script.
Aren't you proud?

Running a script

After you create your first script, you're ready to take it for a test ride:

1. Move the cell pointer to an appropriate position.

For example, if you recorded the example type-your-name script, move
the cell pointer to an empty cell where you want your name to appear.
If you recorded a script to apply formatting, move the cell pointer to a
cell to which you want to apply the formatting.

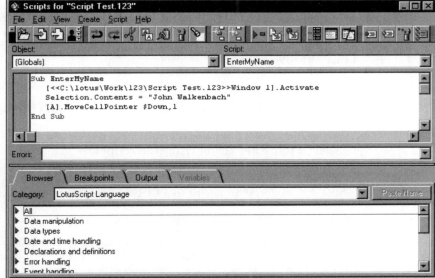

Figure 18-2:
The Scripts
window
enables you
to look at
your script.

2. **Choose Edit⇨Scripts & Macros⇨Run (or just press Alt+F3, which is the shortcut for this command).**

   In response, 1-2-3 displays the Run Scripts & Macros dialog box, shown in Figure 18-3.

3. **Select the name of the script you want to run from the list at the bottom of the dialog box and then click Run.**

   1-2-3 plays back the script — which generates the same actions that you originally recorded. If you recorded the EnterMyName script from the previous example, clicking Run enters your name in the active cell and then moves the cell pointer down one row.

Figure 18-3:
The Run
Scripts &
Macros
dialog box.

The script works! Or at least the script *should* work. If your script doesn't run the way you expected it to, you probably omitted one or more of the steps in the previous section. Just try the steps again. You need to use a different script name for your second attempt, because you can't record a script that already exists.

Assigning the script to a key combination

When your script works the way you want it to, the next step is to make the script easier to run. After all, choosing the script from a dialog box isn't exactly a time-saver.

Here's how you assign your script to a Ctrl+key combination:

1. Choose Edit⇨Scripts & Macros⇨Global Script Options.

1-2-3 displays the Global Script Options dialog box, shown in Figure 18-4. This dialog box lists all the available scripts (if this is your first script, it's the only one that appears) and also shows the options associated with each script. At first, no options are listed for your script.

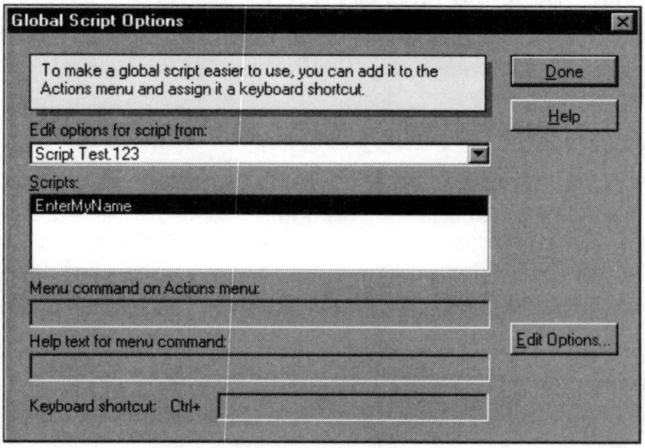

Figure 18-4:
The Global
Script
Options
dialog box.

2. Select the script name and then click Edit Options.

1-2-3 shows the Edit Script Options dialog box (see Figure 18-5).

3. Select the Quick key option and enter whatever letter you choose into the box.

For example, if you enter **N**, you can now press Ctrl+**N** to execute the script.

Figure 18-5:
This dialog
box is
where you
assign a
menu
command
or quick key
to your
script.

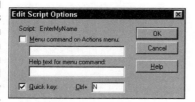

The quick key *must* be a letter. 1-2-3 may appear to accept numbers, but they don't work.

4. Click OK to close the current dialog box and then click <u>D</u>one to close the previous dialog box.

Try out your script. Move around the worksheet and press the Ctrl+key combination that you specified. Lo and behold, 1-2-3 repeats your recorded actions every time.

Be careful when you assign Ctrl+key combinations to scripts. 1-2-3 has its own use for some of these Ctrl+key combinations. For example, Ctrl+B is a shortcut that makes the current selection bold. If you assign Ctrl+B to a script, you can't use the normal Ctrl+B shortcut, because 1-2-3 executes your script instead. This limitation isn't really a big deal, though, because 1-2-3 always provides other ways to perform an action.

In Step 3 of the preceding process, you can also specify a menu command for the script. For example, you can enter **Type My Name** as the menu command. If you do so, 1-2-3 displays a new menu (Actions) with your menu item listed under the new menu. Then you can choose <u>A</u>ctions⇨Type My Name to execute the macro.

In the whole scheme of things, the EnterMyName script that I describe in this section is definitely on the simple end of the spectrum. However, scripts need not be complex to be useful.

Changing Your Point of View

This section shows you how to create a slightly more complex script that you may find quite useful.

When working on a spreadsheet, you may find seeing as much information as possible on the screen helpful. For example, you may perform the following actions:

✔ Set the Zoom factor to 50 percent.

✔ Remove the edit line.

✔ Remove the status bar.

✔ Remove the SmartIcons.

✔ Remove the row and column borders (sheet frame).

Issuing all those commands is a lot of work to go through — and even more work when you consider that you have to reset all these settings when you're ready to return to normal. As you've probably figured out by now, the solution is to record a script that performs all these actions for you. In fact, you need two scripts: one to set up your custom view, and another to return things to normal. In both cases, 1-2-3 executes the script faster than you can say *LotusScript*.

Recording the CustomView script

To create the script that sets the Zoom factor to 50 percent and also removes all extraneous items from the screen:

1. **Choose Edit⇨Scripts & Macros⇨Record.**

2. **Enter a name for the script.**

3. **Click Record.**

4. **Choose View⇨Zoom to⇨50%.**

5. **Choose View⇨Hide SmartIcons.**

6. **Choose View⇨Hide Status Bar.**

7. **Choose View⇨Hide Edit Line.**

8. **Choose Sheet⇨Sheet Properties to access the Sheet InfoBox and then click the View tab.**

9. **Remove the check mark from the Sheet frame option.**

10. **Click the Stop Script Recording SmartIcon.**

Recording the NormalView script

To create the NormalView script, repeat the same steps as for the CustomView script — but name the script NormalView and put the settings back to normal.

Assigning the scripts to a key combination

After you record the CustomView and NormalView scripts, assign them to key combinations of your choice. Choose Edit⇨Scripts & Macros⇨Global Script Options, and follow the procedures I describe in the section "Assigning the script to a key combination," earlier in this chapter. If you want to, assign a menu command, as well.

Try your new key combinations out, and enjoy switching between the custom view and the normal view in the blink of an eye.

Scripts only work for the workbook in which they were recorded. You can create general-purpose scripts, but you need to edit the recorded script, which is beyond the scope of this book.

Using Other People's Scripts

You may, at some point in your career, receive a workbook from someone who actually knows how to develop complex scripts (or you may purchase a workbook all set up to do something useful). This workbook may have one or more scripts in it, and you've been told that these scripts make the spreadsheet do something useful. In fact, this scenario isn't all that unusual. Some people take great pride in developing scripts that do useful things (and showing off their skills in the process).

If you're lucky, the worksheet has instructions that tell you what to do. For example, the worksheet may say, "To generate the report and print this worksheet, press Ctrl+P" or "Press Ctrl+U to begin updating the monthly sales figures."

The person who creates such a workbook is simply trying to make things easier for you or anyone else who uses the spreadsheet. The scripts may do quite a bit behind the scenes — more than you care to do or know how to do. In this case, running a script is much like issuing a command.

You don't have to know what the script is doing in order to use the script. Just press the appropriate key combination and sit back and relax while 1-2-3 follows the orders in the script.

Yet another scenario involves running scripts that are stored in a special type of workbook called an *add-in*. If you acquire an add-in, chances are this add-in includes scripts. In almost every case, the scripts are tightly integrated into 1-2-3. For example, you may execute the scripts by using new menu commands, or the add-in may display a new SmartIcon bar.

If the concept of scripts interests you, the best way to find out more about scripts is by experimenting with them. Start with an empty workbook, turn on the script recorder, and see what happens. Before long, you are going to have a good understanding of how scripting works. And eventually, you may even get so involved that you want to find out how to write scripts manually, rather than rely on recording them. This can happen to the best of us.

Chapter 19
Worksheet Outlining

- -

In This Chapter

▶ Determining which types of worksheets may benefit from an outline

▶ Creating a row outline or a column outline

▶ Expanding or collapsing an outline to show more or less detail

▶ Hiding outline symbols

▶ Removing an outline completely

- -

*B*ack in high school, you probably had at least one teacher who insisted that you develop an outline before you wrote your reports. An *outline* is essentially an overview of your report that shows the headings and subheadings and presents the general structure of the document.

If you're a fan of outlines, have I got news for you: 1-2-3 has a handy feature that enables you to create outlines using the data in a worksheet.

In high school, you first wrote an outline, and then you wrote your report. With 1-2-3, you take the opposite approach: First you create your report (with all the gory details included), and then you create the outline from the report. Although the 1-2-3 outlining feature wouldn't have helped out much in your high school classes, this feature can do wonders when you try to organize and present a large quantity of information.

Outline? In a Worksheet? Surely You Jest . . .

If you're like most people, you may have a hard time grasping the concept of a worksheet outline. Allow me to clear things up. The best way to understand how worksheet outlining works is to look at an example. Figure 19-1 shows a worksheet that's a perfect candidate for an outline. This worksheet shows sales by state and by month. I inserted formulas to calculate subtotals for each region and subtotals for each quarter.

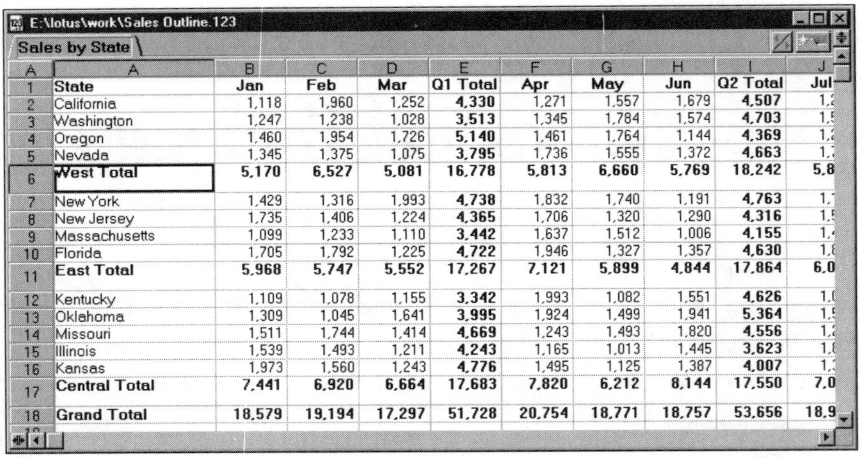

State	Jan	Feb	Mar	Q1 Total	Apr	May	Jun	Q2 Total	Jul
California	1,118	1,960	1,252	**4,330**	1,271	1,557	1,679	**4,507**	1,
Washington	1,247	1,238	1,028	**3,513**	1,345	1,784	1,574	**4,703**	1,
Oregon	1,460	1,954	1,726	**5,140**	1,461	1,764	1,144	**4,369**	1,
Nevada	1,345	1,375	1,075	**3,795**	1,736	1,555	1,372	**4,663**	1,
West Total	**5,170**	**6,527**	**5,081**	**16,778**	**5,813**	**6,660**	**5,769**	**18,242**	**5,8**
New York	1,429	1,316	1,993	**4,738**	1,832	1,740	1,191	**4,763**	1,
New Jersey	1,735	1,406	1,224	**4,365**	1,706	1,320	1,290	**4,316**	1,
Massachusetts	1,099	1,233	1,110	**3,442**	1,637	1,512	1,006	**4,155**	1,
Florida	1,705	1,792	1,225	**4,722**	1,946	1,327	1,357	**4,630**	1,
East Total	**5,968**	**5,747**	**5,552**	**17,267**	**7,121**	**5,899**	**4,844**	**17,864**	**6,0**
Kentucky	1,109	1,078	1,155	**3,342**	1,993	1,082	1,551	**4,626**	1,
Oklahoma	1,309	1,045	1,641	**3,995**	1,924	1,499	1,941	**5,364**	1,
Missouri	1,511	1,744	1,414	**4,669**	1,243	1,493	1,820	**4,556**	1,
Illinois	1,539	1,493	1,211	**4,243**	1,165	1,013	1,445	**3,623**	1,
Kansas	1,973	1,560	1,243	**4,776**	1,495	1,125	1,387	**4,007**	1,
Central Total	**7,441**	**6,920**	**6,664**	**17,683**	**7,820**	**6,212**	**8,144**	**17,550**	**7,0**
Grand Total	**18,579**	**19,194**	**17,297**	**51,728**	**20,754**	**18,771**	**18,757**	**53,656**	**18,9**

Figure 19-1: A sales worksheet with subtotals.

The worksheet shown in Figure 19-1 is great if you're interested in seeing all the details. But the folks in upper management often don't care about the details. For example, what if your boss only wants to see the quarterly subtotals? Or maybe just the regional subtotals? Or she's really bottom-line oriented and only cares to see the grand total?

One solution to the "displaying too much detail" problem is to hide the rows and columns that you don't want to see (to hide rows or columns, you can use the Basic tab of the Range InfoBox). Hiding rows and columns is fine, but doing so is a great deal of work. Creating an outline is a better solution.

Collapsing the columns

Figure 19-2 shows the sales worksheet after I created an outline. In this figure, the outline is *collapsed* by columns to hide the monthly details and show only the quarterly subtotals. The visible columns are those that contain the formulas that sum up the monthly data.

Collapsing the rows

Figure 19-3 shows what happens when I collapse the outline by rows to hide the state sales details and show only the regional subtotals. The visible rows are those that show the sum of the state sales figures.

TIP

When to use an outline

Outlines are most useful for creating summary reports in which you don't want to show all the details. After you create an outline, you can show as much or as little of the supporting information as you want. Some worksheets are better suited for outlines than others. If your worksheet uses data with subtotals, then that worksheet is probably a good candidate for an outline.

However, you can create an outline from any worksheet you like. In fact, you may want to create an outline simply to provide an easy way to hide and unhide rows or columns. After you create the outline, you hide rows or columns by collapsing the outline. You unhide rows or columns by expanding the outline.

Figure 19-2:
The sales worksheet after creating an outline and collapsing the columns to show only the quarterly subtotals.

E:\lotus\work\Sales Outline.123

Sales by State

State	Q1 Total	Q2 Total	Q3 Total	Q4 Total	Grand Total
California	4,330	4,507	4,722	5,554	19,113
Washington	3,513	4,703	5,139	4,721	18,076
Oregon	5,140	4,369	3,786	4,239	17,534
Nevada	3,795	4,663	4,667	4,624	17,749
West Total	16,778	18,242	18,314	19,138	72,472
New York	4,738	4,763	3,915	4,289	17,705
New Jersey	4,365	4,316	4,051	4,526	17,258
Massachusetts	3,442	4,155	4,882	5,376	17,855
Florida	4,722	4,630	5,062	4,734	19,148
East Total	17,267	17,864	17,910	18,925	71,966
Kentucky	3,342	4,626	4,306	4,526	16,800
Oklahoma	3,995	5,364	4,338	4,449	18,146
Missouri	4,669	4,556	4,203	4,279	17,707
Illinois	4,243	3,623	4,889	4,330	17,085
Kansas	4,776	4,007	4,322	4,299	17,404
Central Total	17,683	17,550	17,752	17,357	70,342
Grand Total	51,728	53,656	53,976	55,420	214,780

Collapsing the outline by rows and by columns results in a very concise report. However, the details are still available — all you need are a few mouse clicks to show more information

REMEMBER

In the state sales example, both the rows and the columns are outlined. 1-2-3 enables you to create row outlines, column outlines, or both (as in the preceding example).

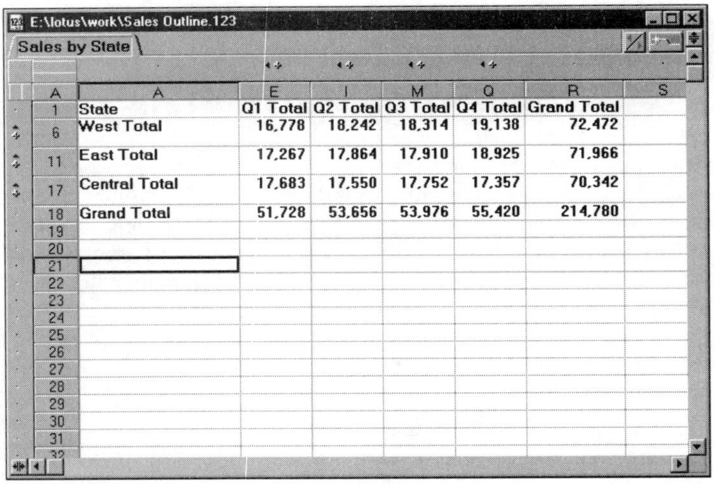

Figure 19-3:
The sales
worksheet
after
creating an
outline and
collapsing
the rows to
show the
quarterly
and regional
subtotals.

Creating an Outline

Creating an outline isn't difficult, but your job is much easier if the worksheet is very well structured and consistent.

Before creating an outline, you need to make sure that the summary formulas are all entered correctly and consistently. By *consistently,* I mean in the same relative location. Generally, you enter formulas that compute summary information (such as subtotals) below the data that they refer to. However, in some cases, you may enter the summary formulas above the referenced cells. 1-2-3 can handle either method — but for best results you want to be consistent throughout the worksheet.

Creating a row outline

Creating a row outline consists of creating groups of rows that contain the details. Each group you create forms a part of the outline that can be collapsed (or hidden) to hide the details or expanded (or unhidden) to show the details. For example, the sales worksheet (which I present at the beginning of this chapter) contains three groups of rows: West, East, and Central.

The following steps show you how to create a group of rows for an outline:

1. **Select the rows that you want to include in the group — but do *not* select the row that has the summary formulas.**

   See Figure 19-4.

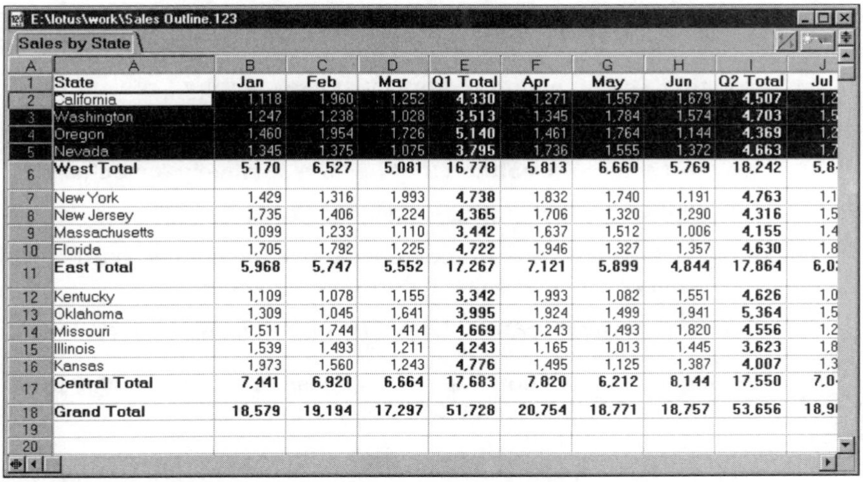

E:\lotus\work\Sales Outline.123 — Sales by State

	A	B	C	D	E	F	G	H	I	J
1	State	Jan	Feb	Mar	Q1 Total	Apr	May	Jun	Q2 Total	Jul
2	California	1,118	1,960	1,252	4,330	1,271	1,557	1,679	4,507	1,2
3	Washington	1,247	1,238	1,028	3,513	1,345	1,784	1,574	4,703	1,5
4	Oregon	1,460	1,954	1,726	5,140	1,461	1,764	1,144	4,369	1,2
5	Nevada	1,345	1,375	1,075	3,795	1,736	1,555	1,372	4,663	1,7
6	**West Total**	**5,170**	**6,527**	**5,081**	**16,778**	**5,813**	**6,660**	**5,769**	**18,242**	**5,8**
7	New York	1,429	1,316	1,993	4,738	1,832	1,740	1,191	4,763	1,1
8	New Jersey	1,735	1,406	1,224	4,365	1,706	1,320	1,290	4,316	1,5
9	Massachusetts	1,099	1,233	1,110	3,442	1,637	1,512	1,006	4,155	1,4
10	Florida	1,705	1,792	1,225	4,722	1,946	1,327	1,357	4,630	1,8
11	**East Total**	**5,968**	**5,747**	**5,552**	**17,267**	**7,121**	**5,899**	**4,844**	**17,864**	**6,0**
12	Kentucky	1,109	1,078	1,155	3,342	1,993	1,082	1,551	4,626	1,0
13	Oklahoma	1,309	1,045	1,641	3,995	1,924	1,499	1,941	5,364	1,5
14	Missouri	1,511	1,744	1,414	4,669	1,243	1,493	1,820	4,556	1,2
15	Illinois	1,539	1,493	1,211	4,243	1,165	1,013	1,445	3,623	1,8
16	Kansas	1,973	1,560	1,243	4,776	1,495	1,125	1,387	4,007	1,3
17	**Central Total**	**7,441**	**6,920**	**6,664**	**17,683**	**7,820**	**6,212**	**8,144**	**17,550**	**7,0**
18	**Grand Total**	**18,579**	**19,194**	**17,297**	**51,728**	**20,754**	**18,771**	**18,757**	**53,656**	**18,9**
19										
20										

Figure 19-4: Selecting rows is the first step in creating a row group for an outline.

2. **Choose Sheet⇨Outline⇨Demote Rows.**

   1-2-3 displays an outline frame to the left of the column border. The frame contains an outline symbol for each row group that you create. Figure 19-5 shows what this outline frame and outline symbols look like. I describe how to use these symbols in the next section, "Expanding and Collapsing an Outline."

3. **Repeat Steps 1 and 2 for each group that you want to create.**

When you *collapse* the outline (that is, show less detail), rows in the group are hidden. But the summary row, which is not in the group, isn't hidden.

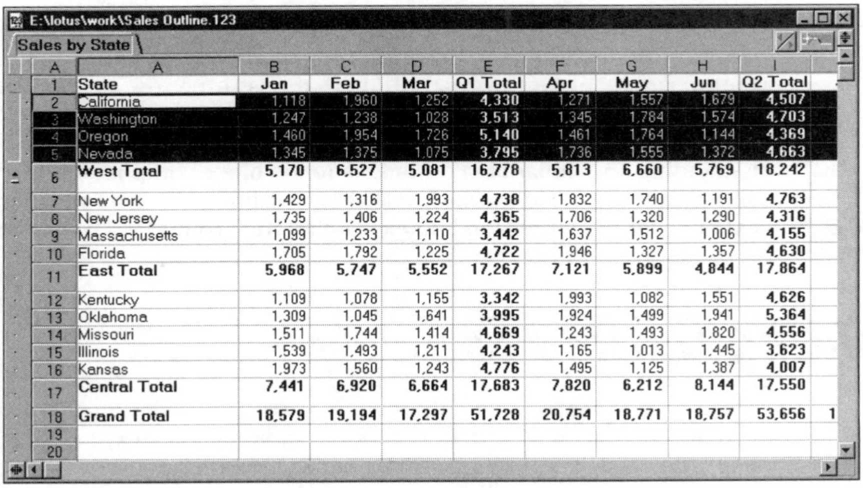

E:\lotus\work\Sales Outline.123 — Sales by State

	A	B	C	D	E	F	G	H	I	
1	State	Jan	Feb	Mar	Q1 Total	Apr	May	Jun	Q2 Total	
2	California	1,118	1,960	1,252	4,330	1,271	1,557	1,679	4,507	
3	Washington	1,247	1,238	1,028	3,513	1,345	1,784	1,574	4,703	
4	Oregon	1,460	1,954	1,726	5,140	1,461	1,764	1,144	4,369	
5	Nevada	1,345	1,375	1,075	3,795	1,736	1,555	1,372	4,663	
6	**West Total**	**5,170**	**6,527**	**5,081**	**16,778**	**5,813**	**6,660**	**5,769**	**18,242**	
7	New York	1,429	1,316	1,993	4,738	1,832	1,740	1,191	4,763	
8	New Jersey	1,735	1,406	1,224	4,365	1,706	1,320	1,290	4,316	
9	Massachusetts	1,099	1,233	1,110	3,442	1,637	1,512	1,006	4,155	
10	Florida	1,705	1,792	1,225	4,722	1,946	1,327	1,357	4,630	
11	**East Total**	**5,968**	**5,747**	**5,552**	**17,267**	**7,121**	**5,899**	**4,844**	**17,864**	
12	Kentucky	1,109	1,078	1,155	3,342	1,993	1,082	1,551	4,626	
13	Oklahoma	1,309	1,045	1,641	3,995	1,924	1,499	1,941	5,364	
14	Missouri	1,511	1,744	1,414	4,669	1,243	1,493	1,820	4,556	
15	Illinois	1,539	1,493	1,211	4,243	1,165	1,013	1,445	3,623	
16	Kansas	1,973	1,560	1,243	4,776	1,495	1,125	1,387	4,007	
17	**Central Total**	**7,441**	**6,920**	**6,664**	**17,683**	**7,820**	**6,212**	**8,144**	**17,550**	
18	**Grand Total**	**18,579**	**19,194**	**17,297**	**51,728**	**20,754**	**18,771**	**18,757**	**53,656**	1
19										
20										

Figure 19-5: 1-2-3 displays outline symbols after you create a row group.

Creating a column outline

Creating a column outline works just like creating a row outline:

1. **Select the columns that you want to include in the group — but do *not* select the column that has the summary formulas.**

2. **Choose Sheet➪Outline➪Demote Columns.**

    1-2-3 displays an outline frame above the column border, with an outline symbol for each column group that you create.

3. **Repeat Steps 1 and 2 for each column group that you want to create.**

If you plan to have both a row outline and a column outline in your worksheet, you can create them in any order.

When you collapse the outline, columns in the group are hidden. But the summary column, which is not in the group, isn't hidden.

Expanding and Collapsing an Outline

As I describe in the previous section, 1-2-3 displays outline symbols after you create row groups or column groups. Use these outline symbols to expand (show detail) or collapse (hide detail) an outline.

When a group (either a row group or a column group) is expanded, the outline symbol displays as a minus sign. Click the minus sign to collapse the group. When a group is collapsed, the outline symbol displays as a plus sign. Click the plus sign to expand the group.

You can expand or collapse any row or column group that you like. In other words, you don't have to expand every row group or expand every column group. Figure 19-6 shows an outline that has three row groups, but only one of the row groups is expanded.

Expanding and collapsing outlines sounds more complicated than it really is. The best way to understand worksheet outlining is to create an outline and experiment by collapsing and expanding the groups.

Hiding Outline Symbols

The symbols that 1-2-3 displays when a worksheet outline is present can take up quite a bit of screen real estate. If you want to see as much data as possible on-screen, you can temporarily hide these outline symbols without removing the outline. To do so, follow these steps:

	A	B	C	D	E	F	G	H	I
1	State	Jan	Feb	Mar	Q1 Total	Apr	May	Jun	Q2 Total
6	West Total	5,170	6,527	5,081	16,778	5,813	6,660	5,769	18,242
7	New York	1,429	1,316	1,993	**4,738**	1,832	1,740	1,191	**4,763**
8	New Jersey	1,735	1,406	1,224	**4,365**	1,706	1,320	1,290	**4,316**
9	Massachusetts	1,099	1,233	1,110	**3,442**	1,637	1,512	1,006	**4,155**
10	Florida	1,705	1,792	1,225	**4,722**	1,946	1,327	1,357	**4,630**
11	East Total	5,968	5,747	5,552	17,267	7,121	5,899	4,844	17,864
17	Central Total	7,441	6,920	6,664	17,683	7,820	6,212	8,144	17,550
18	Grand Total	18,579	19,194	17,297	51,728	20,754	18,771	18,757	53,656

E:\lotus\work\Sales Outline.123
Sales by State

Figure 19-6:
This outline
has only one
of its row
groups
expanded.

1. **Bring up the Sheet InfoBox (choose** <u>S</u>heet⇨Sheet <u>P</u>roperties), and **click the Outline tab.**

2. **Remove the check mark from the Show outline frame check box for either the row outline, the column outline, or both.**

When you hide the outline symbols, the outline is still in effect, and the worksheet displays the data at the current outline level. That is, some rows or columns may be hidden.

Removing an Outline

If you decide that you no longer need an outline on your worksheet, you can remove the outline (the data remains, but the outline goes away). Just choose <u>S</u>heet⇨<u>O</u>utline⇨Clea<u>r</u> Outline. The outline is then fully expanded (all hidden rows and columns are unhidden), and the outline symbols disappear.

Creating Multilevel Outlines

Some worksheets may require a *multilevel outline.* When you create a row outline, for example, you create row groups. A multilevel row outline consists of groups of row groups.

To create a group of row groups, start by collapsing the row groups to hide the detail. Then select the rows that you want to group for the higher level group. Choose <u>S</u>heet⇨<u>O</u>utline⇨<u>D</u>emote Rows, and 1-2-3 creates a group of row groups. Then the outline symbols display in two levels, and you can hide even more detail.

Figure 19-7 shows the sales workbook, fully collapsed, after creating a multilevel row outline and a multilevel column outline. As you can see, all the detail is hidden; the only data that's visible is the grand total — the real bottom line.

No need to skimp; you can create as many levels as you need.

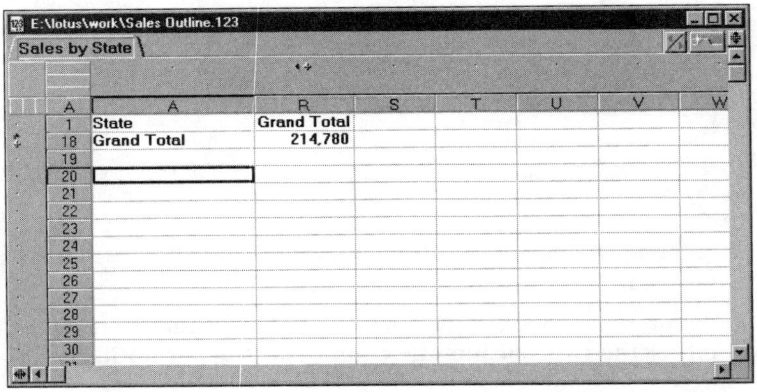

State	Grand Total
Grand Total	214,780

Figure 19-7: A multilevel outline, fully collapsed.

Chapter 20

What-If Analysis: Using the Version Manager

*O*ne of the more appealing aspects of 1-2-3 (or any spreadsheet, for that matter) is that you can create formulas that use values in other cells. If you change any of the values used by a formula, the formula recalculates and displays a new result. When you change values used by formulas in a systematic manner, you're performing a type of *what-if analysis*.

This chapter introduces the concept of what-if analysis, and describes how to use the powerful 1-2-3 Version Manager feature to help you manage your what-if scenarios.

What-If Analysis: An Example

The best way to understand what-if analysis is with an example. A company manufactures three products, and making each product requires a certain number of hours and a certain amount of materials. I created a worksheet (see Figure 20-1) to calculate the net profit for the company.

For example, Product A requires 6 hours of labor and 12 units of materials. The cost to produce Product A is $750. The formula in cell B10 is

```
(B8*$B$4)+(B9*$B$5)
```

Creating the product manufacturing model

The product manufacturing model, used in the examples in this chapter, is a good example of a simple what-if model. The worksheet uses formulas that calculate results using data in two input cells. If you want to follow along with the example I present in this chapter, you can create the worksheet by following these steps:

1. **Enter the items in rows 1–9, row 11, and row 13 as they appear in Figure 20-1.**

   All these entries are either labels or values.

2. **Enter the following formula into cell B10:**

   `(B8*$B$4)+(B9*$B$5)`

   Cell B10 calculates the cost to produce one unit of Product A by using the hourly cost and materials cost values.

3. **Select cell B10 and copy this formula into cells C10 and D10.**

4. **Enter the following formula into cell B12:**

   `+B11-B10`

   Cell B12 calculates the profit for one unit of Product A by subtracting the cost to produce the product from the selling price of the product.

5. **Copy the formula from cell B12 to cells C12 and D12.**

6. **Enter the following formula into cell B14:**

   `+B13*B12`

   Cell B14 calculates the net profit for Product A by multiplying the number of units produced by the profit per unit.

7. **Select cell B14 and copy this formula to columns C and D.**

8. **Enter the following formula into cell B16:**

   `@SUM(B14..D14)`

   Cell B16 computes the sum of the net profit values for the three products.

Figure 20-1: This worksheet is set up to forecast profit for three products, based on resource costs.

	A	B	C	D
1	Product Manufacturing Model			
2				
3	Resource Costs			
4	Hourly cost:	$25.00		
5	Materials cost:	$50.00		
6				
7		Product A	Product B	Product C
8	Hours per unit:	6	12	18
9	Materials per unit:	12	10	16
10	Cost to produce:	$750	$800	$1,250
11	Selling price:	$850	$975	$1,375
12	Unit profit:	$100	$175	$125
13	Units produced:	125	90	60
14	Net profit:	$12,500	$15,750	$7,500
15				
16	Total net profit:	$35,750		
17				
18				

Because the product sells for $850, the net profit for Product A is $100. The company plans to manufacture 125 units of Product A, so that product is going to generate a net profit of $12,500. The other products require different amounts of labor and materials, and they have different selling prices. The company also plans to produce different quantities of the products. As you can see in the figure, the total net profit is $35,750 — the sum of the net profit values for the three products.

If you want to re-create the product manufacturing workbook to follow along on your own computer, refer to the sidebar, "Creating the product manufacturing model."

The manufacturing model worksheet has two input cells, which contain the cost of the two resources: the hourly cost of the labor (cell B4) and the unit cost for the material (cell B5). Changing the value in either or both of these input cells causes the formulas to recalculate and display different net profit values.

Asking what-if questions

In Figure 20-1, the worksheet shows a net profit of $35,750. This profit, of course, depends on the cost of the resources.

You may be in a situation in which you need to predict the total profit, but you're uncertain of what the hourly labor cost and material costs are going to be. In fact, you can ask "what-if" questions like these:

✔ What if labor costs increase?

✔ What if the cost of material goes down?

✔ What if the labor costs and the material costs both increase?

Business always involves uncertainty, and the management team for this company has identified three possible situations, or *scenarios,* that can occur. Think of a scenario as a set of assumptions that you make. Table 20-1 summarizes these scenarios.

Table 20-1	Three Scenarios for the Manufacturing Model	
Scenario	*Hourly Cost*	*Material Cost*
Best Case	$23.50	$45.00
Worst Case	$27.00	$52.50
Most Likely Case	$25.00	$50.00

. . . *Getting well-then answers*

Because the product manufacturing worksheet is all set up with formulas, seeing the effects of the three scenarios I describe in the preceding section is an easy task. Simply plug in new values for cells B4 and B5 and see the results in the formula cells.

The preceding example shows a what-if scenario involving values in only two input cells (hourly cost and material cost). But scenarios can get more complex and use dozens or even hundreds of input cells. Such a what-if scenario can be a nightmare. Fortunately, 1-2-3 offers a tool called the *Version Manager* to help you keep track of various scenarios.

Introducing Version Manager

So what is the Version Manager? In a nutshell, this feature enables you to name various scenarios and display a named scenario with only a few mouse clicks. In 1-2-3 terminology, a scenario is known as a *version*. Your workbook can have different named versions for a set of input cells.

After you create two or more versions, you can switch to an alternate version and observe the effects on your formulas. In other words, Version Manager is a handy tool that makes keeping track of different scenarios an easy task.

Using Version Manager

The nice thing about Version Manager is that this feature is very flexible. You can use Version Manager for simple problems (like the manufacturing model I describe in the previous section) or for extremely complex problems that require multiple input ranges and dozens of versions.

A version is a set of specific values in your input cells. Each version that you define has a different set of values for the input cells. However, not all cells need to be different across all versions.

Creating your versions

The first step in using Version Manager consists of creating various named versions for a range of input cells. After you create the versions, you can display any version you want.

Creating the first version

Before you start creating different versions of your input range:

1. **Make sure that your worksheet is set up with formulas that use a range of input cells.**

   An *input cell* is a cell that you change. You then see the results of the change in your formulas.

   The input cell range can consist of any number of cells, but the cells should be adjacent.

2. **Select the range of input cells and name it by choosing Range➪Name, entering the name in the Name box, and clicking OK.**

   This step is optional, but providing a name for the input cells is a good idea.

3. **Enter the values for the first scenario into the input cells.**

   The first version is always named Original (the 1-2-3 default name). You can change this name after you create the first version (see the section "Changing the name or comments for a version," later in this chapter).

A version's name is not the same as a range name. A single named range may have many versions, and each version has a unique name.

Creating the second version

To create the second version of your input range, follow these steps.

1. **Select the input range and choose Range➪Version➪New Version.**

   1-2-3 displays the New Version dialog box (see Figure 20-2). The first tab, labeled Step 1. Basics, is displayed.

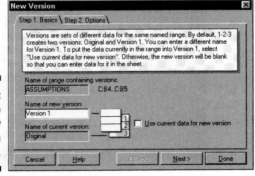

Figure 20-2:
The first tab
of the New
Version
dialog box.

2. Enter a name for the version in the box labeled Name of new version:.

This step is optional, and you can use the default name (Version 1) if you like. However, renaming the version to something descriptive is a good idea because you use that name to select which version to display.

3. Click Next.

1-2-3 displays the second tab (Step 2. Options) of the New Version dialog box. Figure 20-3 shows this dialog box.

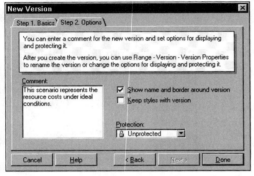

Figure 20-3: The second tab of the New Version dialog box.

4. Enter a comment that describes the version that you are going to enter.

This step is optional, but adding a description is helpful if you want to describe the version or provide notes to yourself.

5. Click Done to close the New Version dialog box.

1-2-3 clears input cells and surrounds the cells with a frame, as shown in Figure 20-4.

6. Enter the values for the scenario.

At this point, the input range has two versions defined: the original values (named Original), and the version you created in the preceding steps.

Creating more versions

If you want to create additional versions for your input range, simply repeat the steps I outline in the preceding section, providing a new version name in Step 2 and new values for the version in Step 6.

Manufacturing Model

A \ B \ C \

	A	B	C	D
1	Product Manufacturing Model			
2				
3	Resource Costs	Best Case		
4	Hourly cost:			
5	Materials cost:			
6				
7		Product A	Product B	Product C
8	Hours per unit:	6	12	18
9	Materials per unit:	12	10	16
10	Selling price:	$850	$975	$1,375
11	Units to produce:	125	90	60
12	Cost to produce:	$0	$0	$0
13	Unit profit:	$850	$975	$1,375
14				
15	Net profit:	$106,250	$87,750	$82,500
16				
17	Total net profit:	$276,500		
18				

Figure 20-4:
1-2-3 inserts
a frame
around the
input cells.

When you create a version, you give the version a name and 1-2-3 clears out the cells in the input range. Then you enter the values for the version in the empty cells.

Displaying a version

After you create some versions for your input range, you can display any of the versions. To display a version, click the icon in the upper-right corner of the frame surrounding the input range. You get a drop-down list of all your named versions, as shown in Figure 20-5. Select the desired version from the list and 1-2-3 places the values for that version into the input cells. And, of course, the formulas recalculate to show new results.

Manufacturing Model

A \ B \ C \

	A	B	C	D
1	Product Manufacturing Model			
2				
3	Resource Costs	Worst Case		
4	Hourly cost:	$27	Best Case	
5	Materials cost:	$52	Original	
6			Worst Case	
7		Product A	Product B	Product C
8	Hours per unit:	6	12	18
9	Materials per unit:	12	10	16
10	Selling price:	$850	$975	$1,375
11	Units to produce:	125	90	60
12	Cost to produce:	$792	$849	$1,326
13	Unit profit:	$58	$126	$49
14				
15	Net profit:	$7,250	$11,340	$2,940
16				
17	Total net profit:	$21,530		
18				

Figure 20-5:
1-2-3
displays a
list of all
named
versions.

Changing the values for a version

After you create a particular named version, you may want to change one or more of the values for the input cells. To change a value, just replace the old value with the new value.

Changing the name or comments for a version

You may want to change the name of a version or edit the comment that describes a version. For example, the first version is always named Original — which isn't a very good name. To change the name of a version or edit its comment, right-click anywhere within the input range and choose Version Properties from the shortcut menu. Doing so displays the Range InfoBox, with the Version tab selected (see Figure 20-6). Make the changes in the appropriate box.

Figure 20-6:
The Version tab of the Range InfoBox enables you to change a version's name or edit a version's comments.

Deleting a version

To delete a version, start by displaying the version you want to delete (refer to the section "Displaying a version" earlier in this chapter). Then right-click anywhere within the input range and choose Delete Current Version from the shortcut menu.

Producing a summary report

After you define your versions, you may find it helpful to have 1-2-3 generate a report that shows the effects of your scenarios on selected formulas.

To generate a summary report, follow these steps:

1. Choose Range⇨Version⇨Report.

1-2-3 displays its Version Report dialog box, shown in Figure 20-7.

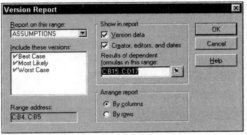

Figure 20-7:
The Version
Report
dialog box.

2. In the box labeled Include these versions:, place a check mark next to each version that you want to include in the report.

You probably want to include all versions, but you can omit one or more if you want.

3. In the range selection box (labeled Results of dependent formulas in this range), specify the range that contains the formulas that you are interested in.

You can either type the range address or point to the range in the worksheet. To point to the range of formulas, click the arrow button on the right side of the range selection box and drag in the worksheet.

4. Click OK.

1-2-3 opens a new workbook and generates the report. After the report is generated, 1-2-3 reactivates your original workbook, so you need to activate the report workbook to examine the report.

Figure 20-8 shows an example of a version summary report.

Unfortunately, 1-2-3 doesn't do such a great job generating these reports. 1-2-3 uses cryptic cell addresses for the labels even if you define names for the cells. To make the report easier to read, you may want to copy the labels from your original worksheet and paste them into the cells that display cell references.

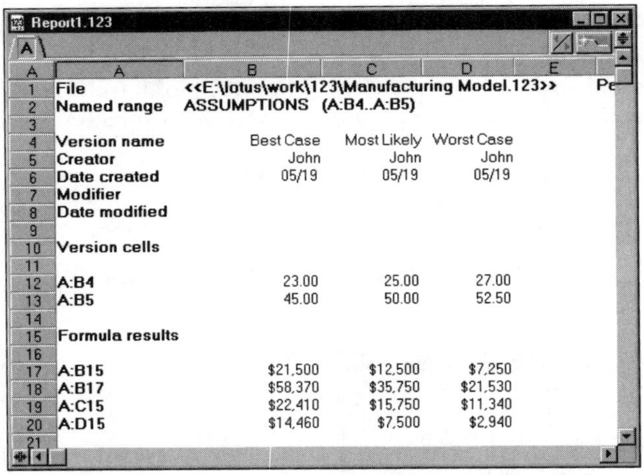

Report1.123

	A	B	C	D
1	File	<<E:\lotus\work\123\Manufacturing Model.123>>		
2	Named range	ASSUMPTIONS (A:B4..A:B5)		
3				
4	Version name	Best Case	Most Likely	Worst Case
5	Creator	John	John	John
6	Date created	05/19	05/19	05/19
7	Modifier			
8	Date modified			
9				
10	Version cells			
11				
12	A:B4	23.00	25.00	27.00
13	A:B5	45.00	50.00	52.50
14				
15	Formula results			
16				
17	A:B15	$21,500	$12,500	$7,250
18	A:B17	$58,370	$35,750	$21,530
19	A:C15	$22,410	$15,750	$11,340
20	A:D15	$14,460	$7,500	$2,940

Figure 20-8: This report, generated by 1-2-3, summarizes the versions.

Tell Me More

Version Manager is a powerful feature. The simple example in this chapter doesn't really do this feature justice. The example I present uses three versions of a single range. In fact, Version Manager can handle any number of versions of any number of ranges. This flexibility enables you to do some pretty awesome what-iffing and scenario management.

If you're interested in this feature, my suggestion is that you tackle it slowly and don't try to do too much at once. Make sure that you understand what's going on before you progress to more complex analyses.

Chapter 21

Bouncing from 1-2-3 to the Internet and Back Again

- -

In This Chapter

▶ Introducing the Internet

▶ Finding information on the Internet

▶ Accessing the Internet from 1-2-3

- -

C hances are, you're already familiar with the Internet. Perhaps you use e-mail or spend time surfing the *World Wide Web* (the graphical branch of the Internet). The Internet is probably the most exciting thing happening these days in the world of computing. In fact, the Web reaches well beyond the computer community, with Web-site addresses (called *URLs*) becoming commonplace on TV commercials, magazine ads, and even billboards.

Well, guess what: 1-2-3 includes features that enable you to access the Internet directly from your spreadsheet. In this chapter, I present an over-view of the Internet and briefly describe some of the Internet features built into 1-2-3.

The features I discuss in this chapter may not be enabled on your copy of 1-2-3, for one reason or another. For example, some companies choose not to enable these features for security reasons. Check with your employer to find out whether your version of 1-2-3 is enabled for Internet access.

Launching into Cyberspace

The Internet, in short, is a global collection of connected *(networked)* computers that can pass information back and forth. Strange as it may seem, the Internet is essentially a noncommercial system, and no single entity controls it.

Still, most people don't think of the Internet as a collection of computers. Rather, the Internet has taken on a unique persona as an information resource that anyone with a computer can access. The millions of computers connected to the Internet simply do the grunt work of passing the information from point A (which may be a computer in Hamburg, Germany) to point B (which may be the computer in your cubicle).

Starting to use the Internet can be like opening a can of worms — or, to be more precise, a can of alphabet soup. Internet parlance is chock-full of new terms (many of which are cryptic acronyms) that are likely to send your head spinning. Use the following definitions to keep your head planted firmly in place:

- **Browser:** Software that downloads HTML documents, interprets them, and displays their contents. You can also use a browser to download files from an FTP site. The two leading Web browsers are Microsoft Internet Explorer and Netscape Navigator.

- **E-mail:** A method of sending and receiving messages *(electronic mail)* via the computer. Depending on how your system is set up, you may be able to send and receive e-mail only within your company using the company intranet, or you may be able to send and receive e-mail all over the world using the Internet.

- **FTP:** An abbreviation for File Transfer Protocol. FTP is a common method for transferring a file from one computer to another.

- **FTP site:** An area on one computer where files are available for other computers to download. Lotus, for example, maintains an FTP site with loads of files you can download.

- **HTML document:** A computer file that may contain words, pictures, sounds, and so on, formatted in Hypertext Markup Language (HTML). Because people use many different kinds of computers to view HTML documents, Hypertext Markup Language relies on embedded codes (called tags) to tell your computer how to display the information. Your computer must have Web-browsing software to interpret these tags and display the information properly. (HTML documents are also called *Web pages.*)

- **HTTP:** An abbreviation for Hypertext Transfer Protocol, the method by which people transfer documents over the Web.

- **Hyperlink:** Special text or images in an HTML document (Web page) that you can click to load a new Web page into your browser.

- **Internet:** A worldwide network of computers that can communicate with each other and pass information back and forth.

- **Intranet:** A private network of computers not available to the general public. Intranets use the same file types (such as HTML documents) as the Internet, but access to intranets is limited. For example, your company may have an intranet that only its employees can access.

✓ **URL:** An abbreviation for Uniform Resource Locator. A URL is a series of characters that uniquely describes a resource on the Internet. For example, the following URL describes the home page for my Web site, which happens to deal with spreadsheets: `www.j-walk.com/ss/`.

✓ **Web site:** A collection of HTML documents (Web pages) located on a particular computer. The files on a Web site are available to anyone in the world. For example, Lotus maintains a Web site where you can find information about its products, technical support, and many other interesting tidbits.

✓ **WWW:** The World Wide Web, one of many parts of the Internet that support the free transfer of information between computers throughout the world. The WWW uses HTML as its primary file format, and the documents are connected using hyperlinks.

What's available on the Internet?

The amount and variety of information available on the Internet is simply mind-boggling. The Internet contains information on virtually any topic you can imagine; finding that information is the tricky part.

Information on the Internet is available from four primary sources:

✓ **Web sites:** The Web has rapidly become the most popular part of the Internet. Using Web-browsing software, you can access millions of Web sites. For example, Lotus has a Web site located at `www.lotus.com`.

✓ **FTP sites:** An FTP site is a computer that has files available for download. You can download these files using Web-browsing software or other software designed specifically to get files from FTP sites. Lotus has an FTP site located at `ftp.support.lotus.com/`.

✓ **Newsgroups:** A *newsgroup* is like an electronic bulletin board. People post messages or questions, and other people respond to the messages and answer the questions. Thousands of newsgroups are available, spanning just about any topic you can imagine. You need special news-reader software to read or post messages to a newsgroup, but most Web browsers include such software. For an example of a newsgroup that deals with 1-2-3, visit `news:comp.apps.spreadsheets`. Figure 21-1 shows a few messages posted to this newsgroup.

✓ **Mailing lists:** If you have access to Internet e-mail, you can subscribe to any of several thousand mailing lists that address a broad array of topics. Subscribers send e-mail to the mailing list, and then every other subscriber to the list receives that e-mail. Currently, no mailing list is devoted to 1-2-3 (although such a mailing list may appear at any time).

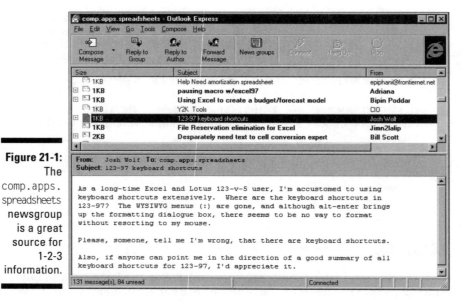

Figure 21-1:
The
comp.apps.
spreadsheets
newsgroup
is a great
source for
1-2-3
information.

How do you get on the Internet?

You can access the Internet in a number of ways, including the following:

- ✔ **Through your company:** Your company may already be connected to the Internet. If it is, just fire up your Web browser, and you're there!

- ✔ **Through an Internet Service Provider (ISP):** Most communities have several companies that are glad to set up an Internet account for you. For a small monthly fee (usually around $20.00), you can have unlimited (or almost unlimited) access to the Internet.

- ✔ **Through a commercial online service:** Several companies have taken the concept of ISPs a step further, supplementing Internet access with additional features, such as their own e-mail server, chat rooms, games, and more. If you subscribe to an online service such as America Online (AOL), CompuServe, The Microsoft Network (MSN), or Prodigy, you can access the Internet through that service.

Using the 1-2-3 Internet Tools

Not to be left out of the cyber-revolution, 1-2-3 contains several built-in tools for accessing the Internet. More specifically, you can

✔ Jump directly to any of several Lotus sites on the Internet.

✔ Add a hyperlink to a cell in a worksheet, or create a button that activates a hyperlink.

✔ Convert a worksheet to a Web page. The cells in your worksheet are converted to an HTML table or to a jDoc document. You can save the document to your hard drive or directly to an Internet FTP server.

✔ Open a Web page directly into 1-2-3. Unless the Web page consists only of an HTML table, the result is usually pretty disappointing.

✔ Import a table from a Web page into a 1-2-3 worksheet. These tables are "linked," so you can refresh them at any time to get the latest information.

✔ Search the Internet for text contained in a worksheet cell.

If you plan to use any of the Internet features of 1-2-3, take a moment to get acquainted with the Internet Tools SmartIcon bar, shown in Figure 21-2. To display this SmartIcon bar, choose View⇨Show Internet Tools.

In order for your Internet Tools SmartIcon bar to work, your copy of 1-2-3 must be configured properly and you must have all the necessary software, hardware, and connections to access the Internet. A book like this one can't possibly cover all the steps involved in getting your system hooked up to the Internet. But don't worry — in most cases, if you need to access the Internet via 1-2-3, someone in your company will be responsible for doing the necessary preparation.

Figure 21-2:
With the Internet Tools SmartIcon bar, the Internet is just a click away.

—Convert to Web pages

—Open a file from the Internet

—Save current file to the Internet

—Create or edit hyperlink

—Create a hyperlinked button

—Create a Web table

—Refresh one or more Web tables

—Go to Lotus home page

—Go to Lotus Customer Support page

—Go to Customer Support FTP server

—Go to Lotus SmartSuite reference library

—Search Internet for selected text

Visiting Lotus on the Internet

While using 1-2-3, you may want to check out some material at the Lotus Internet sites — at least the folks who designed 1-2-3 think that you may. They included shortcuts to four sites on the Internet Tools SmartIcon bar:

SmartIcon	Corresponding Menu Command
🏠	Help⇨Lotus Internet Support⇨Lotus Home Page
❓	Help⇨Lotus Internet Support⇨Lotus Customer Support
💻	Help⇨Lotus Internet Support⇨Lotus FTP Site
📚	(no menu command)

Clicking the SmartIcon (or choosing the corresponding menu command) awakens your Web browser and displays the appropriate Internet site. From there, you simply click the hyperlinks until you find the information you need.

If you want to access these sites directly from your Web browser, use the following URLs:

Lotus Home Page:	www.lotus.com
Lotus Customer Support:	www.support.lotus.com
Lotus FTP Site:	ftp.support.lotus.com/

Figure 21-3 shows how the Customer Support site looked when I checked in.

Adding a hyperlink to a worksheet

A new feature in the latest version of 1-2-3 lets you add an Internet hyperlink directly to a worksheet. You can then click the hyperlink to load a Web document into your browser. Figure 21-4 shows a worksheet with a hyperlink added.

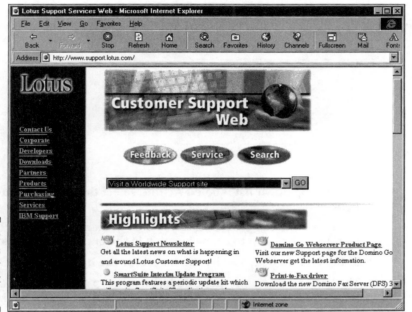

Figure 21-3:
The Lotus
Customer
Support
site.

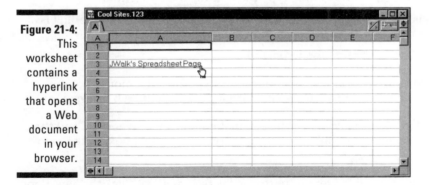

Figure 21-4:
This
worksheet
contains a
hyperlink
that opens
a Web
document
in your
browser.

A hyperlink can also be linked to a different 1-2-3 workbook or to a different location in the current workbook.

To add a hyperlink to a worksheet:

1. **Choose Create➪Hyperlink (or click the SmartIcon labeled Create or edit a hyperlink).**

   1-2-3 displays the Create Hyperlink dialog box, shown in Figure 21-5.

Figure 21-5:
Use the
Create
Hyperlink
dialog box
to add a
hyperlink
to your
worksheet.

Create Hyperlink

Create a hyperlink to a range or an object in this workbook, another file of any type, or to an Internet location.

OK
Cancel

Action: Go to an Internet location

Link to: http://www.j-walk.com/ss

Examples: http://www.lotus.com, ftp://ftp.lotus.com

Help

Attached to: A:A3

Cell contents: J'Walk's Spreadsheet Page

2. **In the drop-down list labeled Action, select the action for the hyperlink.**

   The hyperlink can open an Internet Web document, load another 1-2-3 workbook, or jump to a new location in the current workbook.

3. **In the Link to box, specify the target for the hyperlink.**

   The link can be an Internet URL (such as http://www.lotus.com), a file specification (such as c:\work\myfile.123), or a workbook location (such as a cell reference).

4. **In the Cell contents box, type the text for the hyperlink.**

   This text will appear in the cell. If you leave it blank, the hyperlink is created, but it will be "invisible."

5. **Click OK to create the hyperlink.**

When you move the mouse pointer over a hyperlink, the mouse pointer turns into an image of a hand — just like it does in your Web browser.

To remove a hyperlink, select the cell that contains the hyperlink, and then choose Create⇨Hyperlink. In the Create Hyperlink dialog box, click Remove Link.

If you prefer, you can create a button for your hyperlink. Click the SmartIcon labeled Create a hyperlinked button, and then click and drag in the worksheet to draw the button. When you release the mouse button, the Create Hyperlink dialog box appears. Fill in the details and you've got yourself a hyperlink button.

Saving data to a Web document

What if your 1-2-3 worksheet contains data that you need to publish on the Web or on your company's intranet? Good news: Converting 1-2-3 data to a Web document is a piece of cake.

The scoop on jDoc documents

The HTML format is the standard for Web documents. HTML files are plain text files that contain special tags. These tags tell your browser how to display the information. 1-2-3 Millennium Edition lets you save data as an HTML file, or in a special format called jDoc.

The advantage of saving your work in a jDoc file is that the browser will display an exact replica of your worksheet — including charts, maps, and other graphics. An HTML file, on the other hand, displays worksheet data in tabular format, and the information may not look the same as it does in 1-2-3. The disadvantage of a jDoc file is that it is quite a bit larger, and therefore takes longer to load into the browser. Also, a jDoc document requires a Java-enabled browser (which includes Microsoft Internet Explorer and Netscape Navigator).

Bottom line? In general, use the HTML format whenever possible. It creates smaller files and offers greater compatibility.

To convert your 1-2-3 data to one or more Web pages, follow these steps:

1. **Choose File⇨Internet⇨Convert to Web Pages, or just click the Convert to Web Pages SmartIcon.**

   1-2-3 displays the first of a series of dialog boxes (see Figure 21-6).

2. **Specify a name for the Web document.**

3. **Specify what you want to convert by clicking the appropriate option button.**

4. **Specify the format for the Web document.**

   1-2-3 can create two types of Web documents: standard HTML files and jDoc files. Refer to the sidebar, "The scoop on jDoc documents."

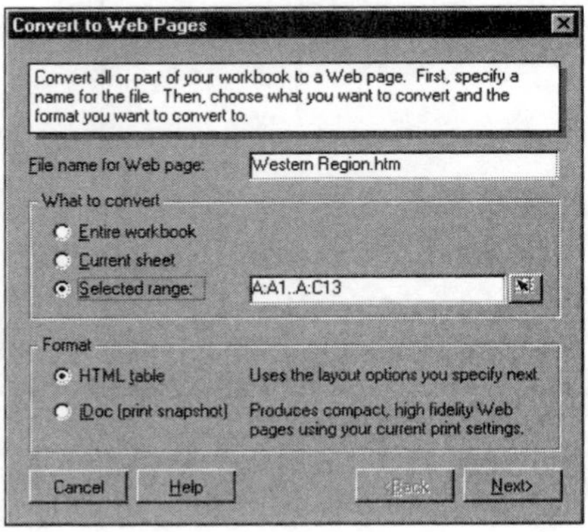

Figure 21-6:
1-2-3 lets you convert a range, a worksheet, or an entire workbook to a Web document.

Convert to Web Pages

Convert all or part of your workbook to a Web page. First, specify a name for the file. Then, choose what you want to convert and the format you want to convert to.

File name for Web page: Western Region.htm

What to convert
- ○ Entire workbook
- ○ Current sheet
- ● Selected range: A:A1..A:C13

Format
- ● HTML table   Uses the layout options you specify next.
- ○ jDoc (print snapshot)   Produces compact, high fidelity Web pages using your current print settings.

Cancel   Help   <Back   Next>

5. **Click Next to display the next dialog box.**

6. **Specify your options in the dialog box.**

   The options you see in the second dialog box depend on the format you choose in the first dialog box. If you're saving the data in the jDoc format, you don't have as many options because the document will closely resemble the original file.

7. **Click Next to display the final dialog box.**

8. **In the final dialog box, specify a location for saving the document.**

   You can save the document to your hard drive, or directly to an Internet FTP server (probably on your corporate intranet).

Note: Before you can save a file to an FTP server, you must set up the FTP connection using the File⇨Internet⇨Setup command. The procedure varies, but if you need to use this feature, odds are that your technical support person has it all set up for you and ready to go.

Creating a linked HTML table in 1-2-3

A new feature in 1-2-3 lets you insert a table from an HTML document directly into a worksheet. Figure 21-7 shows an example. The table is "linked" directly to the Internet URL, so if the data changes, you can refresh the table in your worksheet to see the latest updates.

Figure 21-7: You can insert a linked HTML table into a worksheet.

Month	Northern	Southern
January	987	983
February	1023	982
March	883	873
April	2122	1091
May	893	883
June	1033	1032
July	2311	398
August	1132	144
September	1090	122
October		
November		
December		
Total		

Source: http://jwalk/data/index.html

Web Table 1

To create a linked HTML table, follow these steps:

1. **Choose File⇨Internet⇨Get Data from Web, or just click the Create a Web Table SmartIcon.**

   1-2-3 displays the Get Data from Web dialog box.

2. **Enter the URL into the Web address box.**

   For example, `http://intranet/data/index.html`.

3. **Specify a worksheet range for the table.**

   A single cell is sufficient.

4. **If you like, put a check mark next to Adjust column widths to fit Web data.**

5. **Click OK to retrieve the data and create the table.**

   Notice that the table also displays the original URL (the table's source).

The Web table is a "one-way" table. In other words, if you make changes in the table, these changes are not stored in the Web page.

When a Web table is activated, a new menu (Web Table) appears. You can use this menu to change various properties, refresh the Web table, or break the connection — making it a static table.

To refresh a Web table, click the arrow icon in the lower-right corner of the Web table (or click the SmartIcon labeled Refresh one or more Web tables).

Searching the Internet

Yet another new feature lets you search the Internet for text contained in a cell. Just activate the cell that contains the text you want to search for, and then click the SmartIcon labeled Search Internet for selected text. Your browser is activated and takes you to the Yahoo! search site, with the search results displayed.

This feature is pretty much useless as far as I'm concerned. Personally, I'd rather choose my own Internet search engine and have more flexibility with my searches. But it's there if you want it.

Part VI
The Part of Tens

The 5th Wave — By Rich Tennant

SOFTWARE APPLICATION TESTING CENTER

EXIT

"WE TEST FOR COMPATIBILITY, PERFORMANCE, SERVICE, AND FORMATTING. IF IT FAILS THESE, THEN IT'S TESTED FOR THE DISTANCE IT CAN BE SAILED ACROSS THE PARKING LOT AND ONTO THE EXPRESSWAY."

In this part . . .

For reasons that are historical (as well as helpful), all the books in the ...*For Dummies* series contain chapters with lists of ten. I went along with this tradition and prepared three top-ten lists: good 1-2-3 habits to acquire, concepts essential to mastering 1-2-3, and a huge list of ready-made formulas. The Part of Tens — the tradition lives on!

Chapter 22

Top Ten Good 1-2-3 Habits to Acquire

*H*abits that you form early tend to stick with you over the years. All 1-2-3 users should try to develop the following ten habits as they gain experience using the program.

Use the SmartIcons, Status-Bar Buttons, and Shortcut Keys

Many people completely ignore all the ease-of-use features that spreadsheet designers work so hard to include (and their ad agencies charge so much to promote). Using the InfoBox for routine things like aligning the contents of a cell is not only slower, but it also invites more opportunities for you to make mistakes.

Use Your Hard Disk Wisely

Don't save your worksheet files to a floppy disk; always use your hard disk as your primary file storage place. You can save and retrieve worksheets faster when you save them on your hard disk, and hard disks are less likely than floppy disks to go bad. However, you *should* use floppies to store backup copies of all your important files, just in case your hard disk does decide to fly south for the winter.

Take Advantage of Multisheet Workbooks

Many users tend to ignore the fact that they can insert as many sheets as they need into a workbook. Using these extra sheets is a great way to organize your work; the extra sheets provide a quick way to jump to a particular part of your worksheet by simply clicking a tab.

Use Cell and Range Names Whenever Possible

If you have some cells or ranges that you use frequently in formulas, you should take a few seconds to give them names with the Range⇨Name command. By naming your frequently used cells or ranges, you can use their names (rather than obscure addresses) in formulas. Doing so makes the formulas easier to read and understand. A side benefit is that you can use the range navigator icon in the edit line to quickly add a range name to a formula or to jump directly to a named cell or range.

Remember to Multitask: Work with More Than One Program at Once

When you're working away in your spreadsheet and need to do something else (like compose a memo in your word processor), you don't need to close 1-2-3. Just click the Windows Start button and execute the program you need. 1-2-3 remains in the background. If the program is already running, you can just click its icon from the Windows Task list. Also, save your work before jumping over to another application. The other program may crash your system. Such things happen far too often.

Take Advantage of the Online Help in 1-2-3

Great as this book is, it doesn't tell you *everything* about 1-2-3. If you get stuck, your first line of attack should be to press F1 and see what the online help has to say. Even better, choose Help⇨Ask the Expert. You can type your question in plain English, and you have an excellent chance that the Expert will lead you to the answer you need.

Be Adventurous: Try New Things

Dozens of weird commands lurk within the bowels of the 1-2-3 menu system and dialog boxes. Don't be afraid to try out these unfamiliar commands to see what happens. But to be on the safe side, have an unimportant worksheet open when you do so. And don't forget to use Edit⇨Undo if the command messes things up.

Be a Good Citizen — Use Print Preview

All too often, people print draft after draft of their worksheets, making only minor changes before each printing. A better approach is to use the handy Print Preview feature, which shows you exactly how your printed output will look. You even can zoom in to examine various parts more closely.

So remember to use Print Preview often and with much joy. Your office manager, your coworkers, and your local environmentalist will thank you.

Keep It Simple

Don't go overboard with fancy formatting. I know that spending hours trying to get your worksheet to look perfect is very tempting — experimenting with fonts, type sizes, colors, borders, and the like is actually kind of fun. But the final product is probably not worth this much attention. Unless you have lots of time on your hands, focus on the content of your worksheet rather than on the worksheet's appearance.

Warm Up to Scripts

After you get comfortable with using the basic features of 1-2-3, you may want to explore the world of scripts. Even a rudimentary knowledge of scripting can save you lots of time when you're doing repetitive tasks. Check out Chapter 18 to find out more about how to use scripts to improve your quality of life in 1-2-3.

Chapter 23

Top Ten Essential Concepts for 1-2-3 Users

To be a true 1-2-3 user, you should live, breathe, and become one with the concepts I discuss in this chapter.

Many Versions of 1-2-3 Are Available

When people talk about using 1-2-3, don't assume that they're referring to the same version that you use. Generally, the different versions of 1-2-3 are *very* different from each other. So someone who only knows how to use 1-2-3 Millennium Edition doesn't necessarily know how to use 1-2-3 Release 4 for Windows or 1-2-3 Release 5 for Windows. And when you start considering the various DOS versions of 1-2-3, you're talking about a completely different animal altogether. Even worse, different 1-2-3 versions also use different file formats. So if someone asks you to send her a 1-2-3 file, make sure that you know which file format she wants.

Your choices of formats are WKS, WK1, WK3, WK4, and 123. Your program, 1-2-3 Millennium Edition, saves files in the newest 123 format. But you can save your work as a WK1, WK3, or WK4 file by using the File⇨Save As command. Be forewarned, however, that you may lose some formatting or formulas during the translation.

It's important to understand that 1-2-3 97 also uses the 123 extension for its files. However, 1-2-3 97 cannot read a file generated by 1-2-3 Millennium Edition unless you save the file in 1-2-3 97 format.

1-2-3 Is Compatible with other Windows Applications

Windows programs are like beer and pretzels — they go well together. You should know that you can run more than one Windows program at a time and switch among them whenever you need to.

Furthermore, the Windows Clipboard is the language interpreter of the bunch. You can easily copy information between different programs by using the Clipboard. When you use the Windows Clipboard, you can copy a range of cells from 1-2-3 and paste that range into your Windows word processor. You also can use the Clipboard for copying and pasting graphics. The Clipboard is one of the most useful features in Windows, so don't ignore it!

1-2-3 Has Other Windows in Its Window

Believe it or not, many users don't understand this Windows concept: Each program that you run, including 1-2-3, has its own window, which you can resize, move, minimize, or maximize within the Windows environment. Within the 1-2-3 program window, each workbook also has its own window, which you can resize, move, minimize, or maximize. (I see some potential for a window-washing business out there. . . .) Understand this concept thoroughly, and you'll see your productivity level start to rise.

You Can Select Ranges in Myriad Different Ways

For a small range that doesn't extend beyond the current screen, dragging the mouse over the range may be the fastest way to select that range. But using the keyboard is often more efficient. To select a range with the keyboard, press Shift and use the navigation keys. You also can combine this process with the End key, followed by an arrow key (this entry moves to the end of the range). And don't forget that you can select an entire row or column by clicking the row number or column letter in the worksheet frame. Finally, you can select noncontiguous ranges by holding down the Ctrl key while you make your selections.

You Have Many Command Options

1-2-3 is a flexible program and usually offers several ways to execute a particular command. You can execute most operations by using the menu system, but that way isn't always the most efficient. Many menu commands have shortcut keys or SmartIcon equivalents. The status bar at the bottom of the screen is often the fastest way to change fonts, text sizes, and numeric formatting. And of course, you have the InfoBox — your one-stop shopping spot for working with just about any object. In almost every situation, you can right-click with your mouse to get to a shortcut menu. And don't forget about drag-and-drop — for simple copy and move operations, this method can't be beat.

Cell Comments Are Free — Use Them with Abandon

1-2-3 lets you insert cell comments to document your work or leave messages and reminders for yourself (or others). This feature, which is accessible via the Cell comment tab of the Range InfoBox, is extremely useful. The main advantage is that you can add all sorts of text without cluttering up your worksheet cells.

1-2-3 Has More @functions Than You Ever Need

If you ever have a few spare minutes (like when someone puts you on hold during a telephone call), why not pass the time by browsing through the @function list in the 1-2-3 online help? I guarantee that you'll find something you can use. The little @ icon on the edit line is one of the handiest tools in 1-2-3. Clicking this icon inserts an @function into your formula and even tells you exactly what arguments the @function needs. And don't forget that you can click the Help button in the @Function List dialog box to get help on the selected @function.

The Online Help System Is Comprehensive

If you get stuck, your first course of action should be to press F1, the express route to the online help system (or you can use the new Ask the Expert feature). The 1-2-3 online help system is extremely thorough and is loaded with examples. And don't overlook the Help⇨Quick Demos command — it's a good way to kill some time and maybe even discover something in the process.

Hard Disks Crash for No Apparent Reason

With all the computers out there, you need to know that hard disks crash thousands of times a day. People turn on their computers and get a strange message followed by a screen full of nothingness. In other words, everything stored on the hard disk is gone! Kaplooey! You can reinstall the software, but all the data files (including your 1-2-3 workbooks) are pushing up daisies. This, of course, will never happen to you, because either you are extremely lucky or you have taken the advice that I offer in several places throughout this book: *Make a backup copy of your workbook files on a floppy disk, a network drive, or a removable device such as a Zip drive!*

The More You Use 1-2-3, the Easier It Gets

I can understand how new users may be overwhelmed and intimidated by this program — it can do many things and has tons of commands. But just wait; you will soon be very comfortable with the commands that you use frequently. And as your comfort level increases, you'll find yourself wondering what some of those other commands can do. Before you even realize what's happening, you progress from being a beginning user to feeling very comfortable in the 1-2-3 environment. And you owe it all to this book. . . .

Chapter 24

More Than Ten Formulas You Can Pilfer

*P*eople who use spreadsheets tend to want to do the same general sorts of tasks. Many of these procedures are built right into the spreadsheet in the form of menu commands or @functions. But many other popular spreadsheet actions require formulas.

I can't develop formulas just for you (unless the price is right . . .). However, I can share with you some formulas that I find useful. Most of these formulas involve @functions, so this chapter serves double-duty by also demonstrating some realistic uses of these functions. You may find one or two formulas that are just what you need for getting that report out on time. Or a formula you see here may give you an idea for a similar formula that you can create yourself.

In any case, feel free to do what you want with these formulas: Study them diligently, ignore them completely, or handle them in any way that suits your needs.

The formulas in this chapter use names for @function arguments, which means that you can't simply enter the formulas into a worksheet and expect them to work. You have to make some minor changes to adapt the arguments to your own needs. When you incorporate these formulas into your worksheets, you must do one of the following:

- ✔ **Substitute the appropriate cell or range reference for the range name I use.** For example, the formula @SUM(expenses) uses a range named expenses. If you want to sum the values in A12..A36, substitute that range reference for expenses. Your adapted formula becomes @SUM(A12..A36).

- ✔ **Name cells or ranges on your worksheet to correspond to the range names used in the formulas.** Following the previous example, you can simply choose Range⇨Name and assign the name *expenses* to the range A12..A36.

- ✔ **Use your own range names and make the appropriate changes in the formulas.** If your worksheet has nothing to do with tracking expenses, define a more appropriate name.

Formulas for Everyone

The formulas in this section are relatively simple (and perhaps even trivial). But they show up again and again in spreadsheets all over the world.

Calculating a sum

To calculate the sum of a range named expenses, use the following formula:

```
@SUM(expenses)
```

The summation SmartIcon can write a formula like this one for you automatically. Just move the cell pointer to the cell in which you want to place the @SUM formula and click the SmartIcon (it's the one that says 1+2=3). 1-2-3 inserts the formula in a jiffy.

1-2-3 has a slick feature that smacks of artificial intelligence. When you type the text *Total* into a cell, 1-2-3 quickly analyzes your worksheet and inserts appropriate @SUM formulas. For example, Figure 24-1 contains some information that needs to be totaled. The fastest way to accomplish this task is simply to enter the word *Total* in cell A6 and again in cell E2. 1-2-3 inserts @SUM formulas in row 6 and column E.

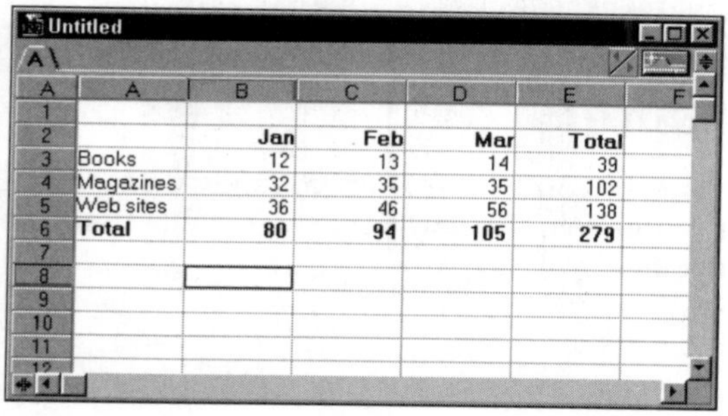

Figure 24-1:
Use the
secret
word, and
1-2-3
creates
formulas
for you.

Computing subtotals and grand totals

Some applications — budgets, for example — include subtotals as well as grand totals. Figure 24-2 shows an example that uses subtotals and a grand total at the bottom. Rather than use the @SUM function, you should know about the @SUBTOTAL and @GRANDTOTAL functions. The @SUBTOTAL function works just like the @SUM function. The @GRANDTOTAL function, however, adds only the cells that have an @SUBTOTAL function in them.

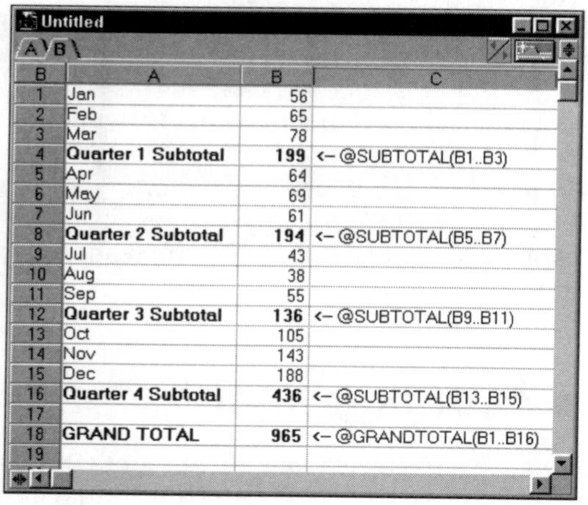

Figure 24-2:
Dealing
with
subtotals
and grand
totals is
easy.

In the example shown, the @GRANDTOTAL function's argument is B1..B16, but the result includes only the four cells that have @SUBTOTAL functions in them.

Counting the number of nonblank cells in a column

If you have a list of items in your worksheet, you may want to keep a running count of the number of items in the list. Here's a formula that returns the number of nonblank cells in column A:

```
@COUNT(A1..A65536)
```

Calculating a percentage change

Calculating the percentage change between two values is a common task. For example, you may want to compare last month's sales with the current month's sales and express the result as a percentage change. If the value for last month is in a cell named old and the value for the current month is in a cell named new, use the following formula:

```
+(new-old)/old
```

If old is greater than new, the percentage change value is positive. Otherwise, the value is negative. You probably want to use the Range InfoBox to format this cell to appear as a percentage.

If a chance exists that old equals 0, use the following formula instead:

```
@IF(old=0,@NA,(new-old)/old)
```

This revised formula displays NA rather than ERR, which shows up if you attempt to divide by zero.

Calculating a loan payment

This example assumes that you have cells named amount (the loan amount), term (the length of the loan, in months), and rate (the annual interest rate). The following formula returns the monthly payment amount:

```
@PMT(amount,rate/12,term)
```

Notice that this formula divides the annual interest rate (named rate) by 12. Doing so produces a monthly interest rate. If you are making payments every other month, divide rate by 6.

If you want to determine the amount of a loan payment that's applied to the principal, use the @PPAYMT function. To determine the amount that's applied to interest, use the @IPAYMNT function. I demonstrate these functions in Figure 24-3. Cell B5 contains the payment number (from 1 to 48 in this case). The amount allocated to principal and interest varies with the payment number — more goes to interest earlier in the loan.

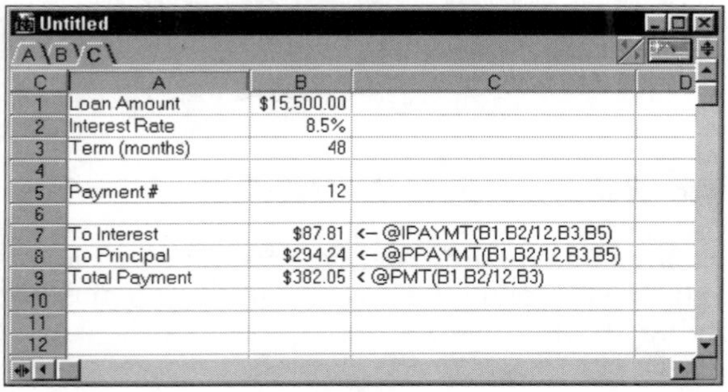

Figure 24-3:
@functions
calculate
the amount
of a loan
payment
that's
applied to
principal
and the
amount
paid to
interest.

	A	B	C	D
1	Loan Amount	$15,500.00		
2	Interest Rate	8.5%		
3	Term (months)	48		
4				
5	Payment #	12		
6				
7	To Interest	$87.81	← @IPAYMT(B1,B2/12,B3,B5)	
8	To Principal	$294.24	← @PPAYMT(B1,B2/12,B3,B5)	
9	Total Payment	$382.05	< @PMT(B1,B2/12,B3)	
10				
11				
12				

Mathematical Formulas

The formulas in this section deal with mathematical operations: square roots, cube roots, random numbers, and so on.

Finding a square, cube, or other root

You remember square roots. The square root of a number is the number that, when multiplied by itself, results in the original number. For example, 4 is the square root of 16 because $4 \times 4 = 16$. 1-2-3 has a handy @SQRT function that calculates the square root of a number.

In addition to square roots, you may need to find other roots (no, not carrots and potatoes). For example, the cube root of a number is the number that, when multiplied by itself twice, results in the original number. For example, 4 is the cube root of 64, because $4 \times 4 \times 4 = 64$. You can also calculate fourth roots, fifth roots, and so on.

To place the cube root of a number in a cell named value, use the following formula:

```
+value^(1/3)
```

To place the fourth root of a number in that same cell, use the following formula:

```
+value^(1/4)
```

Calculate other roots in a similar manner by changing the bottom half of the fraction.

Generating a random number

Spreadsheet users often use random numbers to simulate real events. For example, if you're trying to predict next year's sales, you may want to add some random numbers to this year's sales.

To get a random number between 0 and 1, use the following formula, which displays a new random number every time the worksheet is recalculated or every time you make a change to a cell:

```
@RAND
```

If you need a random integer (a whole number) that falls in a specific range, the formula gets a bit trickier. The following formula returns a random integer between two numbers stored in low and high. For example, if low contains 7 and high contains 12, the formula returns a random number between (and including) 7 and 12. The formula reads:

```
@INT((high-low+1)*@RAND+low)
```

If you want a formula that simulates the toss of a six-sided die, here it is:

```
@INT(6*@RAND+1)
```

Rounding numbers

To round a number in a cell named amount to the nearest whole number, use the following formula:

```
@ROUND(amount,0)
```

To round the number to two decimal places, substitute a 2 for the 0 in the formula. In fact, you can round the number to any number of decimal places by changing the value of the second argument.

1-2-3 includes three other rounding @functions: @ROUNDUP, @ROUNDDOWN, and @ROUNDM. If your work involves rounding numbers, check out the 1-2-3 online help for a detailed explanation (and examples) of these @functions.

Text Formulas

As you know, 1-2-3 can deal with text (or labels) as well as numbers. Here are a few formulas that enable you to manipulate text.

Changing the case

1-2-3 has several @functions that you can use to change the case of text in a cell. For example, if you want to convert the text budget forecast (assumed to be in cell A1) to BUDGET FORECAST, use a formula like the following example:

```
@UPPER(A1)
```

Related functions that may be of interest include @PROPER (makes the first letter uppercase, everything else lowercase) and @LOWER (makes the text lowercase).

Joining text

Joining two strings together is called *concatenation*. Assume the cell named first contains the text Liz and the cell named last contains Phair. The following formula concatenates these strings into the name of a superb female recording artist:

```
+first & " " & last
```

The ampersand is the concatenation operator. Note that I concatenated a space character to separate the two names (otherwise, the result would be LizPhair, not Liz Phair). You can concatenate text with text, but not text with a value. However, you can get around this restriction, as I show in the following examples.

Working with text and values

If you want to concatenate text with a value, you must first convert the value to text. In this example, the cell named word holds the text AMOUNT:. The cell named answer holds the value 125. The following formula displays the text and the value in a single cell:

```
+word&" "&@STRING(answer,0)
```

The @STRING function converts a value to text, and the second argument for the @STRING function gives the number of decimal places to be displayed (in this case, none).

The result of this formula appears as

```
AMOUNT: 125
```

Here's another example. Assume that you have a range of cells named scores. The following formula displays a label and the maximum value in scores in one cell:

```
+"Largest: "&@STRING(@MAX(scores),0)
```

If the largest value in scores is 95, this formula displays:

```
Largest: 95
```

The @STRING function converts the value returned by the @MAX function into a label. This label is then concatenated with the string Largest.

Date Formulas

This section contains a few formulas dealing with dates.

The date and time @functions get their information from your computer's clock. If you rely on any of these functions for serious work, make sure that the date and time are set properly in your computer. Use the Windows Control Panel to set your system clock.

Inserting today's date

If you want a cell in your worksheet to display the current date, enter the following formula into that cell:

```
@TODAY
```

This formula returns a date serial number, so you need to use Range InfoBox to format the result as a date. (You may also have to make the column wider so that the date shows up.)

The 1-2-3 date serial number system is fairly simple to understand. The numbering system starts with January 1, 1900 (which has a value of 1). January 2, 1900 has a value of 2, and so on.

Determining the day of the week

The following formula returns the current day of the week as text:

```
@CHOOSE(@WEEKDAY(@TODAY),"Mon","Tue","Wed","Thu","Fri","Sat","Sun")
```

You can replace @TODAY in the preceding formula with a reference to a cell that has a date serial number in it so that you can find the day of the week for any date.

Determining the last day of the month

In business situations, knowing the last day of the month (which is usually the day that you have to produce the monthly reports) is often necessary. The following formula returns the last day of the current month:

```
@DATE(@YEAR(@TODAY),@MONTH(@TODAY)+1,1)-1
```

To figure out the last day of the month for any date, substitute a reference to a cell that has a date for both occurrences of @TODAY.

Still More Formulas

Here are a few more miscellaneous formulas for your computing pleasure.

Showing the workbook's name and location

When looking at a worksheet printout, many people like to be able to recognize the filename and exactly where the file is stored. The solution is to insert the following formula somewhere in your workbook:

```
@CELLPOINTER("filename")
```

The @CELLPOINTER and @CELL functions can tell you lots of other interesting information. Refer to the online help for a complete list of arguments that you can use.

Determining the time you spent on a workbook

You may be interested to know how long (hours and minutes) you worked on a particular workbook. To find out, just insert the following formula anywhere in the workbook:

```
@INFO("editing-time")
```

This formula returns a time value that corresponds to the total amount of time that the workbook has been open. But then again, maybe you don't really want to know. . . .

Check out the online help for the other valid arguments for the @INFO function. This function can tell you quite a bit!

Looking up a corresponding value

Many spreadsheets need to look up a value in a table that is based on another value. Examples include parts lists and income tax tables: You need to look up the tax rate from a table, and the tax rate is based on a person's taxable income.

Figure 24-4 shows an example of a small lookup table. In this worksheet, the user can enter a part number into cell B3, which is named partnum. The formulas in cells B4 and B5 return the corresponding price and discount. The lookup table is in D2..F13 and has the name partlist. The values in the first column of any lookup table must be in ascending order (smallest to largest).

The formula in cell B4, which displays the price, is

```
@VLOOKUP(partnum,partlist,1)
```

The formula in cell B5, which displays the discount, is

```
@VLOOKUP(partnum,partlist,2)
```

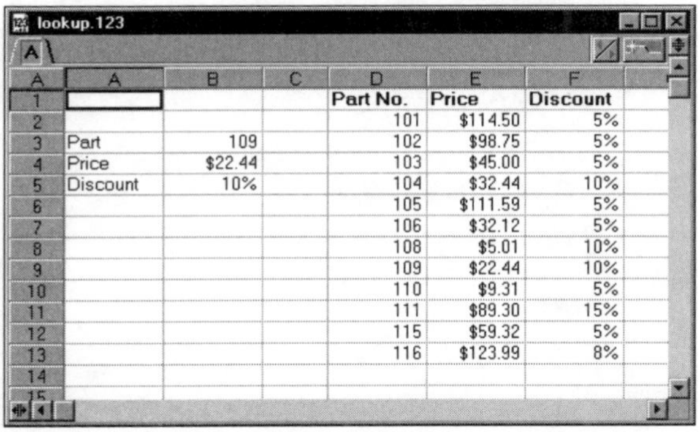

	A	B	C	D	E	F
1				Part No.	Price	Discount
2				101	$114.50	5%
3	Part	109		102	$98.75	5%
4	Price	$22.44		103	$45.00	5%
5	Discount	10%		104	$32.44	10%
6				105	$111.59	5%
7				106	$32.12	5%
8				108	$5.01	10%
9				109	$22.44	10%
10				110	$9.31	5%
11				111	$89.30	15%
12				115	$59.32	5%
13				116	$123.99	8%
14						

Figure 24-4: Looking up a value in a table.

The @VLOOKUP function looks for the first argument (here, partnum) in the first column of the range specified by the second argument (here, partlist). The function then returns the value in the column represented by the third argument (0 corresponds to the first column in the table, 1 to the second column, 2 to the third column, and so on). If the formula doesn't find an exact match, it simply uses the first row that's not greater than what it's looking for.

Appendix

Glossary

● ●

This appendix contains terms that you may encounter while using 1-2-3, reading this book, or listening to people talk about computers. Although this glossary doesn't substitute for a real computer dictionary (try the *Illustrated Computer Dictionary For Dummies,* 2nd Edition; IDG Books Worldwide, Inc.), you may find that it contains enough terms so that you can hold your own at the water cooler.

@function: A special process (preceded by an "at" sign) that performs some calculation for you in a formula. 1-2-3 has hundreds of @functions, some that are very useful to real people, and others that are designed for scientists and mathematicians. Most @functions use arguments. (See also *formula.*)

absolute cell reference: A cell reference in a formula that always refers to a specific cell (as opposed to a relative cell reference). After the formula is copied to another cell, it still refers to the original cell. Use dollar signs to specify an absolute cell reference — for example, $A$1. (See also *relative cell reference.*)

active cell: The cell in a worksheet that's ready to receive input from you. The current contents of the active cell appear in the edit line.

active workbook: The workbook that you're currently using. You can have several workbooks in memory, but only one of them can be the active workbook. The active workbook's title bar is a different color from the title bars in the other windows.

active worksheet: The worksheet that you're currently working on. Each workbook can have several worksheets, but only one of them is the active worksheet. You activate a worksheet by clicking its sheet tab.

address: The way you refer to a cell. Every cell has its own address (some are on the wrong side of the tracks). An address consists of a sheet letter, a colon, a column letter, and a row number. (The sheet letter is optional. If you omit it, also leave out the colon.) Here are some examples of addresses: A:C4, C:Z12, A1, and K9, also known as the dog cell. (See also *cell reference.*)

arguments: The information you provide that gives the details for a particular @function. The arguments are in parentheses, separated by commas.

ASCII file: See *text file.*

backsolving: Also known as *goal seeking.* This is the process of letting 1-2-3 determine the value of a cell that gives you a desired result in a cell that has a formula.

backup: An extra copy of a file, which is usually stored on some other disk. Making a backup copy of every important file and keeping the backup copy on a floppy disk is a good idea. That way, if you turn on your computer and discover that your hard disk died during the night, it won't ruin your whole day (just your morning).

borders: The different types of lines you can put around a cell or range. You have a good choice of border types, and you can even specify different colors and thicknesses.

browser: Software that downloads HTML documents, interprets them, and displays their contents. You can also use a browser to download files from an FTP site. The two leading Web browsers are Microsoft Internet Explorer and Netscape Navigator.

bug: To bother or pester. This is what you do to the office guru when you need his or her help. This term also refers to a software problem that causes strange things to happen or crashes your system.

button: A rectangular box, usually found in a dialog box, that causes something to happen after you click it with your mouse. You also can put a button directly on a worksheet and attach a script to it.

byte: The amount of memory or disk space needed to store one character, such as a letter or number. (See also *memory.*)

CD-ROM: CD-ROM (an acronym for Compact Disc Read-Only Memory) is a popular storage medium. This technology requires a special drive, and it uses CDs that look exactly like audio CDs. These discs can hold massive amounts of information — the equivalent of about 300,000 typewritten pages (three stories tall). Unlike hard and floppy disks, however, you cannot write information to CDs. After you buy one, you can't change anything on it. Also, accessing data on a CD-ROM is slower than accessing data on normal disks.

cell: The basic building block of life. Also, the intersection of a row and a column in a worksheet. A cell can hold a value, a label, a formula, a prisoner, or nothing at all.

Cell comment: A note to yourself that is stored along with a cell. Use the Cell comment tab of the Range InfoBox to insert or read cell comments.

cell pointer: A heavy outline that tells you which cell in the worksheet you selected. To move the cell pointer, press the cursor movement keys or click another cell with your mouse.

cell reference: Identifies a cell by giving its column letter and row number. For example, C5 refers to the cell at the intersection of column C and row 5. If you refer to a cell on a different sheet, you need to tack on a sheet letter before the cell reference. For example, B:C5 refers to the cell at the intersection of column C and row 5 on the second sheet (B). You can have relative cell references (most common) or absolute cell references.

central processing unit: Your computer's *central processing unit* (CPU) is located on the motherboard. The CPU is your computer's brain and determines how fast and powerful your computer is. Your CPU is probably made by Intel and labeled 80486 or Pentium. (See also *motherboard.*)

chart: A graphic representation of a range of values in a worksheet. Charts (or graphs) are stored on the draw layer of a worksheet. 1-2-3 has many different chart types — probably more than you'll ever need.

check box: In a dialog box, an option that can be turned either on or off by clicking the mouse (not the same as a radio or option button). You can activate more than one check box at a time.

circular reference: An error condition in which the result of a formula depends on the formula itself (either directly or indirectly). For example, if you put @SUM(A1..A10) in cell A10, the formula refers to its own cell in a circular reference. If your worksheet has a formula with a circular reference, you see CIRC displayed in the status bar.

click: To press and release the left mouse button. (See also *right-click.*)

clip art: An image stored in a file, which can be used by various software (including 1-2-3). Thousands and thousands of clip-art files are available, which you can use freely in your work.

Clipboard: An area of memory, managed by Windows, that stores information (usually to be pasted somewhere else). To put information on the Clipboard, choose Edit⇨Copy or click a SmartIcon designed for that purpose.

collection: A group of noncontiguous cells, ranges, stamps, or baseball cards. To select a collection, hold down the Ctrl key while you select the cells or ranges that you want. (See also *range.*)

column: A vertical group of 8,192 cells in a worksheet. Columns are identified by letters. (See also *row.*)

command: What your wish is to me. Also, an order that you give to 1-2-3 by using the menu system, a SmartIcon, or a shortcut key.

crash: The term for what happens when your computer stops working for no apparent reason. If you're running Windows, you get a message that tells you a serious error has occurred and asks if you want to continue or ignore it. Ignoring it never does any good, so you may as well kiss your work good-bye. The possibility of a crash is a good reason to save your work often. Usually, a system crash is the result of a software bug.

cursor movement keys: The keys on your keyboard (such as the arrow keys and the Home, End, PgUp, and PgDn keys) that cause the cell pointer to move.

database: An organized list made up of records (rows) and fields within records (columns). You can work with a database by performing a query or by sorting. (See also *list.*)

default: Settings that come automatically with a computer program, designed to include the most popular choices that people make. If you don't specify some options, your work looks the way it does because of its default settings. (For example, the default type size may be 12 points.) When something goes wrong, you can always say, "It's not my fault. It's default of the software."

dialog box: A box that pops up (after you choose a command) and gives you more choices. After you make the choices, you close the dialog box by clicking the OK button. If you change your mind or if you want to undo any change you make in the dialog box, simply click the Cancel button.

disks: Every computer has at least one disk drive. Most computers have two, and many computers have three. Two types of disks exist: hard disks and floppy disks. Both types store information as a series of magnetic impulses. (See also *hard disk* and *floppy disk.*)

double-click: To click the left mouse button twice in rapid succession.

drag-and-drop: To use the mouse to grab an item, move it, and drop it somewhere else. You can use drag-and-drop to move a cell, a range, or a graphics object.

drawing tools: SmartIcons that let you draw or manipulate graphic objects on the draw layer.

draw layer: The invisible layer (on top of every 1-2-3 worksheet) that holds charts and drawn objects.

drop-down listbox: In a dialog box, a listbox that normally shows only one option but has an arrow next to it, indicating that more options are available. If you click the arrow, the listbox drops down to show more options.

DumbIcon: A SmartIcon that doesn't do what you thought it would do.

e-mail: A method of sending and receiving messages *(electronic mail)* via the computer. Depending on how your system is set up, you may be able to send and receive e-mail only within your company using the company intranet, or you may be able to send and receive e-mail all over the world using the Internet.

edit line: The line at the top of the 1-2-3 screen that shows the address of the active cell. The contents of the active cell also appear in the edit line.

endless loop: See *infinite loop.*

extension: The part of a file's filename that follows the period. For a file named budget.123, the 123 part is the extension. Usually, a filename's extension tells you what type of file it is (files created by 1-2-3 Millennium Edition have a 123 extension).

field: In a database, this is a column that holds a particular part of a record.

file: An entity stored on a disk. A 1-2-3 workbook, for example, is stored in a file that has a 123 extension on the filename. A file is also used to help prisoners escape from a cell.

floppy disk: Floppy disks are removable disks (used for memory storage) and come in two sizes: $3^1/_2$-inch and $5^1/_4$-inch — although the latter size is becoming increasingly rare. Contrary to popular belief, $3^1/_2$-inch disks are not floppy; they have a sturdy, plastic case. Your primary floppy disk drive is known as drive A. If you have another floppy drive, it's called drive B.

font: The combination of a typeface and a type size.

formatting: The process of changing the way your information looks. You can have two general types of formatting: numeric formatting and stylistic formatting.

formula: Information that you put into a cell that performs a calculation. A formula can use the results of other cells in its calculation, and it can also use @functions.

frozen titles: The process of keeping certain top rows or left columns always displayed, no matter where the cell pointer is. You can freeze titles by choosing View⇨Titles.

FTP: An abbreviation for File Transfer Protocol. FTP is a common method for transferring a file from one computer to another.

FTP site: An area on one computer where files are available for other computers to download. Lotus, for example, maintains an FTP site with loads of files you can download.

function: See *@function*.

graph: See *chart*.

graphic object: Something that you draw on the draw layer of a worksheet. You can move and resize graphic objects.

handles: The little square objects, at the corners and on the sides of graphics, that you can drag with a mouse to change the size of the graphics objects.

hard disk: A hard disk is fixed inside your computer, and normally you can't remove it, although removable hard disks do exist. Hard disks store a large amount of information, and they transfer the information quickly. Hard disks come in a variety of sizes, from small 40MB drives up to several gigabytes or more. Your hard disk is known usually as Drive C. You can have more than one hard disk in a PC, and a single hard disk can be partitioned so that it appears as more than one disk.

HTML document: A computer file that may contain words, pictures, sounds, and so on, formatted in Hypertext Markup Language (HTML). Because people use many different kinds of computers to view HTML documents, Hypertext Markup Language relies on embedded codes (called tags) to tell your computer how to display the information. Your computer must have Web-browsing software to interpret these tags and display the information properly. (HTML documents are also called *Web pages*.)

HTTP: An abbreviation for Hypertext Transfer Protocol, the method by which people transfer documents over the Web.

hyperlink: Special text or images in an HTML document (Web page) that you can click to load a new Web page into your browser.

IBM: If you've never heard of IBM, you probably just arrived from the planet Zordox. IBM owns Lotus, the company that manufactures 1-2-3.

infinite loop: See *endless loop*.

InfoBox: A floating dialog box that makes applying formatting or working with a selected object very easy. 1-2-3 has tons of InfoBoxes — one for just about anything you can select. Each InfoBox has a series of tabs. Click a tab and the InfoBox changes to display new controls. Unlike a normal dialog box, an InfoBox remains on-screen while you go about your business.

insertion point: The position where new text is inserted when you're editing the contents of a cell. You can tell the insertion point, because the cursor looks like a vertical bar.

installation: The process of copying the files needed by 1-2-3 from a CD-ROM or floppy disks to your hard disk.

Internet: A worldwide network of computers that can communicate with each other and pass information back and forth. 1-2-3 enables you to access the Internet without leaving the program.

intranet: A private network of computers not available to the general public. Intranets use the same file types (such as HTML documents) as the Internet, but access to intranets is limited. For example, your company may have an intranet that only its employees can access.

John Walkenbach: The author of this book. Hi!

keyboard: You give information to your software through the keyboard. A number of different keyboard layouts are available, and most people don't really give much thought to which one they choose. Keyboards feel differently; some people prefer clicky keys, while others like a more mushy feel. Pianos also have keyboards, but most of them don't have a Ctrl key.

kilobytes: A kilobyte is 1,000 bytes and is normally abbreviated as KB or K. A kilobyte is used as a measure of storage capacity of disks and memory. 1K of memory stores about 1,024 characters. (See also *memory.*)

label: Also known simply as text. A bunch of letters (and sometimes also numbers) that you put into a cell, basically to provide information about your worksheet or other cells. A label is not a value and it's not a formula, but it's handy to have in your worksheet for clarity.

laptop computers: Laptop computers (also called *notebooks*) come with all different types of processors. Their diminutive size sets them apart from standard desktop computers and makes them convenient for people who travel a great deal. Notebooks usually run on batteries, and people on airplanes like to show them off. Although notebooks have become very powerful over the years, they're much more expensive than equally powerful desktop models.

lawsuit: A common activity among the lawyers at software companies. This pastime gives them something to do in order to justify their six-figure salaries.

list: A collection of items, each of which is stored in a separate row. Each item may have more than one part (that is, use more than one column). The order of the items may or may not be important. (See also *database.*)

listbox: A feature of many dialog boxes in which you can choose an option from a list of possibilities.

Lotus: Lotus created the original 1-2-3 (for DOS) about a decade ago. Although 1-2-3 wasn't the first spreadsheet for PCs, it was great in its time and became one of the most successful software products ever. The original DOS version of 1-2-3 is no longer anything to write home about, but 1-2-3 Millennium Edition (the latest release) is great.

macro: Previous releases of 1-2-3 used macros to automate various operations and to customize the program. 1-2-3 Millennium Edition still supports macros, but using scripts is the preferred way to go.

map: A graphic representation of a geographic area that uses colors and hatching to represent data values for regions. 1-2-3 enables you to create maps by using data stored in a worksheet.

Maximize button: The button on the title bar of a window that (after you click it with your mouse) makes the window as large as it can be. If the window is already maximized, this button is replaced with a different button (a *Restore button*) that returns the window to its previous size. (See also *Minimize button.*)

memory: Every computer has memory, which usually ranges from 4 to 32 megabytes (or more!). The more memory your computer has, the better off you are.

Computer memory and disk storage come in many different units:

- **Bit:** The smallest unit of computer measurement. A bit is either on (1) or off (0)

- **Byte:** Eight bits

- **Kilobyte:** 1,000 bytes (abbreviated as K)

- **Megabyte:** A million bytes, or 1,000K (abbreviated as MB)

- **Gigabyte:** A billion bytes, or 1,000MB (abbreviated as Gbyte or GB)

menu bar: The group of words at the top of the 1-2-3 screen (File, Edit, and so on). After you select one of these words, its menu drops down to display commands.

Microsoft: The mother of all software companies. Microsoft makes MS-DOS, Windows, Excel, and many other popular software programs. Excel is 1-2-3's biggest competitor. The company's CEO, Bill Gates, is the richest man in the United States.

Minimize button: The button on the title bar of a window that, after you click it with your mouse, turns the window into an icon. (See also *Maximize button.*)

mode indicator: The word at the right corner of the *status bar* that tells you what mode 1-2-3 is currently in.

modem: The device used to communicate directly with other computers. A modem connects your PC (via a serial port) to a normal phone line and — if you're lucky — makes a connection with another computer that has a modem. If you want to connect to the Internet, access online services (such as CompuServe or Prodigy), or send and receive faxes, you need a modem.

monitor: The hardware device that displays information that your software wants you to see. Monitors come in many types and sizes, and they vary in resolution. Your monitor works in conjunction with your video card, and the combination determines how the information looks on-screen.

motherboard: A printed circuit board (with a bunch of electronic-looking gizmos sticking out) that sits at the bottom of the inside of your computer. It contains all the circuitry that makes a computer a computer. The motherboard also contains chips that hold your computer's memory, and it also contains a number of slots.

mouse: The device that probably looks like a bar of white soap-on-a-rope connected to your computer.

mouse pointer: A representation of the mouse on-screen. Normally, the mouse pointer is an arrow, but it often changes shape to let you know that you can do certain things.

multisheet workbook: A workbook consisting of least two worksheets.

named range: A range of cells (or even a single cell) that has been given a meaningful name. Naming cells and ranges makes them easier to use in formulas and makes the formulas more readable. Choose Range⇨Name to name the cell or range.

numeric formatting: The process of changing the way a number looks when it's displayed in a cell (for example, displaying a number with a percent sign). Changing the numeric formatting does not affect the value in any way; it just affects its appearance.

option button: In a dialog box, a group of buttons from which only one can be selected at any time (also known as a radio button).

outline: A way to view data in a worksheet so that it can be collapsed or expanded. Collapsing an outline shows less detail; expanding an outline shows more detail.

pane: One of two (or four) parts of a worksheet window you've split by choosing View➪Split. Splitting a screen into panes enables you to see and work with two (or four) different parts of a workbook without having to do a great deal of scrolling around.

parallel port: A part of your computer that sends and receives information in several different (parallel) streams. This process allows for faster communication. Printers usually use parallel ports. (See also *ports* and *serial port*.)

paste: To copy an item that has been stored on the Windows Clipboard into a worksheet or chart. You can paste a cell, a range, a chart, or a graphics object — but it must be copied to the Clipboard first. (See also *Clipboard*.)

pointing: The process of selecting a range by using either the keyboard or the mouse. When you need to indicate a cell or range address, you can enter it directly, or you can point to it by selecting cells with your mouse or by highlighting cells using the keyboard.

ports: The means by which computers communicate with external devices (such as printers, modems, and mice). Two types of ports exist: serial ports and parallel ports.

preview: Seeing on-screen how your worksheet will look after you print it. Choose File➪Preview➪Page Setup to preview a worksheet. Also, what movie theaters force you to sit through so that you buy more popcorn.

printer: That device that spits out paper with black stuff on it.

query: The process of locating specific records in a database. You can specify the exact criteria that you want.

quick menu: See *shortcut menu*.

radio button: See *option button*.

random access memory (RAM): A type of memory that can be written to and read from; commonly referring to the internal memory of your computer. The *random* means that any one location can be read at any time; it's not necessary to read all of the memory to find one location.

range: Where the deer and the antelope play. Also two or more contiguous cells. (See also *collection*.)

recalculation: The process of evaluating all the formulas in a worksheet. Normally, this is all done automatically. But if your worksheet is in manual recalc mode, you have to specify when to recalculate (by pressing F9).

record: In a database, one unit (row) that comprises fields (columns). It is also an obsolete (albeit nostalgic) method of storing music.

relative cell reference: A normal cell reference in a formula. If the formula is copied to another cell, the cell references adjust automatically to refer to cells in their new surroundings. (See also *absolute cell reference*.)

resolution: What you make on New Year's Eve and forget about by January 3rd. This term also refers to the number of pixels a monitor has. The more pixels, the higher the resolution, and the higher the resolution, the better the picture.

Restore button: On a maximized window, the button on the title bar that returns the window to its previous size.

right-click: To press and release the right mouse button. In 1-2-3, right-clicking displays a shortcut menu that's relevant to whatever you have selected at the time.

row: A horizontal group of 256 cells. Rows are identified by numbers. (See also *column.*)

scroll bar: Not your neighborhood pub, but one of two bars (either the vertical or horizontal scroll bar) on the worksheet window that enables you to scroll through the worksheet quickly by using the mouse.

selection: The cell, range, collection, chart, or graphics object that is affected by the command you choose.

serial port: A computer device that sends and receives information in a single stream of bits. These ports are sometimes known as COM ports. Modems, mice, and some printers use serial ports. (See also *ports* and *parallel port.*)

sheet: See *worksheet.*

shortcut key: A Ctrl+key combination (such as Ctrl+C) that is a shortcut for a command.

shortcut menu: The menu that appears when you right-click the mouse after an item is selected. Most of the time, you find the command that you need here.

SmartIcon: One of the buttons (or elements) on a SmartIcon bar that is usually a quicker way of issuing a menu command when clicked.

SmartIcon bar: A collection of SmartIcons. Also known as a toolbar.

sorting: The process of rearranging the rows of a range by using one or more columns in the range as the sort key. Choose Range⇨Sort.

sound card: A device that is inserted into a slot on your motherboard, and is capable of generating much better sound than the normal, tiny speaker.

spreadsheet: The generic word for a worksheet or a program like 1-2-3.

status bar: The line at the bottom of the 1-2-3 screen that shows the status of several items in the program or on-screen. You also can use the status bar to quickly change the font, type size, numeric format, or number of decimal places displayed.

stylistic formatting: The process of changing the appearance of cells and ranges, which involves changing colors, modifying type sizes and fonts, and adding borders. This formatting is best done by using the InfoBox.

tab: What you hope your friend picks up when you go out to dinner. In a multisheet workbook, it's the item that displays the sheet letter (or the name you gave to the sheet by double-clicking it). To activate another sheet, click its tab.

text box: In a dialog box, a small box in which you type letters or words.

text file: A "generic" computer file that holds information but holds no special formatting commands. Most programs (including 1-2-3) can read and write text files.

title bar: The colored bar at the top of every window. You can move a nonmaximized window by dragging its title bar with the mouse.

undo: To reverse the effects of the last command. Choose Edit➪Undo (or press Ctrl+Z).

URL: An abbreviation for Uniform Resource Locator. A URL is a series of characters that uniquely describes a resource on the Internet. For example, the following URL describes the home page for my Web site, which happens to deal with spreadsheets: www.j-walk.com/ss/.

value: A number entered into a cell.

version manager: A feature in 1-2-3 that enables you to keep track of different scenarios in a worksheet. Access this feature by choosing Range➪Version.

Web site: A collection of HTML documents (Web pages) located on a particular computer. The files on a Web site are available to anyone in the world. For example, Lotus maintains a Web site where you can find information about its products, technical support, and many other interesting tidbits.

window: Where a worksheet is displayed or held. 1-2-3 is also a window that holds other windows. (See also *Windows*.)

Windows: The software product made by Microsoft. Windows is required in order to run 1-2-3.

WITTGOOHOT: An acronym for "Whatever It Takes To Get Out Of Here On Time." People often use this term close to quitting time.

worksheet: Where your cells are stored. A worksheet appears in a workbook. You add a new worksheet to a workbook by choosing Create➪Sheet or by clicking the New Sheet button.

WYSIWYG: An acronym for "What You See Is What You Get." This refers to the fact that the formatting you perform on-screen also applies to what gets printed.

WWW: The World Wide Web, one of many parts of the Internet that support the free transfer of information between computers throughout the world. The WWW uses HTML as its primary file format, and the documents are connected using hyperlinks.

x-ray: The only word I could think of that starts with *x*.

Y2K: An abbreviation for Year 2000. Some computer systems will have major problems on January 1, 2000.

zoom: The process of changing the size of the information displayed in a worksheet. You can zoom in or out by choosing View➪Zoom To.

Index

(continued)

• *Q* •

Discover Dummies Online!

The Dummies Web Site is your fun and friendly online resource for the latest information about ...*For Dummies*® books and your favorite topics. The Web site is the place to communicate with us, exchange ideas with other ...*For Dummies* readers, chat with authors, and have fun!

Ten Fun and Useful Things You Can Do at www.dummies.com

1. Win free ...*For Dummies* books and more!
2. Register your book and be entered in a prize drawing.
3. Meet your favorite authors through the IDG Books Author Chat Series.
4. Exchange helpful information with other ...*For Dummies* readers.
5. Discover other great ...*For Dummies* books you must have!
6. Purchase Dummieswear™ exclusively from our Web site.
7. Buy ...*For Dummies* books online.
8. Talk to us. Make comments, ask questions, get answers!
9. Download free software.
10. Find additional useful resources from authors.

Link directly to these ten fun and useful things at
http://www.dummies.com/10useful

For other technology titles from IDG Books Worldwide, go to
www.idgbooks.com

Not on the Web yet? It's easy to get started with *Dummies 101*®: *The Internet For Windows*®*95* or *The Internet For Dummies*®, 5th Edition, at local retailers everywhere.

Find other ...*For Dummies* books on these topics:
Business • Career • Databases • Food & Beverage • Games • Gardening • Graphics • Hardware
Health & Fitness • Internet and the World Wide Web • Networking • Office Suites
Operating Systems • Personal Finance • Pets • Programming • Recreation • Sports
Spreadsheets • Teacher Resources • Test Prep • Word Processing

IDG BOOKS WORLDWIDE. BOOK REGISTRATION

Register This Book and Win!

We want to hear from you!

Visit **http://my2cents.dummies.com** to register this book and tell us how you liked it!

- ✔ Get entered in our monthly prize giveaway.

- ✔ Give us feedback about this book — tell us what you like best, what you like least, or maybe what you'd like to ask the author and us to change!

- ✔ Let us know any other ...*For Dummies*® topics that interest you.

Your feedback helps us determine what books to publish, tells us what coverage to add as we revise our books, and lets us know whether we're meeting your needs as a ...*For Dummies* reader. You're our most valuable resource, and what you have to say is important to us!

Not on the Web yet? It's easy to get started with *Dummies 101*®: *The Internet For Windows*® *95* or *The Internet For Dummies*®, 5th Edition, at local retailers everywhere.

Or let us know what you think by sending us a letter at the following address:

...*For Dummies* Book Registration
Dummies Press
7260 Shadeland Station, Suite 100
Indianapolis, IN 46256-3945
Fax 317-596-5498

BUSINESS AND GENERAL REFERENCE BOOK SERIES FROM IDG

COMPUTER BOOK SERIES FROM IDG

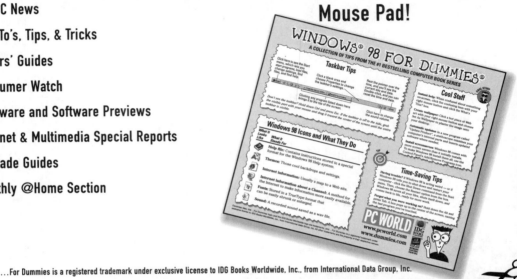